A History of Qarabagh

A History of Qarabagh

An Annotated Translation of
Mirza Jamal Javanshir Qarabaghi's
Tarikh-e Qarabagh

by
George A. Bournoutian

Mazda Publishers
1994

The publication of this volume was made possible in part by a grant from the AGBU Alex Manoogian Cultural Fund

Library of Congress Cataloging-in-Publication Data

Javānshīr Qarabāghī, Jamāl, d. 1853.
  [Tārīkh-i Qarabāgh. English & Persian]
  A History of Qarabagh: an annotated translation of Mirza Jamal
  Javanshir Qarabaghi's Tarikh-e Qarabagh/by George A. Bournoutian.
    p.   cm.
  Includes bibliographical references (p.) and index.
  1-Nagarno-Karabakh (Azerbaijan)—History. I. Bournoutian.,
  George A., II. Title.
  DK699.N34J3813   1993
  947'.91—dc20   93-356
  88
                                                                CIP
                                                                NE

Mazda Publishers, P.O. Box 2603, Costa Mesa, California 92626 U.S.A.

ISBN 1-56859-011-3

*To Dr. Armenak Alikhanian of Mush
who practiced medicine but loved history*

Contents

Maps

Preface

For the past twenty years my research has focused on the eighteenth-
and nineteenth-century history of that part of Transcaucasia which
formed the eastern segment of historic Armenia. In the course of this
research it has become obvious to me that in order to present a fair and
balanced view of the history of the region, one must rely not only on
Russian, Armenian, and European primary sources but on the work of
Iranian and local Turkic chroniclers as well.

The majority of Iranian primary sources are chiefly concerned with
the political history of Iran during the Safavid, Afshar, Zand, or Qajar
dynasties. Unless the shah deemed it necessary to make an appearance
there, events occurring in outlying regions such as Qarabagh, are, for the
most part, allotted a cursory paragraph in these writings. The search for
regional histories, however, led me to a number of chronicles dealing
exclusively with Qarabagh. Although the authors were Transcaucasian
Turks, later known as Azerbaijanis, they all, with one exception, wrote
their histories in Persian, which remained until the latter part of the
nineteenth century the primary literary language of the Muslims of
Transcaucasia.

The earliest chronicle on Qarabagh is the history of Mirza Jamal
Javanshir Qarabaghi, which concerns itself with political and, to some
extent, socioeconomic conditions in Qarabagh from the 1740s until 1806.
It presents a fascinating account of the khanate of Qarabagh, an impor-
tant, albeit short-lived, entity, which was formed by the Javanshir khans
following the death of Nader Shah in 1747 and which ended with
Russian control of the province in 1806 and its formal annexation into
Russia in 1822.

The struggle for the throne of post-Safavid Iran and its effects on
Qarabagh and the rest of Transcaucasia are vividly described in *Tarikh-e
Qarabagh*. The history begins with the campaigns of Nader Shah Afshar
in Transcaucasia and his forced relocation of Qarabaghi tribes. The

struggle among Nader's successors and the emergence of new contenders, such as Fath 'Ali Khan Afshar and Mohammad Hasan Khan Qajar,
are depicted, as are their campaigns in Qarabagh. The rise of Panah Khan
and his son Ebrahim Khan of Qarabagh, King Erekle II of Georgia, and
Hajji Chelebi of Shakki during this interregnum and their struggles
against each other for supremacy in the region is detailed as well. Mirza
Jamal also relates the temporary unification of Iran under Karim Khan
Zand and its effect on Qarabagh and the rest of Transcaucasia. Finally,
the emergence of the Qajar dynasty, the invasions of Aqa Mohammad
Khan, and the efforts of Fath 'Ali Shah and 'Abbas Mirza to halt the
Russian penetration into the region completes the narrative.

Of additional interest to scholars of the region is the information on
the Armenians of Qarabagh presented by Mirza Jamal and the other
Qarabaghi chroniclers. Modern Azeri historians have generally not com-
mented on passages in these works which relate to the Armenians.
Armenian historians, who have written a great deal about the Armenians of Qarabagh, have used mainly Armenian, Russian, and Western
sources. What is significant about Mirza Jamal's history is that it is a
primary source which, to a great extent, corroborates Armenian, Russian, and Western travel accounts of the position, influence, and the
continuous presence of Armenians in Qarabagh.

Russian, Azeri, and Turkish translations of Mirza Jamal's history have
already appeared. They have included, however, but meager annotations; more grievously, they have omitted certain passages contained in
the original manuscript, as well as made errors in their translations.
Students of the history of Transcaucasia, I believe, would certainly
benefit from a fully annotated English translation. To be truly valuable,
and to convey a more complete picture, however, any new study had to
incorporate in its annotations information from the other Qarabaghi
chroniclers, as well as the accounts of Iranian historians of that period.
Since one of my objectives was to concentrate solely on these sources, I
have excluded from this study, except for a few references in the footnotes, all Armenian, Russian, and west European primary sources.

The completion of this study owes much to many. I wish to express
my sincere gratitude to the late Marie Manoogian, who encouraged me
to undertake this project, as well as to Edmond Azadian and the AGBU
Alex Manoogian Cultural Fund, for providing a research grant.

Special thanks are due to my teacher, Professor Amin Banani of
UCLA, in whose graduate courses I learned how to read and interpret
Persian manuscripts, an art no longer taught in most universities. He

was kind enough to check this translation against the original manuscript and make a number of corrections and suggestions.

Two individuals performed miracles in obtaining hard-to-find sources: Levon Avdoyan of the Library of Congress and Adrienne Franco of Iona College. Eugene Beshenkovsky of the Lehman Library of Columbia University helped locate the Azeri translation of *Tarikh-e Qarabagh* and the Hatcher Library of the University of Michigan, Ann Arbor, provided the microfilm of the newspaper *Kavkaz*. The Academy of Sciences of Azerbaijan was kind enough to provide a copy of the Persian text of *Tarikh-e Qarabagh* during my IREX fellowship in 1973-74.

Robert Hewsen of Rowan College not only sent me a copy of the Russian translation of *Tarikh-e Qarabagh* but, as always, selflessly provided invaluable information on the geography of the region. In addition, his wide knowledge and studies of the *meliks* of Qarabagh helped in identifying those mentioned in the manuscript.

Muriel Atkin of George Washington University read the translation, providing insightful comments as well as valuable information on the Russian military and administrative figures in Transcaucasia. James Reid of the Vryonis Center in Sacramento supplied information on some of the tribes of Qarabagh. Haideh Sahim and John Walbridge of the Center for Iranian Studies, Columbia University, checked this English translation for inconsistencies. Richard Hovannisian of UCLA and Rosalyn Ashby of Yavapai College made useful suggestions concerning the introduction. Ann Cammett produced the maps, Nancy Girardi and Patti Besen of the Information Technology Resource Center at Iona College prepared the computer discs, and Lois Adams edited the final draft.

Finally, there is a debt that cannot be repaid. My wife Ani not only spent many hours on this project, but gave up her vacation, occupied the children in my physical and mental absences, tolerated a house full of notes, and patiently endured my occasional bouts of frustration.

George Bournoutian
Iona College, 1993

Abbreviated Titles

Alamara-ye Naderi	Mohammad Kazem Marvi, Alamara-ye Naderi. Tehran, 1990. 3 vols.
Bamdad	Mahdi Bamdad, *Sharh-e hal-e rejal-e Iran (dar qarn 12 va 13 va 14 hijri)*. Tehran, 1968-1972. 6 vols.
Farsname-ye Naseri	Haj Mirza Hasan Hoseini Fasa'i, Tarikh-e *Farsname-ye Naseri*. Tehran, 1896/9.
Garabagh Tarikhi	Mirzä Jamal Javanshir Garabaghi, *Garabagh Tarikhi*. Baku, 1959.
Golestan-e Eram	'Abbas Qoli Aqa Bakikhanov, *Golestan-e Eram*. Baku, 1970.
Golshan-e Morad	Mirza Mohammad Abo'l-Hasan Ghaffari Kashani, *Golshan-e Morad*. Tehran, 1990.
Istoriia Karabaga	Mirza Dzhamal Dzhevanshir Karabagskii, *Istoriia Karabaga*. Baku, 1959.
"Karabag"	First Russian translation of Mirza Jamal's history by A. Berzhe in the newspaper *Kavkaz*. Tiflis, 1855.
Karabagh Tarihi	Mirza Cemal Cevansir Karabaghli, *Karabagh Tarihi*. Ankara, 1990.
Karabakhskogo khanstva	Akhmedbek Dzhavanshir, *O politicheskom sushchestvovanii Karabakhskogo khanstva (s 1747 po 1805 god)*. Baku, 1961.
Ma'ser-e Soltaniye	'Abd or-Razzaq Beg Donboli, *Ma'ser-e Soltaniye*. Tehran, 1973.
Mojmal ot-Tavarikh	Abo'l-Hasan b. Mohammad Amin Golestane, *Mojmal ot-Tavarikh*. Tehran, 1965.
Montazam-e Naseri	Mohammad Hasan Khan E'temad os-Saltane, *Tarikh-e Montazam-e Naseri*. Vols. II-III Tehran, 1984-85.

Nasekh ot-Tavarikh	Mirza Mohammad Taqi Sepehr, *Nasekh ot-Tavarikh*. Vols. I-II. Tehran, 1965.
Qarabagh-name	Mirza Adigezal'-Bek, *Karabag-name*. Baku, 1950.
Rouzat os-Safa	Reza Qoli Khan Hedayat, *Tarikh-e Rouzat os-Safa-ye Naseri*. Vol. IX. Qom, 1960.
Tarikh-e Giti-gosha	Mirza Mohammad Sadeq Musavi Nami Esfahani, *Tarikh-e Giti-gosha*. Tehran, 1984.
Tarikh-e Jahangoshay	Mirza Mohammad Mahdi Koukabi Astarabadi, *Tarikh-e Jahangoshay-e Naderi*. Facsimile of the 1757/58 manuscript. Tehran, 1991.
Tarikh-e Mohammadi	Mohammad Fathollah Saru'i, *Tarikh-e Mohammadi*. Tehran, 1992.

a27271

Terms, Names, Dates, and Transliteration

The term *Turk* refers to the Ottomans or to the present-day Turks. Turkic groups who inhabited Transcaucasia prior to the twentieth century are grouped under the general rubric of *Transcaucasian Turks*, and are primarily identified by their tribal affiliation and geographic location. The term *Azerbaijani* or *Azeri* refers to this entire group in the twentieth century. The use of the term *Azerbaijan* requires clarification, as well. Although Azerbaijan was not a political entity in the eighteenth and nineteenth centuries, the term had long been used to identify a geographical region, denoting the northwestern province of Iran. The Safavids, at one time, for revenue purposes, included the lands north of the Arax River as part of the province of Azerbaijan. This practice gradually fell out of use after the fall of the Safavids. Mirza Jamal, as well as most other eighteenth- and nineteenth-century Persian sources, viewed Azerbaijan as the Iranian region located south of the Arax (see map 2). Except for the preface and introduction, where Azerbaijan denotes the present-day Republic of Azerbaijan, I shall observe Mirza Jamal's use of the term.

Despite the fact that many of the rulers and military leaders of Iran, as well as a large number of its nomadic tribes, were of Turkic background, Iranian culture was distinct from that of its Arab and Turkish neighbors. Therefore, the term *Persian* will denote the written and spoken language of Iran. The terms *Iran* and *Iranian* will refer to the land and its people.

The term *Transcaucasia* betrays a Russian bias, *Transaraxia*, a Persian bias. *Eastern Caucasus* is the neutral term; however, to avoid confusion and to maintain uniformity with most historians, I have decided to retain *Transcaucasia*.

I have modernized or corrected all personal and place names in the manuscript to appear as they would in their own language or as they are referred to today. Hence *Vorontsov* instead of *Varansof*, *Erevan* instead of

Iravan, Nakhichevan instead of *Nakhjavan*. There are a few exceptions; one of which is *Teflis*, which instead of its current name of *Tbilisi*, will be referred to by its more common eighteenth- and nineteenth-century designation of *Tiflis*. For the sake of accuracy, I have retained Mirza Jamal's geographical terms the first time they appear in the text, with the currently-used or more accepted names in parenthesis.

All dates in the text are based on the Arabic lunar calendar (354/5 days, beginning in 622 A.D.). The publication dates of the Iranian sources after 1925, however, are in the solar calendar of 365 days based on the same starting point as the lunar calendar. In both cases the Gregorian dates are given in parentheses. Dates involving Russian history, unless specified, are in the old-style or Julian calendar, which in the eighteenth century was eleven days, and in the nineteenth century, twelve days, behind the Gregorian calendar used in the West.

In transliterating from the Persian I have indicated the way the word is pronounced in Persian, rather than trying to reconstruct it in its Arabic pronunciation. Persian terms which appear in Russian translations of Persian sources have presented a problem, because of the many Persian sounds which do not exist in Russian. When the term or meaning was obvious I have transliterated it according to the original Persian; in other instances, I have retained the Russian transliteration with an approximate rendering in parenthesis, followed by a question mark. With few exceptions, all Arabic and Turkish titles have been transliterated according to a simplified IJMES system. I have transliterated Russian according to the simplified Library of Congress system. The phonetic values of eastern Armenian are used for transliterating Armenian names. For Azeri, I have used a modified Library of Congress system for Cyrillic, with certain adjustments for letters not found in that alphabet. Diacritical marks, ligatures, and other symbols have been eliminated for the sake of simplicity. Finally, I have used the familiar English form for terms such as *bazaar, sultan, hijri, Azerbaijan* (instead of bazar, soltan, hejri, and Azarbaijan), among others.

Introduction

An Assessment of Mirza Jamal Javanshir Qarabaghi's *Tarikh-e Qarabagh* and Other Primary Persian-Language Sources Relating to the History of Qarabagh

Armenian and Russian sources notwithstanding, the primary sources on the history of Qarabagh in the eighteenth and nineteenth centuries are almost all written in Persian. Although the majority of the Muslim population of Qarabagh and Transcaucasia spoke a Turkish dialect, until the later part of the nineteenth century the administrative and literary language was Persian, with Arabic reserved for religious studies. The knowledge of Persian is, therefore, essential to any serious study of the region prior to the twentieth century. It is also necessary to read Persian manuscripts written in the styles of handwriting known as *shekaste* and *nasta'liq*, if one is to examine the original sources of the period.

The Persian sources, themselves, fall into two categories: The first, all written by Transcaucasian Turks, deal primarily with Qarabagh, the second encompass chronicles of Iranian history during the rule of the late Safavids, Afshars, Zands, and early Qajars.

1) Primary Sources Dealing Mainly with Qarabagh
There are four translated and published sources and a number of unpublished manuscripts dealing mainly with the history of Qarabagh.[1] The earliest of these is the present work by Mirza Jamal Javanshir Qarabaghi, entitled *Tarikh-e Qarabagh*, of which Azeri, Russian, and

---

[1] More material is available in the archives of Azerbaijan and may be on its way to being published. The current political situation in Baku precluded any correspondence with the Academy of Sciences of Azerbaijan (also see note 51).

Turkish translations, albeit inadequate, are available. The facsimile of the Persian text has also been published.[2]

Mirza Jamal's career was long and eventful, especially by the standards of his time. He was born in 1187 hijri (1773/74) in the Javanshir district near Dizak in the village of Khajalu (Khojalu?).[3] He was the son of Mohammad-khan Beg, the grandson of Salif Beg Minbashi, and the great-grandson of Sharif Beg Javanshir. His grandfather, a *minbashi*, or "head of one thousand," was a tribal chief. After the death of his grandfather, his father became the chief of the Javanshir tribe, inheriting the position given to his father by Ebrahim Khan, the ruler of Qarabagh. His father was soon transferred to the Shushi fortress as its commander.

Mirza Jamal studied Persian and Turkish, and in 1202 hijri (1787/88), at age fifteen, became one of the scribes in Ebrahim Khan's chancery, through which passed all of the correspondence of Qarabagh.[4] After a few years, probably during the initial threat from Aqa Mohammad Khan,[5] he left Shushi with other members of the khan's household and settled in the village of Khoznak (Khunzakh?).[6] He became secretary to one of the wives of the khan, Bike Khanum, the sister of 'Umma Khan, the ruler of the Avars of Daghestan.[7] After six years, during which he studied Arabic, he and Bike Khanum returned to the Shushi fortress, upon the death of Aqa Mohammad.

Ebrahim Khan, in gratitude for the courageous acts of Mohammad-khan Beg and his followers during the siege of Shushi by Aqa Mohammad Khan, appointed Mohammad-khan Beg's son, Mirza Jamal,

---

[2] The facsimile is an 1877/78 copy of an 1847 version, see below. The manuscript is reproduced here, beginning with the last page of this study.

[3] The following biographical information is based on material supplied by Mirza Jamal's son, Reza Qoli, to Mirza Fath 'Ali Akhundov (or Akhundzade, who worked as a translator in the Tiflis chancellery in the 1830s, and later wrote satirical works) at the request of A. Berzhe, the first Russian translator of *Tarikh-e Qarabagh* (see below). It was published in the newspaper *Kavkaz*, 61 (1855), p. 259. Additional information, based on an unnamed manuscript written by Mirza Jamal's son, Reza Qoli, was gathered from the introductions of the Russian and Azeri translations of *Tarikh-e Qarabagh* (see below).

[4] This was not unusual at that time, since most scribes began their careers after finishing the *maktab* and *madrase* at about age fifteen.

[5] Aqa Mohammad Khan was the founder of the Qajar dynasty in Iran (1796-1924). In the late eighteenth century he began the conquest of Iran and Transcaucasia. See text for more details.

[6] The probable date is 1792.

[7] For information on 'Umma Khan see pages 84-85 and note 223 in text.

to the post of his personal secretary and the vizier of Qarabagh. Mirza Jamal was thus present during the signing of the Russo-Qarabaghi treaty between Ebrahim Khan and Prince Tsitsianov,[8] which made Qarabagh a protectorate of Russia.[9] In 1805, during the First Russo-Iranian war (1804-1813),[10] he acted as secretary to Mohammad Hasan Aqa, the elder son of Ebrahim Khan, who led the Qarabaghi cavalry under the command of General Nebol'sin.[11] Mirza Jamal was present during the battle of Khonashin between the forces of Nebol'sin and 'Abbas Mirza[12] and reported on that war to Ebrahim Khan.[13] Soon after, he went to Nakhichevan, from which he carried dispatches to General Gudovich at the Erevan border. Later he was sent to General Kotliarevskii[14] in Agh-Oghlan, where he was put in charge of provisions for the army. During the entire period of the Russo-Iranian wars, he and his clan of some one hundred persons were supported by the Russian state.

After the murder of Ebrahim Khan, he remained in the service of

---

[8] The treaty was signed in 1805. Paul Tsitsianov was a descendant of a Tsitsishvili prince who had emigrated to Russia during the reign of Peter the Great. He was born about 1754. He served under Valerian Zubov during the reign of Catherine. Like most of her officers, he retired from service during the reign of Paul (1797-1801). He returned to government service when Alexander I (1801-1825) named him Commander-in-Chief in the Caucasus in 1802. He was killed in 1806.

[9] See pages 116-117 in text.

[10] The First Russo-Iranian war ended with the Treaty of Golestan (Gulistan). Iran lost the khanates of Baku, Shirvan, Ganje, Shakki (Sheki), Qarabagh, Qobbe (Kuba), and parts of Talesh (see map 5), and renounced all its claims to Georgia as well.

[11] Peter Fedorovich Nebol'sin began his career in the Russo-Turkish wars of the late eighteenth century. He rose through the ranks, and by 1804 was promoted to major general. In 1806 he was transferred to Transcaucasia where he participated in a number of battles during the First Russo-Iranian war. He died in 1810.

[12] 'Abbas Mirza was the son of Fath 'Ali Shah Qajar and the crown prince of Iran. He was born in 1788/89 and died in 1833. See note 351 in text for more details.

[13] For more details on that conflict, see pages 125-126 in text.

[14] General Peter Kotliarevskii (1782-1852) served in the infantry division in Mozdok, on the Caucasian line, under General Lazarev, becoming his adjutant in 1799. He swiftly rose through the ranks, became Tsitsianov's adjutant and served during the First Russo-Iranian war. He commanded the Russian troops that won the battles of Aslanduz (1812) and Lenkoran (1813). He was badly wounded at Lenkoran and had to retire from service.

Ebrahim's son, Mahdi Qoli Khan, the last khan of Qarabagh.[15] When the latter fled to Iran in 1822,[16] Mirza Jamal retired, and on orders from General Ermolov, the governor general of the Caucasus,[17] received an annual pension of 510 silver rubles, 120 bushels of wheat, and 30 bushels of rice. After the khan's departure, Ermolov came to Shushi in 1822, ordered an official survey and began gathering information about the province, which had by then officially been annexed to Russia. Mirza Jamal was called out of retirement and was probably asked to provide his notes and documents on the past administration. In 1823 he was appointed by the Russian commandant of Shushi to the post of chancery secretary, in which he served Colonel Ermolov, Colonel Mogilevskii, Prince Madatov, and General Reutt'.[18] In 1826 during the Second Russo-Iranian war (1826-1828), Mirza Jamal accompanied Prince Madatov

---

[15] Russia took control of Qarabagh after the death of Ebrahim Khan in 1806. Mahdi Qoli Khan held the title of "Khan of Qarabagh," but for all intents and purposes, he was an administrator in the Russian empire.

[16] Realizing his inferior position, Mahdi Qoli probably made overtures to Iran. Russian suspicions and their degrading attitude forced him to flee in 1822. Russia then officially abolished the khanate. He joined Iranian forces and fought against the Russians in the Second Russo-Iranian war. In 1836 he was allowed to return to Qarabagh, where he spent the rest of his life as a pensioner of the state. He died in 1845 and is buried in Aghdam.

[17] Alexei Petrovich Ermolov (1777-1861) came from a noble family and embarked on a military career early in his life. By 1792 he was already a captain. Four years later he joined General Zubov's campaign in Transcaucasia. Following Catherine's death he returned to Russia. He fought against Napoleon and participated in the Battle of Borodino under the command of General Kutuzov. He became the head of the Russian artillery and took part in the wars against Napoleon in 1813 and 1814. By 1816 he was named Chief of the Georgian or Caucasian Corps and served as extraordinary and plenipotentiary envoy to Iran. In 1819 he became the supreme commander in Transcaucasia. He remained in this post until the new tsar, Nicholas I, not trusting Ermolov's Decembrist sympathies, forced his resignation in 1827.

[18] Peter Nikolaevich Ermolov (first cousin of General Alexei Ermolov) and Paul Ivanovich Mogilevskii were both senior officials in the chancellery of General Ermolov in Tiflis. In 1823, they conducted the first survey of the Qarabagh khanate. Lieutenant General and Prince Valerian Grigor'evich Madatov was descended from the Qarabagh *meliks*. He joined the Russian army and fought in the Napoleonic wars. In 1816 he was transferred to the Caucasus serving in Shakki, Shirvan, and Qarabagh. In 1826 he defeated the Persian army at Shamkhor. He was recalled from the Caucasus with Ermolov and died in 1829 in the Balkans during the Russo-Turkish war of 1828-1829. Lieutenant General

across the Arax, where, with the help of his nephew, Karim Beg, he managed to move the entire village of Seyyed-Ahmadlu from Qaradagh to the Dizak district in Qarabagh.[19]

In 1840, already in his late sixties, Mirza Jamal again retired from service. Subsequently, his pension was terminated and he was in financial difficulties, until Viceroy Vorontsov [20] presented him with the income from the village of Kargah-bazar, a right which his descendants continued to enjoy at least up to 1855 when A. Berzhe [21] published his biography in the newspaper *Kavkaz*. Mirza Jamal knew some Arabic, the Lezgi and Avar languages, had some knowledge of astronomy, and an excellent knowledge of history and geography. He was also familiar with medicine; it is reported that he saw patients in his old age and even prescribed medicine. Mirza Jamal composed a number of Persian poems as well. He died on April 20, 1853.

The date of composition of *Tarikh-e Qarabagh* is unknown. The manuscript used in this translation states only that Shahamir Beglarov came to Shushi in 1847 and asked that a history of Qarabagh be provided for the viceroy's new administration. A careful reading of the manuscript makes it clear that Mirza Jamal already possessed such a work. Internal

---

Iosif Antonovich Reutt' (sometimes spelled Reutte) was born in 1786. In 1801 he took part in the war against the Lezgis and in 1804 he participated in the siege of Erevan and the battle of Edjmiadsin. In 1805 he took part in the campaign against the khan of Shirvan and in 1806 he took part in the siege of Baku. He was one of the defenders at Shushi when that fortress was attcked by Iran at the start of the Second Russo-Iranian war. He crossed the Arax together with the Russian army and after the conclusion of that war stayed in the Caucasus as an administrator. He died in Tiflis in 1855.

[19] The Second Russo-Iranian war ended with the Treaty of Torkmanchay (Turkmenchai), by which Iran lost the Khanates of Erevan and Nakhichevan (see map 5).

[20] M. S. Vorontsov was the first viceroy of the Caucasus, see note 7 in text for more details.

[21] Adol'f Petrovich Berzhe was born on July 28, 1828. He was the son of a French nobleman who, in 1805, came to Russia and assumed the post of Lecturer in French at the University of St. Petersburg. Berzhe attended the same university, graduating in 1851 with a degree in Oriental languages. Soon after he joined the administration of Viceroy Vorontsov in Tiflis. He wrote numerous articles in Caucasian journals and newpapers. He conducted research in Iran (1853-1855) and throughout Transcaucasia, resulting in a number of studies on the history, geography, archeology, and languages of the region. His best known work is his *French-Persian Dictionary*. In 1864 he was appointed the editor-in-chief of the *Akty* (see note 24), a post in which he served until his death on January 31, 1886 in Tiflis.

evidence suggests that he simply added the introductory and concluding remarks, as well as a number of short chapters, in order to please the
viceroy and to reinstate his pension from the Russian government.[22] The
repetitive nature of some of the material, as well as the sudden appearance of socioeconomic information listed in catalog fashion, also supports the notion that the additional material must have been written in
response to specific questions on taxation, land tenure, and administration which were of great interest to the Transcaucasian administrators
in Tiflis.

There is other evidence to suggest that an earlier version of the history
existed. A number of paragraphs of Mirza Jamal's history appear almost
verbatim in Adigozal Beg's *Qarabagh-name* of 1845, a detailed political
narrative which ends in 1828.[23] The question, then, is who borrowed
from whom? An examination of both works shows that no material
from Adigozal's much larger work appears in the *Tarikh-e Qarabagh*. It
is clear that Adigozal, who was writing a comprehensive history of the
region, borrowed material from various sources, including *Tarikh-e
Qarabagh*. In addition, there are certain passages in the *Tarikh-e Qarabagh*,
that only an eyewitness, such as Mirza Jamal, could have written.

Our biographical information on Mirza Jamal indicates that General
Ermolov made use of Mirza Jamal's knowledge of the history of the
region. As already noted, Ermolov began gathering statistical and other
data on Qarabagh immediately after the flight of Mahdi Qoli Khan to
Iran in 1822, and his successors continued this process throughout
Transcaucasia. All of this data was collected in the state archives in Tiflis
and St. Petersburg; some of it was later printed in various collections and
histories.[24] It is, therefore, certain that it was during the period of
information gathering (1823-1840) or immediately after his retirement,
sometime between 1840 and 1844, that Mirza Jamal wrote his history of

---

[22] The best indication of this is the fact that throughout the text Mirza Jamal
refers to both crown prince 'Abbas Mirza and Mahdi Qoli Khan without the
adjectival "the late." On pages 53, 57, 62 of the Persian text (pp. 128, 131, 138
English translation), in the short, additional chapters, however, they are referred
to as "the late 'Abbas Mirza" and "the late Mahdi Qoli Khan."

[23] For information on Adigozal Beg's work, see below.

[24] The best and most useful of these is the famous *Akty sobrannye Kavkazskoiu
Arkheograficheskoiu Kommissieiu*, 12 vols. (Tiflis, 1866-1904), generally referred to
as the *Akty*.

Qarabagh.[25] In any case, Mirza Jamal's work must have been available prior to 1845, the date of Adigozal Beg's *Qarabagh-name*.[26]

A second puzzle is the number of different manuscript versions of the *Tarikh-e Qarabagh* that existed. The manuscript used for this translation is an 1877/78 copy by an unknown scribe, made years after the death of Mirza Jamal.[27] The scribe clearly states that it is a copy of the 1847 version presented to Vorontsov, made, he admits, in great haste and without checking against the original. It is the only version listed, as MS. B-712/11603, by the Academy of Sciences of Azerbaijan. With one exception,[28] the Russian, Azeri, and Turkish translators have all used this manuscript with no mention that they have seen any other manuscripts of this work. Thus, there were at least three manuscripts: manuscript A, the earliest version, written sometime between 1823 and 1844; manuscript B, the 1847 version, presented, with some additions, to Vorontsov; and manuscript C, the 1877/78 copy, the facsimile of which is reproduced in this study.

The story does not end here. In 1855, Berzhe translated Mirza Jamal's work into Russian and published it in the newspaper *Kavkaz*, under the title of "Karabag."[29] His is a simplified translation, minus the colorful honorifics, blessings, and complimentary terms. Berzhe's translation does not include the preface and dedication to Vorontsov, nor the short concluding chapters, which are contained in manuscript C. The final chapter, detailing the Russian arrival in the region, is also condensed. Interestingly, Berzhe's translation has a number of paragraphs which do not appear in manuscript C.[30] The information in these paragraphs, however, appear almost *verbatim*, in Adigozal Beg's *Qarabagh-name*. It is possible that Berzhe used manuscript A, the same version used by Adigozal Beg. Berzhe, whose veracity and care in presenting documents

---

[25] Internal evidence once again supports this contention. 'Abbas Mirza, who died in 1833, and Mahdi Qoli Khan, who died in 1845, are both described as living persons in the main body of the text. This suggests that Mirza Jamal wrote the core of his history before 1845 (see also note 22).

[26] *Qarabagh-name*, p. 44.

[27] The date of this copy is 1294 hijri, corresponding to the year 1877/78. The Russian, Azeri, and Turkish translators have erroneously calculated it as 1875.

[28] Berzhe's earlier translation, as will be noted, uses a different version, see below.

[29] Issues numbered 61, 62, 63, 65, 68, and 69, published from August 6 to September 3, 1855, pp. 259-298.

[30] These paragraphs are collated within the text of this translation and appear in *italics* to distinguish them from Mirza Jamal's text (manuscript C) used in this translation.

is evident in the *Akty*, does not indicate that he had consulted other sources in preparing his translation.

In 1959 Russian and Azeri translations of manuscript C were published together by the History Institute of the Academy of Sciences of Azerbaijan.[31] The translator F. Babaev, made a number of errors and omitted several words, as well as a significant passage.[32] The two translations themselves differ slightly, errors in one not being repeated in the other, and vice versa. The major problem with these translations, however, is the absence of notes. Except for a few remarks, the text has no annotations. The editors did include a biography of Mirza Jamal and the facsimile of the manuscript, as well as Berzhe's translation, which make it a useful work.

Following the onset of the Armeno-Azeri conflict in Nagorno-Karabakh, a Turkish translation was printed in 1990 in Ankara.[33] Prepared by Tahir Sünbül, and included in the series *Kök Sosyal ve Stratejik Arastirmalar Serisi*, the text is a Turkish translation of the 1959 Azeri translation, including its introduction and few remarks, but also all of its errors and omissions. It does not include the Berzhe material, however.

The copy of *Tarikh-e Qarabagh* used in this translation is the same manuscript C, which is written in the *nasta'liq* script, occasionally combined with the *shekaste* script. The conversion of dates from the Muslim calendar to the Christian presented problems for Mirza Jamal, who did not possess the conversion charts developed later. The value of Mirza Jamal's history, however, is that events which occurred in Qarabagh from the 1740s to 1806 are described in great detail. It is, in fact, solely a history of the khanate of Qarabagh and its two khans, Panah and Ebrahim. Mirza Jamal does, of course, occasionally exaggerate the accomplishments of the khans, as well as praise his new patrons, the Russians. Unlike Adigozal Beg's history, however, which is openly biased in favor of the Russians, Mirza Jamal focuses his narrative on the Javanshir khans. He does not shy away from discussing the murder of Ebrahim Khan by the Russians, a subject avoided by Adigozal Beg. His details provide rare information and

---

[31] Mirza Dzhamal Dzhevanshir Karabagskii, *Istoriia Karabaga* (Baku, 1959); Mirzä Jamal Javanshir Garabaghi, *Garabagh Tarikhi* (Bakï, 1959). Since the work is in Persian, I have retained the Persian pronunciation of Mirza Jamal Javanshir Qarabaghi, and *Tarikh-e Qarabagh*.

[32] The passage in question involved the killing of Armenians and the construction of a tower from their heads. The translator has added an ellipsis, clearly indicating that something has been omitted. There was no attempt, however, to delete this passage from the Persian original, which is attached in its entirety.

[33] Mirza Cemal Cevansir Karabaghli, *Karabagh Tarihi* (Ankara, 1990).

valuable insight into the history of a province which are not to be found in other sources or general histories of Iran.

The second primary source on Qarabagh is the work by Mirza Adigozal Beg (ca. 1780-1848) entitled *Qarabagh-name*.[34] The author, the son of Ahvardi-Beg, one of the begs of the Ikirmi-dort[35] tribal confederation, was born in Qarabagh. He completed his education but was forced, together with his family, to flee Qarabagh during Aqa Mohammad Khan's invasion of 1795. By age twenty he was in Tiflis, in the service of Peter Kovalenskii, tsar Paul's envoy to the court of Giorgi XII, the last king of Georgia. Here he began to study Russian. After the Russian annexation of Georgia in 1801, he joined the Russian army under the command of Major General Lisanevich[36] and eventually rose to the rank of captain and served with Prince Madatov. He became a trusted official in the Russian administration, acquired some wealth, and retired in 1830. In the last years of his life he was a member of the provincial court of Qarabagh and was involved in the internal affairs of the province. In 1845, at the request of the vice-governor of Tiflis, Lieutenant Colonel Mikhail Petrovich Koliubakin,[37] he wrote his history of Qarabagh under the Persian title, *Qarabagh-name*, in which he detailed the political history of the province from the coronation of Nader Shah in 1736 to the Treaty of Torkmanchay in 1828.

Adigozal's work has an introduction, twelve chapters, and an autobiography. The value of Adigozal's history is that it contains information on

---

[34] In Azeri it reads: Mirzä Adïgözäl-Bäy, *Garabaghnamä*. The Russian version reads: Mirza Adigezal'-Bek, *Karabag-name*. Since the work was originally written in Persian, I have decided to use the Persian pronunciation of Adigozal Beg and *Qarabagh-name* in the text. The bibliography will contain the Russian transliteration.

[35] According to Sharaf-khan Bidlisi, the Ikirmi-dort was a confederation composed of twenty four Kurdish tribes who lived in the plains of Qarabagh, *Sharaf-name*, I (Moscow, 1967), p. 370; see also note 69 in the text.

[36] Major General Dimitri Tikhonovich Lisanevich was born in 1780. At the age of twenty he was stationed in the Caucasus and served under Tsitsianov, where he was promoted several times. Following the death of Tsitsianov he became the commandant of the Shushi fortress. In 1807 he returned to Russia and fought in the Napoleonic wars. In 1824 he returned to the Caucasus. A year later, on July 22, 1825, he was killed by a Chechen whom he had insulted.

[37] N. P. Koliubakin was born in 1810. Between 1836 and 1863 he was in the Caucasus serving in various non-military posts, including administering the Erevan and Kutais provinces. In 1863 he left for Moscow, where he was appointed a senator. He died in 1868.

both the khans and the Armenian *meliks* of Qarabagh that is not included in Mirza Jamal's history, and which together with the latter presents a more complete picture of the region. It is valuable as well for its information on the years 1806-1828, a period not covered by Mirza Jamal.

The original Persian manuscript is to be found in the Literature Institute of Azerbaijan. It was translated into Russian and edited by V. N. Leviatov, and published in 1950, without the facsimile of the Persian original, by the History Institute of the Academy of Sciences of Azerbaijan.[38] Leviatov, has provided adequate annotations, but has omitted several passages.[39]

The third primary source is by Ahmad Beg Javanshir (1828-1903).[40] He was born in the village of Kahrizli in the Kebirli district of the Shushi region. The village was originally a *toyul* [41] of his father, Ja'far Qoli Beg, and was free from taxation. His grandfather was Mohammad Beg, and his great-grandfather, who, according to Ahmad Beg, was to succeed Panah Khan, was Mehr 'Ali Beg, the brother of Ebrahim Khan of Qarabagh. He studied Persian and Arabic until the age of fifteen. Thanks to the administrative and judicial reforms of the early 1840s, he managed to enroll in a Russian school. In 1843, at the request of Mahdi Qoli Khan, Ahmad Beg was admitted, at government expense, to the Pavlovskii Cadet Corps School at St. Petersburg. He graduated in 1848 and joined the hussars under the command of Constantine, the son of Tsar Nicholas I. He served at the start of the Crimean War, and was decorated and promoted to the rank of captain. A wound he had received during a duel

---

[38] An Azeri translation may have been published at that time, but I have not been able to locate it. An Armenian translation in manuscript form, by an unknown scribe, is in the Matenadaran Archives in Erevan (manuscript number 4463). In addition to the autobiography supplied by Mirza Adigozal, there are two articles on Adigozal Beg, T. I. Ter-Grigorian, "Mirza Adigezal-Bek Karabakhskii," and A. N. Gaziyants, "K biografii Mirza Adigezal-Beka," both in *Doklady Akademii Nauk Azerbaidzhanskoi S.S.R.*, 9 (1948), 405-408. The above biographical information is derived from all these sources.

[39] The deletions are identified by ellipses. One of these deletions is made in a section involving the killing of Armenian *meliks* by Panah Khan.

[40] The Russian transliteration is Akhmedbek Dzhavanshir and the Azeri, Ähmedbäy Javanshir. To be consistant, I have decided to use the Persian pronunciation of Ahmad Beg in the text. The bibliography will contain the Russian and Azeri transliterations.

[41] *Toyul* (*tiyul* or *tuyul*) is a land grant given in compensation for service. For details, see G. Bournoutian, *The Khanate of Erevan under Qajar Rule, 1795-1828* (Costa Mesa, Ca., 1992), pp. 128-132.

in 1850, however, forced him to retire in 1854 and to return to Qarabagh. He became involved in agriculture and in reconstructing the Govur-arkh canal, a project for which plans were drawn but never realized. In the 1870s he was asked to join a commission to verify the ancestry and petitions of those who claimed to be begs or exempt from taxation. His knowledge of important local families helped to expose false claims, and his enemies had him arrested. He later returned to his birthplace and began reading history and literature. In 1883 he wrote his short history, which was published in the newspaper *Kavkaz* in 1884[42] and republished in Shushi in 1901. The work, entitled *O politicheskom sushchestvovanii Karabakhskogo khanstva (s 1747 po 1805 god)*, is in five chapters and was edited by E. B. Shukiurzade, with a modicum of notes, and published in Russian and Azeri by the History Institute of the Academy of Sciences of Azerbaijan in 1961.[43] Ahmad Beg's background makes it clear that his history has a Russian orientation. The pride of his Javanshir heritage comes through, nevertheless, particularly in passages discussing his great-grandfather, Mehr 'Ali Beg, who, he claims, was disinherited by Ebrahim Khan.[44] His work covers the history of the khanate of Qarabagh from the death of Nader Shah and the appointment of Panah Khan as the khan of Qarabagh in 1747/48 to the signing of the Russo-Qarabaghi treaty in 1805. It, therefore, complements Mirza Jamal's chronology, and provides additional information on several topics.

The fourth published primary source is by 'Abbas Qoli Aqa Bakikhanov (1794-1847),[45] referred to by some Azeris as one of their earliest intellectuals and historians. Bakikhanov, who wrote poetry and scientific works as well, was the first to write a scholarly monograph on the history of greater Shirvan, that is, the region which later encompassed most of the Azerbaijan Republic. His work, entitled *Golestan-e Eram*, utilizes histories and geographies written by ancient, medieval, and modern authors and covers the history of the region from ancient

---

[42] Issue no. 139. The only version of this work, including its first publication, is in Russian. It is probable that the author, with his Russian education, wrote the work in that language. This is the only primary source used in this study not written in Persian.

[43] The Azeri title is *Garabagh khanlïghïnïn siyasi väziyyätinä dair [1747-ji ildän 1805-ji ilä gädär]* (Bakï, 1961). The above biographical information on Ahmad Beg was gathered by Shukiurzade and was included in the 1961 edition.

[44] This claim has colored Ahmad Beg's version of certain events, see note 206 in text.

[45] Azeri pronunciation is Abbas Kulu Agha Bakikhanli.

times into the nineteenth century. He wrote this monumental work in Persian. Although a number of manuscripts of his work were available, the first publication was a poor Russian translation in Baku in 1926. The Azeri version published by the Academy of Sciences appeared only in 1951.[46] In 1970 a critical edition based on five Persian manuscripts was published.[47] The project was supervised by 'Abdo'l-Karim Alizadeh, of the History Institute, who deserves praise for his significant contribution to serious scholarship of the region. Although Bakikhanov does not concentrate on Qarabagh, his information is extremely accurate, and is helpful in resolving some of the chronological problems presented in the other sources on Qarabagh.

At the time of this writing, there are a number of unpublished manuscripts in the archives of the Academy of Sciences of Azerbaijan. These include Akhund Sa'id Mir-Mahdi Hashembeg-oglu Musavi's (1811-1893) Ketab-e Tarikh-e Qarabagh,[48] Mirza Yusef Nersesov Qarabaghi's Tarikh-e Safi,[49] Mirza Rahim Fena's Tarikh-e jadid-e Qarabagh, Hasan 'Ali Khan Qarabaghi's Qarabagh-name, and an untitled manuscript by Mirza Jamal's son, Reza Qoli Mirza Jamalbeg-oglu.[50] They are all, presumably, written in Persian.[51]

2) Chronicles of Iranian History

In this category are the chroniclers who detailed the history of the shahs of Iran from the seventeenth through the nineteenth centuries. Although

---

[46] Russian translation reads, Giulistan-i Iram, Azeri translation is Gülistan-i Iräm. Since the work was written in Persian, I have decided to retain the Persian pronunciation of Golestan-e Eram.

[47] The earliest was written in 1844 and the latest in 1866. They are listed as (M-49/6258) and (B-19/3312) in the archives of the Academy of Sciences of Azerbaijan. It is this critical edition which was consulted for the present study.

[48] Thanks to Shukiurzade, some information exists on the author and the content of Ketab-e Tarikh-e Qarabagh. He was born in the village of Mamyrly in Zangezur and later moved to the Togh settlement. He wrote poetry under the name Khazani and was fluent in Arabic and Persian. His manuscript differs from all others in that it discusses economic conditions of the khanate and its administrative divisions. The manuscript is number 14 of the manuscript collection of the Academy of Sciences of Azerbaijan.

[49] This work is MS. number 3935 of the History Institute Archives of the Academy of Sciences of Azerbaijan.

[50] This work is listed under MS. number B-470/5224. Also see note 3 above.

[51] The current conflict in Nagorno-Karabakh has generated new Azeri editions of previously-published primary sources as well as excerpts from some of the above unpublished material. Unfortunately, passages dealing with the Ar-

these primary histories contain little on Qarabagh, their importance is in confirming or contradicting certain facts presented by the Qarabaghi sources. They also enable the reader to observe how central policies affected local conditions. The principal histories of Iran are divided according to dynasties, which do, at times, overlap.

The two sources of the Safavid period used here are *Tarikh-e Alamara-ye 'Abbasi*, by Eskandar Monshi and *Tadhkirat al-Muluk* by an anonymous scribe. The first is the history of Iran during the reign of Shah 'Abbas and was written by his chief secretary. It details not only Shah 'Abbas's reign, but also provides valuable information about earlier rulers and their relations with neighboring states, as well as about the arts and sciences in Iran at that time. The second is a manual of Safavid administration, which contains valuable information on socioeconomic conditions as well as on institutions in the late seventeenth and early eighteenth centuries. Both works have relevant material on Transcaucasia. Although I have examined the Persian originals, I have decided to use their excellent English translations. The former was translated as *History of Shah 'Abbas* by Roger Savory in 1978, and the latter as *Tadhkirat al-Muluk: A Manual of Safavid Administration* by Vladimir Minorsky in 1943.

The rise of the Afshars and the rule of Nader Shah has found its champion in Nader's secretary, Mirza Mohammad Mahdi Koukabi Astarabadi, whose *Tarikh-e Jahangoshay-e Naderi* contains detailed material on Nader's reign. I have used an illuminated manuscript composed in 1171 hijri (1757/58), the facsimile of which was recently reprinted in Tehran in 1991. Mohammad Kazem Marvi's *Alamara-ye Naderi* is finally available in a new edition and sheds additional light on Nader's campaigns in Transcaucasia, as well as his relations with the Armenians of Qarabagh. Mirza Mohammad Khalil Mar'ashi Safavi's *Majma' ot-Tavarikh* (Tehran, 1983) adds some minor details to this period as well.

The events between the death of Nader and the rise of Aqa Mohammad Khan Qajar have been chronicled in a number of histories. All have been published in critical editions. They include, *Mojmal ot-Tavarikh*, by Abo'l-Hasan ibn Mohammad Amin Golestane (Tehran, 1965); *Golshan-e Morad*, by Mirza Mohammad Abo'l-Hasan Ghaffari Kashani (Tehran, 1990); *Tarikh-e Giti-gosha*, by Mirza Mohammad Sadeq Musavi Nami Esfahani (Tehran, 1984); and *Rostam ot-Tavarikh*, by Mohammad Hashem Asef (Tehran, 1973). They all detail the history of

---

menian presence in the region have been deleted or altered. It is hoped that eventually these and other archival materials will be made available to scholars in editions which will include the facsimile of the original text. Also see note 46 in text.

the successors of Nader and particularly the period of Karim Khan Zand and the events involving Mohammad Hasan Khan Qajar, Azad Khan Afghan, and Fath 'Ali Khan Afshar, all of which affected the history of Qarabagh and other parts of Transcaucasia.

The history of the early Qajars (1750-1834) is related by a number of chroniclers. Some were secretaries of the shahs or princes of the realm, other worked in the central or in provincial chanceries. The Qajars were thoroughly involved in Qarabagh and others parts of Transcaucasia; in fact, a branch of the Qajars ruled in Erevan and Ganje from the time of the Safavids. Mohammad Hasan Khan Qajar fought Panah Khan Javanshir; while Aqa Mohammad Khan, Fath 'Ali Shah, and 'Abbas Mirza all campaigned in Qarabagh and other parts of Transcaucasia. An examination of the main sources of Qajar history is, therefore, crucial in affirming or refuting certain facts presented by local historians. The sources used in this study are: *Tarikh-e Farsname-ye Naseri*, by Haj Mirza Hasan Hoseini Fasa'i, an 1314 hijri (1896/97) calligraphic edition reprinted (2 volumes in one) Tehran, n.d. (ca. 1965); *Tarikh-e Rouzat os-Safa-ye Naseri*, by Reza Qoli Khan Hedayat, vol. IX (Qom, 1960); *Ma'aser-e Soltaniye*, by 'Abd or-Razzaq ibn Najaf Qoli Donboli, an 1241 hijri (1825/26) calligraphic edition reprinted in Tehran, 1973; *Tarikh-e Mohammadi* (also known as *Ahsan ot-Tavarikh*), by Mohammad Fathollah b. Mohammad Taqi Saru'i (Tehran, 1992); *Nasekh ot-Tavarikh* by Mirza Mohammad Taqi Lesan ol-molk Sepehr (Tehran, 1965), and Mohammad Hasan Khan E'temad os-Saltane's, *Tarikh-e Montazam-e Naseri*, vols. II-III (Tehran, 1985-88).

3) Other Sources
A number of works written by medieval Arab and Persian geographers are essential to any study of the region, particularly since place names changed with the successive invasions by Arabs, Turks, and Mongols. Hamdollah Mostoufi's *Nozhat ol-Qulub* (Tehran, 1983), Abu-Eshaq Estakhri's *Masalek va Mamalek* (Tehran, 1989), Abo'l-Qasem Ibn 'Abdollah Khordadhbe's, *Al-Masalek va al-Mamalek* (Tehran, 1991) and Vladimir Minorsky's translation of *Hudud al-'Alam* (London, 1970) are among these.

Arab historians give accurate details on the early Muslim period in Qarabagh and the rest of Transcaucasia. These include Ya'qubi's, *Tarikh* (Leiden, 1969) and (Tehran, 1983); Moqaddasi's, *Ahsan al-Taqasim* (Leiden, 1967), Ibn Hauqal's, *Kitab Surat al-Arz* (Leiden, 1938/39), Baladhuri's, *Futuh al-Buldan* (Tehran, 1967). Minorsky's translation of parts of *Jami' al-duwal* (with material from the *Bab al-Abwab*) as *The History of Sharvan and Darband in the 10th-11th centuries* (London, 1958), and his *Studies in Caucasian History* (London, 1953), complete the list of the main primary sources used in this study.

Additional primary and a number of secondary sources, such as Mahdi Bamdad's biographical dictionary of Iranian notables, were used primarily to explicate points raised in the footnotes, and are included in the bibliography.

The Armenians of Qarabagh

The region west and south of the Kur, east of the Hazar, and north of the Arax Rivers had been part of an Armenian state from the second century B.C. and formed parts of the ancient Armenian provinces of Artsakh and Utik. Following the first partition of Armenia between the Byzantine empire and Sasanian Iran in A.D. 387, these provinces were severed from Armenia and combined with Caucasian Albania, which was situated east of the Kur River, to form a new administrative unit called *Ran*. The Armenian population, led by their feudal lords, continued to live in the region until the mid-seventh century, when it was conquered by the Arabs. The Arabs referred to the region as *al-Ran* (pronounced ar-Ran), which in time became *Arran*.[52] The town of Partav, renamed Barda', situated just west of the Kur, became the Arab administrative center. For the next three centuries, the Arabs struggled to dominate the Armenian nobility. Throughout all this period, the Armenians maintained a majority in southern Arran until the eleventh century.[53] Turkish and Mongol invasions from the eleventh to the thirteenth centuries affected, for the first time, the population balance of southern Arran. Death and destruction, forced or voluntary conversions, and, most of all, emigration reduced the Armenian population and caused most of the remaining Armenian nobles and their followers to seek refuge in the mountains of the region. Armenians thus evacuated the lowlands and under the leadership of their princes built fortresses and strongholds known later as *saqnaq* or *seghnakh* in the highlands of Arran. In fact, following the fall of the Armenian Bagratid and Cilician kingdoms between the eleventh and the fourteenth centuries, these districts were among the few areas where Armenians continued to have an active political, military, and intellectual leadership.[54] Between the thirteenth and late fifteenth

---

[52] See note 39 in the text.

[53] See notes 46 and 48 in the text.

[54] The monasteries of Tatev and Gladzor, located in Zangezur, and the See of Gandzasar in the district of Jraberd in Qarabagh were important Armenian intellectual and religious centers for several centuries.

centuries Armenians from many areas to the west, gravitated to these safe havens. Eventually, a number of Armenian nobles, now called *meliks*,[55] ruled in the mountains of Qarabagh and Siunik (Zangezur). The invasions of Timur and the incursion of Turkmen tribes in the fourteenth and fifteenth centuries further reduced the Armenian population of the lowlands.[56] From the fourteenth century onward, the term *Arran* was gradually replaced by the Turko-Persian compound word *Qarabagh*,[57] meaning "Black Garden."[58] Finally, the constant wars between the Ottomans and the Iranians, from the start of the sixteenth through the mid-eighteenth centuries, as well as the dynastic struggles in Iran through most of the eighteenth century, resulted in the forced and voluntary emigration of Armenians from eastern Armenia to neighboring regions, particularly Georgia and Iran. Although the Armenians had become a minority in their homeland, the mountains

---

[55] The term is from the Arabic *malik* which has a variety of meanings including "prince" or "general." See notes 66 and 67 in text. The word entered the Armenian vocabulary as well.

[56] The Armenian presence in the lowlands of Qarabagh was still evident in the late fourteenth and early fifteenth century. H. R. Roemer mentions that Qarabagh in the fourteenth century was still considered an Armenian territory, see "Timur in Iran," in *Cambridge History of Iran*, VI (Cambridge, 1986), p. 59. The German traveler Johannes Schiltberger, who visited Qarabagh in the early fifteenth century, states that although the Muslims had taken possession of Qarabagh, there were still Armenian villages in the region, *The Bondage and Travels of Johann Schiltberger* (New York, 1970), p. 86. By the Safavid era, most Qarabaghi Armenians had taken refuge in the mountains of Qarabagh.

[57] *Qarabagh* is the Persian, *Garabagh* the Azeri, *Gharabagh* the Armenian, *Karabagh* the Turkish, and *Karabakh* the Russian transliteration.

[58] The term first appears in fourteenth-century Persian and Georgian works, see Hamdollah Mostoufi Qazvini, *Ketab-e Nozhat ol-Qulub* (Tehran, 1983), pp. 56, 181-82; *Kart'lis Tskhovreba* (Georgian Chronicle) II (Tbilisi, 1959), p. 240. Although the term is commonly attributed to the rich soil and vegetation of the region, Vladimir Minorsky noted that the name was perhaps connected with some now-extinct Turkic tribe, see *Tadhkirat al-Muluk*, p. 166. Qarabagh's topography divides it into three unique regions: Mountainous Qarabagh, or the highlands west of Aghdam, ranging in elevation from 2000 to 12,000 feet; the central valleys, ranging from 500 to 2000 feet in elevation; and the Qarabagh steppe or south-eastern lowlands between the Arax and Kur Rivers, which join the Moghan Steppe in Iranian Azerbaijan. The Armenians were forced out first from the steppes, then the valleys, and were finally pushed into the mountains.

of Qarabagh and Zangezur remained one of the few areas where they continued to maintain a sizeable majority.[59]

Throughout its history, Armenia was subject to partition between the neighboring empires. The last such division came in 1639, in the treaty of Zohab (Zuhab) between the Safavid shah Safi I and the Ottoman sultan Murad IV. The partition left the historic Armenian lands east of the Arpachay (Akhurian) to the Iranians. The Safavids divided their Armenian possessions into two regions, *Chukhur-e Sa'd* and Qarabagh, each under a governor-general or *beglarbegi*.[60] (See map 1). Eventually travelers, historians, and geographers referred to these *beglarbegis* as *Persian Armenia*. After the fall of the Safavids, the Ottomans invaded the region in 1723 and remained there for over a decade. They succeeded in subduing all of Georgia and *Persian Armenia*, save the mountain regions of Qarabagh and Zangezur. Here, the *meliks* under the leadership of David Beg managed, from their mountain fortresses, to resist until Nader Shah expelled the Turks from Transcaucasia in 1735. Nader rewarded the Armenian *meliks* and broke the power of the Turkmen tribes of Qarabagh by removing a number of their tribes, including the Javanshir, to Iran. He also reorganized *Persian Armenia* into four units, known as the *velayats* or provinces of Erevan, Nakhichevan, Ganje, and Qarabagh. (See map 3.)

After the death of Nader, the Turkic tribes returned to Qarabagh. Panah Khan, the leader of the Javanshir tribe, soon expanded his domain and by 1748 established a khanate which lasted until 1806. His son, Ebrahim Khan, extended the influence of Qarabagh into Zangezur, Nakhichevan, Qaradagh, and Ganje. Both khans clashed with a number of the *meliks*, killing some and forcing others to take refuge in Iran, Ganje and Georgia.[61] The *meliks*, who had sought the assistance of Peter the Great during the Turkish invasion,[62] now petitioned Catherine the Great to oust the khans from their homeland.

---

[59] The five Armenian districts of Qarabagh became known as the *khamse* (*khamsa* or "five" in Arabic), see note 66 in text.

[60] Erevan was the center of Chukhur-e Sa'd and Ganje the center of Qarabagh (also see note 68 in text).

[61] During the second half of the eighteenth century, Panah Khan and especially Ebrahim Khan were responsible for the death or emigration of a large part of the Armenian population. According to a Russian primary source, the Armenians, by the end of 1804, were reduced to 4,000 families, *Akty*, II, 623.

[62] Peter the Great invaded the region in 1723. The Russians, however, concentrated their efforts along the Caspian littoral and did not reach *Persian Armenia* or Georgia. By 1735, the inhospitable climate and the rise of Nader Shah encouraged Russia to withdraw from Transcaucasia.

In the late eighteenth century, during the second Russian penetration into Transcaucasia, a plan for the creation of an Armenian state out of Qarabagh, Erevan, and Nakhichevan, was presented to Catherine. A united Georgia, in the meantime, would take over Ganje. These two large Christian vassal states would act as a buffer against their Muslim neighbors, and would help Russia extend its influence in Transcaucasia (see map 5). It became evident, however, that the Armenians were too scattered and, except for the mountainous regions of Qarabagh-Zangezur, unarmed and leaderless. Furthermore, Georgia had a dynasty and already possessed a significant Armenian population, which was increased daily by immigrants from Erevan, Ganje, and Qarabagh, who were fleeing the unstable conditions in their lands. Georgia, therefore, became the central focus of the Russian expansion in the region.

After annexing Georgia at the start of the nineteenth century, the Russians made a concerted effort to conquer the rest of Transcaucasia. Following a number of armed conflicts, the Russians, assisted by Armenian volunteers, achieved their objective and the lands north of the Arax River became part of the Russian empire at the conclusion of the First and Second Russo-Iranian wars. After Russia gained control of Qarabagh, it became, despite its significant Armenian population, part of the Muslim Province which included the combined territory of the khanates of Shirvan, Shakki, Qobbe, Baku, Qarabagh, and parts of Talesh. There were several reasons for the inclusion of Qarabagh in the Muslim Province. One was the treaty which Russia in 1805 made with Ebrahim Khan of Qarabagh, which guaranteed his family the governorship of the region in exchange for his becoming a Russian vassal. This agreement was, to some degree, honored until 1822. Another was the fact that the Armenian *meliks* of Qarabagh were not a cohesive military or political group. They lacked a leader and their struggle against the Qarabaghi khans was not to create a new Armenia but driven by regional interests. Sentiments of ethnicity, religious unity, and nationalism had yet to be developed among the Armenians. Moreover, the Armenians, except in the mountains of Qarabagh, were a minority in the province.[63]

---

[63] Russian statistics indicate that in 1810 the Armenians composed some 21 percent of the population of Qarabagh, *Akty*, IV, pp. 37-38. In 1823, after the return of those who had fled the region, the Armenian population had increased to an estimated 30 percent, *Opisanie Karabakhskoi Provintsii sostavlennoe v 1823 g.* (no pagination). By 1832, the Armenian population had increased to just a third of the total inhabitants. The overwhelming majority of the Qarabagh Armenians, however, as Mirza Jamal's text indicates, lived in the five mountainous districts. Thus one-third of the population of Qarabagh (or the Armenians), lived in

Finally, the khanates of Erevan and Nakhichevan, or the remainder of *Persian Armenia*, were still under Iranian rule. The conflict over their control was not concluded until both the Second Russo-Iranian and the Russo-Turkish wars had ended in 1828 and 1829 respectively, by which time the administrative configurations were set for the time being.

Although at first Russian administrators generally permitted local customs and administrative practices, this policy was soon reversed. In 1840, Russia began a major provincial reorganization in the Caucasus. The entire region was divided into two large provinces: the Georgian-Imeret'i, with headquarters in Tiflis, and the Caspian, with headquarters in New Shemakha. Qarabagh was included in the Caspian Province. General dissatisfaction prompted the tsar to appoint a viceroy, Vorontsov, who was more sensitive to local problems. Vorontsov reorganized the region into four provinces in 1845: Tiflis, Kutais, Shemakha, and Derbend.[64] Qarabagh became part of the Tiflis and Shemakha Provinces. Vorontsov's successors made other changes in 1862, 1867/68, 1875, and 1880, which partitioned the lands occupied by Transcaucasian Turks, Georgians, and Armenians into new administrative units.[65] Most of the territory of the khanate of Qarabagh was included in the Elizavetpol' Province. Complaints from local officials about these changes began almost immediately and continued periodically until the First World War. With the rise of political and national consciousness, first among the Armenians and Georgians and later among the Turkic population, the tsarist administration adopted three ways of resolving the political and economic demands of Transcaucasia: placating local dissatisfaction with minor reforms or promises of reform; use of force; and creating divisions among the many ethnic and religious groups living there. One of the results was conflict in Qarabagh between the Armenians and the Turkic population, which had begun to refer to itself

---

one-third of the territory of the former khanate. In that mountainous territory, the Armenians constituted an overwhelming majority of the population. In the remaining two-thirds, however, the Turkic groups constituted the majority.

[64] Armenian complaints resulted in the creation of the Erevan Province in 1849. This province essentially recreated the Armenian Province of 1828-1840 (the combined territories of the khanates of Erevan and Nakhichevan), see G. Bournoutian, *The Khanate of Erevan Under Qajar Rule, 1795-1828* (Costa Mesa, 1992), pp. 26-28.

[65] By 1880 the administrative divisions were set and remained unchanged until the Russian Revolution of 1917. Transcaucasia was divided into the following provinces and districts: Tiflis, Kutais, Elizavetpol', Erevan, Baku, Kars, Batum, Daghestan, and Zakatal.

as Azerbaijanis, during the revolutionary years 1905-1907. Both sides, for the first time, divided along cultural, ethnic, linguistic, regional, and religious lines. Armeno-Azeri conflict intensified in the dispute over the Armenian enclave of Qarabagh during the brief period of independence of Armenia and Azerbaijan (1918-1920). By 1923, Qarabagh, despite Armenian protests, became part of Soviet Azerbaijan, but its Armenian enclave, designated as *Nagorno-Karabakh* ("Mountainous Karabakh"), was declared an autonomous region within Azerbaijan. Armenians' dissatisfaction with Nagorno-Karabakh's lack of cultural and political autonomy by 1987 resulted in their demand for the independence of Nagorno-Karabakh.

Mirza Jamal's history and the works of the other Qarabaghi historians cited in this study demonstrate that the Armenian military and economic position in Qarabagh during the eighteenth century was considerable. The Armenian population remained, for the most part, in Mountainous Qarabagh, a region, as noted, known earlier by the name of *khamse* (see map 4). A number of the Armenian *meliks* and their troops fought in several major conflicts against the khans of Qarabagh and were sought after as allies by neighboring khans and by the Persian shahs.[66] Some *meliks* and their followers were killed by the Qarabaghi khans. Others escaped the political and economic pressures and sought refuge in Iran, Ganje and Georgia, waiting for conditions in Qarabagh to improve. The leaders of this self-exiled group, in fact, eventually returned with the Russians to expel the khan, only, as the traveler George Keppel observed, to take on "the milder yoke of Russia."[67]

A Note on the Translation

The manuscript of *Tarikh-e Qarabagh* is only sixty-two pages long.[68] As in most Persian manuscripts, there are chapter headings, but no punctuation marks or paragraphs. Since it is a local history, the number of individuals named are few, especially in comparison to the major Persian chronicles of that period. They are, for the most part, identified in the footnotes. Moreover, due to the brevity of the manuscript, I have

---

[66] See chapters three through seven in the text.

[67] George Keppel, *Personal Narrative of a Journey from India to England*, II (London, 1834), p. 185.

[68] The pagination of the Persian manuscript appears in brackets in this translation.

opted for placing the explanatory comments in footnotes rather than in the introduction or a separate commentary.

A number of Persian terms have more than one meaning; I have on several occasions chosen a slightly different shade of meaning for a particular term, to fit the context of the sentence. *Tarikh-e Qarabagh* maintains the flowery epithets, honorific formulae, hyperbolic expressions, and wearisome repetitions so common in most Persian manuscripts. It does not contain, however, the numerous couplets and other verses or odes to various occasions or seasons. One of my main objectives was to make the translation readable, and to that end I pared down some of the double adjectives, honorifics, and superlatives, without changing the meaning of the text. At the same time, I retained some of Mirza Jamal's repetitiveness and verbosity to convey the flavor of the original.

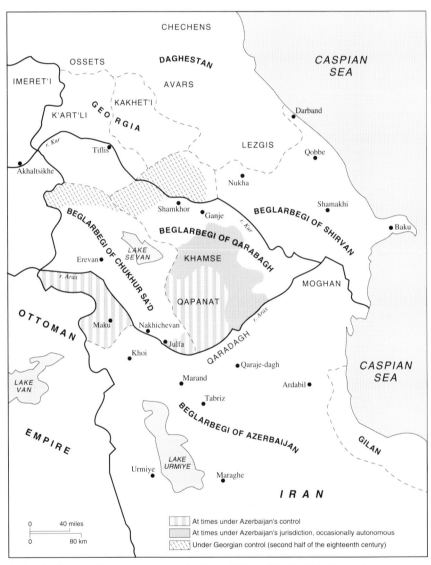

1. Azerbaijan and Transcaucasia in the Late 17th and Early 18th Centuries

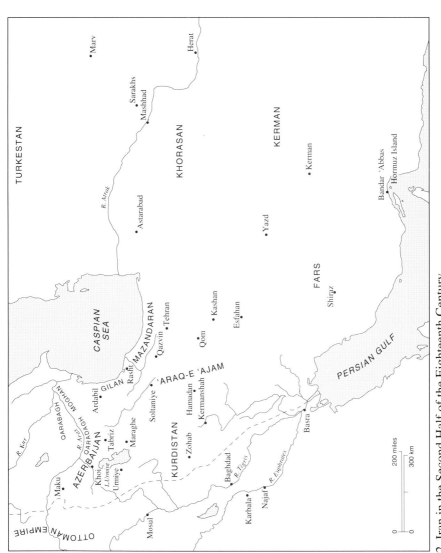

2. Iran in the Second Half of the Eighteenth Century

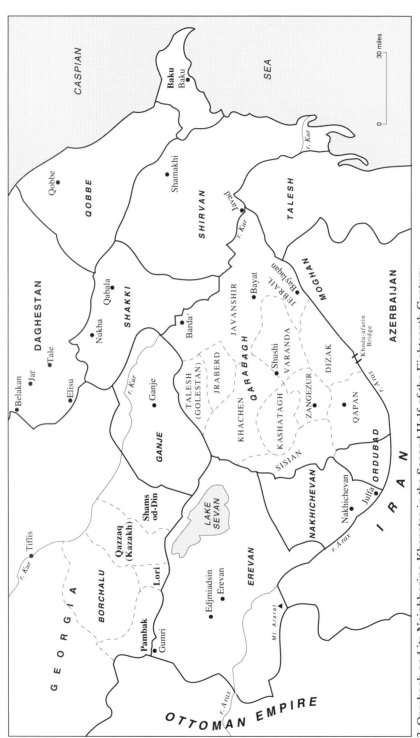

3. Qarabagh and its Neighboring Khanates in the Second Half of the Eighteenth Century

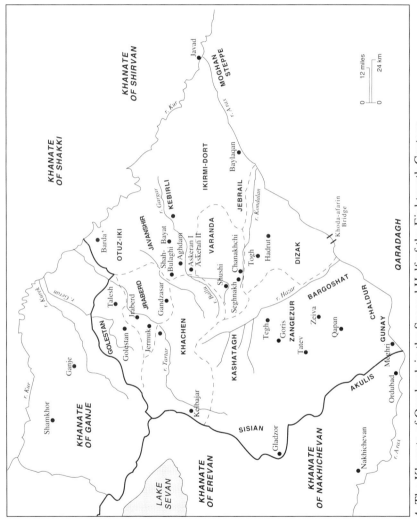

4. The Khanate of Qarabagh in the Second Half of the Eighteenth Century

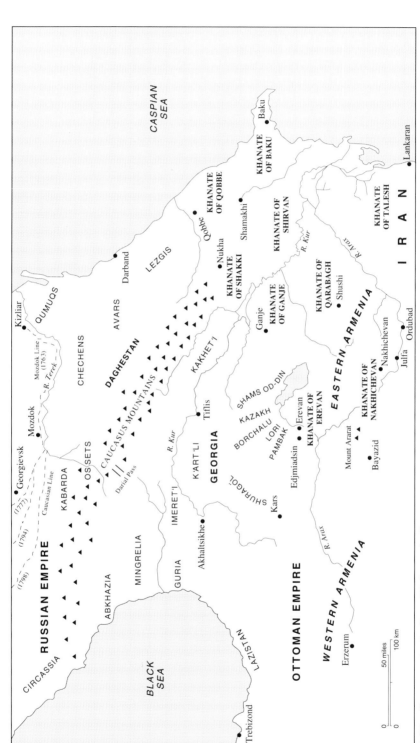

5. The Caucasus in the Late Eighteenth Century

Tarikh-e Qarabagh

English Translation

An Account of the Sovereign Rule[1] of the Late[2] Khans of the *Velayat*[3] of Qarabagh, Panah Khan and Ebrahim Khan, and Other Miscellaneous Events[4]

A copy of the text written by the late[5] Mirza Jamal Qarabaghi at the command of *sardar*[6] Vorontsov.[7]

---

[1] The Persian words *hukumat* and *esteqlal* have a number of common meanings: "absolute authority," "sovereignty," and "dominion," It is important to note that although Panah Khan, and especially, Ebrahim Khan, were the sovereign political authority in Qarabagh, they did, as will be noted, occasionally submit to Iran or Russia. One may argue, therefore, that "autonomous" would be the more correct term. The context of Mirza Jamal's chronicle, however, denotes that "sovereignty" was the meaning he wished to convey.

[2] Mirza Jamal uses the term *marhum* ("the late," or, "of blessed memory") frequently when referring to Panah or Ebrahim Khan. This sign of respect is his way of acknowledging his clan's leaders and his benefactors. In order to maintain the nature of the orginal, the term will be translated every time it appears in the text.

[3] *Velayat* encompasses several meanings, roughly equivalent to "province," "dominion," "kingdom," "state," "region," or "territory." This term will remain untranslated. With few exceptions, which will be noted, Mirza Jamal uses the term to signify a province or *khanate*.

[4] Mirza Jamal does not include the last ruler of Qarabagh, Mahdi Qoli Khan (1806-1822), the son of Ebrahim Khan, in his title. Since Russia occupied Qarabagh in 1806 and made it a protectorate, the tsar, in effect, became the suzerain of the last khan.

[5] The phrase, "written by the late," is a clear indication that this manuscript is a later copy (see introduction).

[6] The term *sardar* has a variety of meanings: "general," "field marshal," "king's lieutenant," and "commander in chief." In this context, it means "king's lieutenant" or "viceroy;" in other parts of the text it signifies "commander," "governor general," or "commander in chief." Hence this term will also remain untranslated.

[7] Prince Mikhail Semenovich Vorontsov (1785-1856) was the first viceroy of the Caucasus. His father was the Russian ambassador to London, where he grew up. Later, he joined the Russian army and fought in the Napoleonic wars. In 1823, Tsar Alexander I appointed him the governor general of southern Ukraine. His success there prompted Nicholas I, on January 30, 1845, to promote him to viceroy with unlimited powers and to extend his authority to include the Caucasus. During his ten-year tenure, Vorontsov made the Caucasian adminis-

In the Name of Allah, the Merciful, the Compassionate[8]
Infinite praise and eternal glory befits the Creator of the universe, Who places the crown of fortune and greatness on whomever He pleases, and removes it from whomever He pleases. In truth, all grandeur, might, and fortune are due to His universal grace and eternal generosity.

beyt (couplet)[9]
You decide who will be a slave and who a king
You grant good fortune to whomever You wish

After the praise and glorification of the Creator of heaven and earth, it should be obvious to all learned persons that knowledge of the past events, conditions, and distinct features of each *velayat* can only be enlightening and profitable [for the present administration].[10]

Thus, in the Muslim year 1263,[11] which corresponds to the Christian

---

tration much more effective by appointing local officials who were knowledgeable about the region, and made a name as an innovator. He resigned his post on November 29, 1854, due to ill health. The viceroyalty of the Caucasus was temporarily assigned to General Murav'ev, and in 1856, given to Prince A. I. Bariatinsky. In 1862, Grand Duke Mikhail, the youngest brother of Tsar Alexander II, was appointed to the post, in which he served until 1882. The viceroyalty was then abolished until 1905, when, due to the political upheavals of the time, a second cousin once removed of Vorontsov, Count Ilarion I. Vorontsov-Dashkov, assumed the post and performed as well as his forebear. For a detailed account of the life and accomplishments of Vorontsov, see Anthony L. H. Rhinelander, *Prince Michael Vorontsov: Viceroy to the Tsar* (Montreal, 1990).

[8] The opening line of the Qur'an's first *Surah* or Chapter (*Surat Fatihat Al-Kitab*), as well as most of the other *Surahs*. It traditionally begins chronicles of Muslim historians.

[9] Persian chroniclers habitually included lines of verse (their own or others'), quotations from the Qur'an, or various invocations within their works. Mirza Jamal, following that custom, has included two sets of verse, one at the beginning and one at the end of the text.

[10] This passage demonstrates Mirza Jamal's subtle way of arguing the value of his history, as well as giving credit to Vorontsov's insight for gathering information on former administrations (see introduction).

[11] Mirza Jamal utilizes the Arabic lunar calendar of 354/355 days starting from the date of Mohammad's departure (*hijrah*) from Mecca to Medina (July 16, 622). The hijri year 1263 began on December 20, 1846, and ended on December 8, 1847.

year 1847, the noble and distinguished colonel of the cavalry[12] Shahamir Khan Beglarov, a native of Qarabagh,[13] came to the fortress of Shushi and met with me, his sincere and old acquaintance, Mirza Jamal Javanshir Qarabaghi. I had been in the service of the khans of Qarabagh, where for many years I performed the duties of *mirza* and *vazir* of Qarabagh.[14] After their rule, I continued [2] as an employee and official of the Exalted and Mighty Russian State, performing all duties assigned to me. During our conversation, due to his kindness to me and his devotion to the general of the infantry, the recipient of many decorations and titles, the lofty Count and Prince[15] Mikhail Semenovich Vorontsov— may the kindness of the all-powerful Allah shine on him—[who is] the protector of renowned *amirs*[16] and of the rich and poor, the viceroy of His Majesty the great *padeshah*,[17] supreme emperor and bountiful *khaqan*,[18] he [Beglarov] stated that His Excellency [Vorontsov] was very eager to familiarize himself with past events in the provinces under his command and the facts about the rule and authority of the past khans.

---

[12] The text reads *bolkovnek* and *qavalir*. Mirza Jamal uses numerous Russian military terms throughout the text. The term *bolkovnek* is *polkovnik* or "colonel." *Qavalir* is the Russian term *kavaler*, literally "cavalier," but in this context, it is more probably *kavalerist*, or "cavalryman," hence colonel of the cavalry. Besides Russian terms, Mirza Jamal at times, uses local Turkish and Arabic terms. Hence, an occasional *chay* instead of the Persian *rud* (river), *qezel* instead of the Persian *qermez* or *sorkh* (red or purple). At times, instead of the customary Arabic *Allah*, he uses the Persian *Khodavand* or *Parvardegar*.

[13] Shahamir Khan came from the Beglarian *meliks* of Golestan. Like many young men from respectable families, he joined the Russian administration. For more details on the Beglarians, see Robert H. Hewsen, "The Meliks of Eastern Armenia: A Preliminary Study," *Revue Des Études Arméniennes* (new series), IX (1972), 319-321. The *meliks* of Qarabagh will be discussed below in more detail.

[14] The title of *mirza* before a name denotes a chancery scribe or secretary; after a name, the title signifies a prince of the royal house. A *vazir* was the head of the civil-financial bureau.

[15] Mirza Jamal uses the Russian terms *graf* (originally German for "count") and *kniaz'* ("prince").

[16] *Amir* or *emir* can be interpreted as "commander," "governor," "chief," "leader," "person of rank or distinction," and "prince." Vorontsov, as the viceroy of the tsar, had authority over all commanders and governors in his jurisdiction.

[17] The title of *padeshah* or "king/emperor" is a Persian one. Mirza Jamal uses it a number of times when describing great or powerful rulers.

[18] The title of *khaqan* was given to the Chinese and Mongol emperors and denoted the most powerful of all rulers.

If someone were to record the history of Qarabagh and give details of the tenure of the previous khans and presented it to this supreme governor, he would be rewarded with kindness and would earn his blessing.[19]

Since I, in my humble respect for the benevolence of the exalted prince viceroy, feel fortunate to be able to perform such a service, and to gain, for even a mere second, the glow emanating from this supreme commander, and to [also] observe his happy and kind countenance, I have therefore, relying on Allah, and without subtracting or adding anything, written the facts as I have discovered them in histories and from wise elders, as well as what I have observed and heard during my fifty years [of service].[20] [3] It is hoped that this copy,[21] presented to his court, will be accepted as a gift and will serve as evidence of my service and sincere devotion. I have divided these pages into a number of chapters. Each chapter is devoted to different events.

[May] Allah provide aid and assure success.

Chapter One:
On the First Settlements, Borders, Ancient Cities, and Rivers of the *Velayat* of Qarabagh[22]

As is recorded in old histories, the borders of Qarabagh are as follows[23]:

---

[19] Mirza Jamal wants to remind everyone, especially the Russians, of his services to the state so that he and his family would continue to receive his income and pension (see introduction).

[20] Since Mirza Jamal was born in 1773/74, it is safe to assume that he means service and not age.

[21] The term *noskhe* signifies a manuscript copy, which means that Mirza Jamal either made a copy of his history and presented it to Vorontsov or prepared an original draft (see introduction).

[22] Berzhe's translation reads, **Chapter One: Borders, Rivers, Climate,** "Karabag," 61 (1855), 260.

[23] Mirza Jamal is in fact describing the borders of the ancient Armenian provinces of Artsakh and Utik, as well as the borders of the Safavid *beglarbegi* of Qarabagh, which at that time included the territory of Ganje, see *Tadhkirat al-Muluk*, translated and explained by Vladimir Minorsky (London, 1943), pp. 101-102 and map 1.

To the south is the Aras (Arax)[24] river, from the Khoda-afarin Bridge
to the Broken Bridge,[25] which today is located within the Qazzaq,
Shams od-Din, and Damurchi-Hasanlu (Damirchi-Hasanli) *mahals*.[26]
Russian state officials call this bridge *Qrasni Mosd,*[27] which means Red
Bridge.[28]

In accordance to ancient histories, Qarabagh extended from the Khoda-afarin
Bridge on the Arax to the Broken Bridge, called by the Russians Red Bridge,

---

[24] Throughout the text Mirza Jamal uses the Iranian designation of "Aras" for
the Arax River.

[25] Mirza Jamal uses the local Turkic dialect and refers to it as *Seneq Korpi*; the
Turkish variant would be *Síníg Köprü.*

[26] The term *mahal* can be translated as "district," "area," or "zone." Occasionally it can be translated as "quarter," although *mahalle* is the more appropriate
term for quarter. "District" is the most accepted translation for *mahal. Mahal* will
also remain untranslated.

[27] The reference is to the Russian term *Krasny Most* (Red Bridge).

[28] Mirza Jamal uses the local Turkic dialect term *Qezel Korpi* or Red Bridge;
the Turkish variant would be *Kízíl Köprü.* The text of this paragraph presents a
problem. The territories of Qazzaq and Shams od-Din lie far to the north, below
Georgia (see map 3), and could not possibly form the southern borders of
Qarabagh. Mirza Jamal, having lived all his life in Qarabagh, was not likely to
make such an error. Bakikhanov also states that the borders of Qarabagh
stretched "from the Khoda-afarin Bridge to the Shulaver (Shulaveri is adjacent
to the Qazzaq and Shams od-Din districts) region of Georgia, further up from
the Broken Bridge," *Golestan-e Eram* p. 173. Adigozal Beg describes the borders
of the province, prior to the reign of Nader Shah, as follows: "from the Broken
Bridge on the Khram river (near Suri-dash) to the Khoda-afarin Bridge on the
border of Azerbaijan (as noted, this term refers to the northwestern province of
Iran, located south of the Arax), *Qarabagh-name*, p. 47. Berzhe's translation of this
passage (see below) correctly identifies the borders, as well. This leaves only two
possibilities: either the scribe made an error when copying the original manuscript, or the manuscript at his disposal was itself a copy which contained this
error. It is clear that Mirza Jamal, like all the above historians, intends to first give
the overall circumference of Qarabagh and then describe its separate borders.

An interesting fact, however, is that all these primary sources describe
Qarabagh's southern border as beginning at the Khoda-afarin Bridge. This does
not include the territory of Zangezur, parts of which, during the rule of Ebrahim
Khan, periodically fell under the control of Qarabagh. Other parts of Zangezur
were controlled by a number of Armenian *meliks*, who were, at times, autonomous, and at other times, under the jurisdiction of the governor of Azerbaijan in
Tabriz. Following the Russian conquest, Zangezur became part of Qarabagh and
remained so (as part of the Elizavetpol' Province) until the Russian Revolution.

presently located in the Kazakh and Demurchi-Hasanlu districts. It bordered on
the west [with] the mountains of Qarabagh, and the Elizavetpol',[29] *Shamshadil,*
and Kazakh districts;[30] *on the south, the Arax; on the north, the Kur; and on the*
east with Javad, where the Kur meets the Arax and flows into the Caspian.[31]

To the east is the Kor (Kur)[32] River, which joins the Arax River at the
village of Javad, and with it flows into the Caspian Sea.

To the north the border of Qarabagh and Elizavetpol'(Ganje)[33] is the
Goran River (Göran-chay), which stretches east to the Kur River, itself
marking the [eastern] border of Qarabagh [and] reaching to the Arax. To
the west are the great mountains of Qarabagh, which are called Koshbeg,
Salvarti, and Eriklu.[34]

At the present, Qarabagh borders to the south with the Arax; to the north the
Kur, flowing near Ganje, which also signifies the width of Qarabagh, covering
some 26 farsakhs (approximately 90 miles) or German miles, as demonstrated
by calculations done during the khanate period; to the east, [the town of] Javad;
and to the west the Qarabagh mountains, [the distance between the two]
measuring some 39 farsakhs (approximately 135 miles), which forms the length
of it.[35]

In centuries past, when there was upheaval and change, the rulers of
Iran, Rum,[36] and Turkestan would sometimes control these *velayats,*

---

[29] See note 33.

[30] Berzhe uses the Russian pronunciation of "Shams od-Din" and "Qazzaq."

[31] "Karabag," 61 (1855), 260. The material in Berzhe's translation which is
absent from the Persian manuscript used in this translation is collated within the
text and appear in *italic*, see note 30 in introduction.

[32] The river has a variety of spellings among which are Kur and Kura. In
ancient times it is referred to as the Cyrus River.

[33] Mirza Jamal assumes that the reader knows that the previous name of
Elizavetpol' (sometimes spelled Elisavetpol) was Ganje. Obviously, at the time
of his writing it bore that name, but not in the historical period to which he is
referring. After conquering the fortress of Ganje in 1804, General Tsitsianov
renamed it Elizavetpol' in honor of the wife of Alexander I, Elizaveta (Elizabeth).
During the Soviet period it was renamed Kirovabad. Following the collapse of
the Soviet regime, the city was once again named Ganja (Persian "Ganje"). Since
Mirza Jamal uses both terms interchangeably, and, as noted, current place names
will be used in this study, Ganje will replace Elizavetpol' every time it appears
in the text.

[34] Part of the Qarabagh Range stretching from north to south.

[35] "Karabag," 61 (1855), 260.

[36] The term *Rum* means Rome; it was given by the Iranians, Arabs, and Turks
to the Byzantine or Eastern Roman Empire. Following the fall of Byzantium to

creating new borders,[37] building fortresses, and designating them by different names [both the fortresses and the *velayats*].[38]

The *velayat* of Qarabagh is part of the country of Arran.[39] During the

---

the Ottomans, the Ottoman Empire was referred to by some Muslim historians as *Rum*. Although Mirza Jamal, throughout the text, equates *Rum* with the Ottoman Empire, in this passage there is a slight possibility that he is referring to the Byzantine Empire, see note 38.

[37] "Turkestan" is the general term for the vast region of Central Asia, from where numerous Turkic and Mongol tribes invaded the Caucasus, Iran, Anatolia, and Mesopotamia. For more information, see W. Barthold, *Turkestan Down to the Mongol Invasion* (London, 1968) and René Grousset, *The Empire of the Steppes: A History of Central Asia* (New Brunswick, 1970).

[38] This paragraph may refer to one of two periods: that which included the wars between the Parthians and Sasanians against the Romans and Byzantines and the eventual invasions of the Seljuk Turks; or, that which included the invasions of Timur, the Aq-Qoyunlu and Qara-Qoyunlu, and the wars between the Safavids and the Ottomans. The term "Turkmen," as well as the rest of the text, may weigh in favor of the second period. In fact, Berzhe has made this assumption, for his translation reads, *the Persian shahs, Turkish sultans, and Turkmen*, "Karabag," 61 (1855), 260.

[39] The term *Arran* is the Arabic *al-Ran* (pronounced ar-Ran), which was their name for the Sasanian province of *Ran*, composed of the former Armenian and Caucasian Albanian provinces. Sources also mention that it derives from a Georgian word (*Rani*), describing the inhabitants of Caucasian Albania (no relation to the Albanians in the Balkans). Arran became the geographic designation of the Arabs for eastern Transcaucasia. There is some confusion as to its exact parameters. The tenth-century historian al-Moqaddasi calls it an island between the Kur and Arax rivers and the Caspian Sea, containing the cities of Tiflis, Darband, and towns in Shirvan, *Ahsan al-Taqasim* (Leiden, 1967), p. 374. Ibn Hauqal mentions two Arrans, one south of the Kur, the other north of it, *Kitab Surat al-Araz* (Leiden, 1938/39), p. 251. Minorsky states that during the tenth and eleventh centuries Arran signified the lands south of the Kur, *A History of Sharvan and Darband in the 10th-11th centuries* (Cambridge, 1958), p. 18. The ninth-century Arab historian al-Ya'qubi includes Arran in what he designates as the Fourth Armenia, *Tarikh* (Tehran, 1983), I, p. 220. The geographer al-Baladhuri includes it in his First Armenia, *Futuh al-Buldan* (Tehran, 1967), p. 197. The *Hudud al-'Alam*, a tenth-century Persian geography, indicates that Arran formed much, but not all of the combined territories of what later became the *beglarbegi* of Qarabagh, and even later, the khanates of Ganje and Qarabagh, *Hudud al-'Alam* (London, 1970), pp. 142-145, commentary pp. 394-403. The term dropped out of use following the Mongol invasions in the thirteenth century and was replaced by "Qarabagh." For more details, see C. E. Bosworth, "Arran," in *Encyclopedia Iranica*, II, 520-522.

time of Noah the prophet—may peace be upon him—the universal deluge occurred. Some time after the flood had subsided, one of the descendants of Noah—may peace be upon him—became the builder and ruler of these *velayats*,[40] which are situated between the rivers Kur and Arax, and include the cities of Teflis (Tiflis), Ganje, Iravan (Erevan), Nakhjavan (Nakhichevan), and Ordubad, as well as Barda' and Baylaghan (Baylaqan),[41] [the last two of] which are in the land of Qarabagh, and which both now lie in ruins, and he called it Arran, for [4] he himself was called Arran.[42]

---

[40] It is interesting to note that Mirza Jamal's account closely parallels the Armenian tradition which states that a descendant of Japheth, a son of Noah, was the father of the Armenians, the inhabitants of the region. Mirza Jamal also seems to confuse a grandson of Noah, Aram, son of Shem, with Arran, see *Genesis*, 10: 21-23. The Armenians claim that Aram was a descendant of Japheth, and not Shem, and was the father of Ara the Handsome, the first king of Armenia, see Moses Khorenatsi, *History of the Armenians*, translated by Robert W. Thomson (Cambridge, 1978), pp. 73-75. The biblical version is somewhat different. Except for naming Mount Ararat as the resting palce of the ark (*Genesis*, 8: 4), it does not follow the Armenian tradition. It is probable that Mirza Jamal learned the Armenian version from the Armenians of Qarabagh, for this tradition does not exist in Islam or in the Russian Orthodox Church. *Hudud al-'Alam* (p. 66), cites a mountain in Mesopotamia as the location of the landing of the ark. The Qur'an mentions Noah and the flood in *Surahs* VII, X, XI, XXI, XXIII, XXVI, XXIX, XXXVII, LIV, and especially LXXI, the *Surat Nuh* (Chapter of Noah), but does not give any geographical location, or name Noah's sons, or what happened to their descendants. *The Qur'an*, translated by Richard Bell, II (Edinburgh, 1960), pp. 607-609.

[41] The manuscript has a "ghain" instead of a "qaf." Other sources, including *Hudud al-'Alam* (p. 149), spell it with a "qaf," hence Baylaqan. It is possible that the unknown scribe who copied the manuscript made the error, for it is easy to mistake the two letters, which look very much alike in calligraphic script. In colloquial Persian, the two letters are pronounced like "ghain" when in an intervocalic position.

[42] The cities of Tiflis, Erevan, Nakhichevan, and Ordubad were not part of Arran, according to most primary sources. Others list Tiflis and Nakhichevan as part of Arran. Mirza Jamal cannot be blamed, however, for the exact parameters of Arran have confused many geographers (see note 39). In fact, the cities of Barda' and Baylaqan appear at times in Arran and at other times as part of medieval Armenia. The geographer and chief astronomer, Ahmad ibn Lutfullah, who, in the eighteenth century, wrote his *Jami' al-duwal*, based on eleventh- and twelfth-century local histories of Darband, Shirvan, and Arran, for example, mentions that Arran's western frontier ran alongside Armenia and among its cities were Ganje, Shamkhor, and Baylaqan. A few lines later, he includes the

...of which the latter is in ruins, while on the site of Barda' there is an insignificant small settlement, populated by the Burdalu tribe.[43]

The first city built in the *velayat* of Qarabagh was the fortress and city of Barda',[44] which is situated by the Terter (Tartar, Tharthar) River, some three *farsakhs* [45] from the Kur River. In ancient times it was populated by Armenians or other non-Muslims.[46] During the period of the past

---

same Baylaqan among the Armenian towns; V. Minorsky, *Studies in Caucasian History* (London, 1953), pp. 6-7.

[43] "Karabag," 61 (1855), 260.

[44] Mostoufi states that Barda' was a city built during the Hellenistic period and rebuilt by Qobad (Kavad II, who ruled for one year in 628) son of the Sasanian king Khosrou Parviz; Hamdollah Mostoufi, *Nozhat ol-Qulub* (Tehran, 1983), p. 91. Barda' is the city of Partav, on the border of Armenia and Caucasian Albania, built around the second century B.C. by the Artashesian kings of Armenia. *Tadhkirat al-Muluk* (p. 167), confirms that it was the ancient Armenian city of Partav. Abo'l-Qasem ibn Khordadhbe, a ninth-century geographer, also confirms this and includes Barda' in his First Armenia, *Al-Masalek va al-Mamalek* (Tehran, 1991), pp. 99-100. *Hudud al-'Alam* (p. 143), describes it as "a large town, very pleasant. It is the capital of Arran and the seat of the king of that province. To it belongs a countryside, flourishing, with many fields and much fruit, densely populated. In it grow numerous mulberry-trees of which the fruit belongs to everybody. The town produces much silk, good mules, madder, chestnuts, and caraway." Abu-Eshaq Ebrahim Estakhri states that Barda' was famous for its silk, figs, hazelnuts, as well as a particular fish taken from the Kur. He confirms that it was a large and pleasant town; *Masalek va Mamalek* (Tehran, 1989), p. 156. Barda', for a time, was the seat of the Arab governor of Armenia and the rest of Transcaucasia. It had its own mint.

[45] *Farsakh* is the same as *parasanga* (from the Latin *parasanga*, Greek *parasanges*, and the Persian *farsang*), an ancient Persian measure of distance equal to about three and a half miles, 18,000 feet, or approximately 12,000 *cubits* [ancient measure of about 18-22 inches, or the length of the arm from the end of the middle finger to the elbow] in length. It can be equated to the *league*, which measures about three statute miles. It is important to note that Mirza Jamal's measurements here were taken from earlier sources, when the *farsakh* was not standardized. It referred to the distance a camel or a horse could cover in an hour at a walking pace.

[46] The new Azeri edition of *Tarikh-e Qarabagh* has deleted the above sentence and most other references to the Armenian presence in Qarabagh, see *Garabaghnamälär* (Baku, 1989), pp. 108, 111, and 112 among others. This collection also contains new Azeri editions of Adigozal Beg's and Ahmad Beg's histories of Qarabagh. "The other non-Muslims," cited by Mirza Jamal were the Caucasian Albanians (*Albanoi* in Greek, *Aghvank* in Armenian) who later crossed the Kur and mingled with the Armenian population. Ancient sources state that Albania,

caliphs of the 'Abbasid dynasty, who built and settled the city of Baghdad and made it the seat of the caliphate, the population of that city [Barda'] in the year 306 hijri, which corresponds to the Christian year 886 (actually 918/19),[47] became Muslims.[48]

---

situated east of the Kur, was a neighbor of Armenia, Strabo, *The Geography of Strabo*, V (Cambridge, Mass., 1969), pp. 187, 223, 321, map XI; Pliny the Elder, *Natural History of Pliny*, II (London, 1890), pp. 17-21; Plutarch, *Lives*, V [Pompey] (Cambridge, Mass,. 1955), pp. 203-209; Ptolemy, *The Geography* (Fankfurt, 1987), pp. 170-171; Dio [Cassius], *Roman History*, III (Cambridge, Mass., 1984), pp. 92-93. It is certain that Christianity was introduced to Caucasian Albania via Armenia and at that times the Albanian Church was subordinate to the Armenian Church. Political and socioeconomic ties between the two people were also strong, with Armenia, overall, playing the dominant role. The only source on the history of the Caucasian Albanians is the Armenian historian Moses Daskhurantsi (also known as Kaghankatvatsi), who describes their history from the earliest times to the eleventh century A.D., see Movses Dasxurantci, *The History of the Caucasian Albanians*, translated by C. J. F. Dowsett (London, 1961). Arab and Persian geographers also state that Armenia's borders stretched to the Kur or to the city of Barda', see Estakhri's *Masalek va Mamalek*, p. 158. Bakikhanov also states that Armenians lived in that region and that the Kur River separated Armenia from Shirvan, *Golestan-e Eram*, pp. 4, 10. In 387, the Iranians and Byzantines partitioned Armenia. Two Armenian provinces were detached by Iran and combined with Caucasian Albania to form a single administrative unit, called *Ran* (see note 39). The city of Partav became the center of that region sometime in the beginning of the sixth century. Located on the border between Armenia and Caucasian Albania, the city had a mixed Armenian and Caucasian Albanian population. Although Zoroastrianism made major inroads in the western parts of Caucasian Albania, it did not have the same success across the Kur, in the eastern regions. Here, the Armenian language, customs, and Christianity held sway until the arrival of the Arabs in the seventh century. Even then, Armenians and Christian Albanians continued to have a dominant presence in parts of what became known as the Arran Province until the Turko-Mongol invasions from the eleventh to the thirteenth centuries.

[47] As noted in the introduction, Mirza Jamal has made a number of errors regarding corresponding Christian dates. The year 306 is, in fact, the equivalent to the year 918/919. The corrected dates will henceforth appear in parenthesis.

[48] During the time of the third caliph 'Othman ibn 'Affan (644-656), Arabs continued their raids into Armenia and Caucasian Albania under the command of generals Salman ibn Rabi'a al-Baheli and Habib ibn Maslama. Around 645 they conquered Partav, which was renamed Barda'. Although Mirza Jamal states that the population of Barda' became Muslim in the early tenth century, other sources indicate that the city achieved a Muslim majority either in the late tenth or early eleventh century. For example, Estakhri, a late tenth-century geographer, men-

In the year 36 hijri (676 A.D.) at the time of the Umayyad caliphs of Damascus, the population of the city of Barda' accepted the Muslim faith.[49]

Next [in importance] is the city of Baylaqan,[50] built some fifteen hundred years ago by King Qobad, one of the monarchs of Iran and

---

tions the fact that Sunday was bazaar day and that the local term for Sunday was *keraki* (the Armenian word for Sunday is *kiraki*), which may signify that the population of Barda' was still predominantly Armenian at that time. The same source also states that the lands from Barda' to Dvin belonged to Smbat, son of Ashot, *Masalek va Mamalek*, pp. 156, 158. Unfortunately Estakhri does not specify which Smbat. Smbat I, son of Ashot I, ruled at the end of the ninth and at the beginning of the tenth century. Smbat II, son of Ashot III, ruled at the end of the tenth century. Ya'qubi includes it in Armenia and adds that as long as it paid tribute, the region remained essentially a frontier province left to its own native princes, *Tarikh* (Leiden, 1969), II, p. 562. Minorsky adds that the Arabs ruled from the city of Barda' from where they spearheaded their expansion into the region, while the local princes retained their lands, see *Sharvan*, p. 18. Moqaddasi, who wrote in the tenth century, mentions that Christians maintained a majority in a number of cities of Arran, *Ahsan al-Taqasim*, p. 376. Finally, Minorsky's work, a translation of a work by an Arab geographer, includes the town of Barda' as part of the Armenian lands, which clearly indicates that the Armenian presence was significant even at that late date. Minorsky's work goes on to describe how Armenian princes ruled alongside Muslim *amirs*, and that, although the two groups fought each other, a number of marriage alliances were made, *Studies in Caucasian History*, pp. 7, 50-52.

[49] "Karabag," 6 (1855), 260. Berzhe's translation has the date of 36 hijri. It is obvious that his copy either missed the dot which signifies a zero (hence 36 instead of 306), or that Berzhe simply did not notice it. The interesting fact is that, realizing that the year did not correspond to the 'Abbasids, Berzhe probably took it upon himself to correct the rest of the paragraph. Unfortunately, he made another error, in that he calculated the year 36 hijri to be the equivalent to 676 A.D. Actually 36 hijri (656-657 A.D.) occurred during the caliphate of 'Ali ibn Abi-Talib, the fourth caliph and the leader of the Shi'is, and not during the Umayyad period.

[50] In the year 332 hijri (943-944), Barda' was sacked by the Scandinavian Rus invaders and never truly recovered. Eventually, Baylaqan became the center of Arran. A century later, in the second half of the eleventh century, the Seljuk Turks arrived in the region. By the year 468 hijri (1075-1076), Sultan Alp Arslan appointed his slave-general Savtigin as governor of Azerbaijan and Arran. From this period began the increasing Turkicization of Arran; for more details see C. E. Bosworth, "The Political and Dynastic History of the Iranian World (A.D. 1000-1217)," in *The Cambridge History of Iran*, V (Cambridge, 1968), pp. 34-133.

Fars.[51] He built a very large canal emanating from the Arax River, along the extensive and dry plain of Baylaqan, and founded that city. In the environs, from the river Kondalan to the river Gargar, he built farms and villages, providing the peasants[52] with a place to live. All around he planted numerous fields, meadows, and orchards, creating [additional] settlements. The canal was called Barlas in ancient times and is now known as Govur-arkhi.[53] Until the time of Genghis Khan the city and its villages continued to be populated and cultivated.[54]

In the year 635 (1237/38),[55] the army of Genghis Khan[56] arrived and laid siege to the city of Baylaqan. After a few months the city was captured and the population was massacred.[57] The people living in the villages and districts of the *velayat* of Qarabagh scattered into the moun-

---

[51] The date and location refer probably to the Sasanian monarch, Kavad I, who ruled 488-496 and again 498-531. The Sasanian family originated in Fars. After revolting against the Parthians, Ardashir defeated the last Arsacid king Artabanus or Ardavan IV (ca. 224 A.D., according to new chronology) and founded the Sasanian dynasty. For further details see Ehsan Yarshater, ed., *The Cambridge History of Iran*, III (pt. 1) (Cambridge, 1983), pp. 99, 116-119. The *Nozhat ol-Qulub* (p. 91), however, states that the city was built by Qobad, son of Parviz, or Kavad II, who ruled for one year in 628. In that case the city was over twelve hundred years old. Khordadhbe confirms the above and includes Baylaqan in his First Armenia, *Al-Masalek va al-Mamalek*, pp. 99-100.

[52] The term *ra'iyat* (pl. *ra'aya*) has a number of meanings such as "people," "subjects," and "peasants." In earlier times, the term implied those who were under the protection of the ruler. In later times, the term became associated with peasants.

[53] Can be also read as Kovur or Gavur, which is the Turkish word for "infidel" or "non-Muslim." There is a remote possibility that the canal was built at the time of the Sasanids by Armenians, who had been constructing canals in Transcaucasia and Anatolia since Urartuan times.

[54] The *Hudud al-'Alam* (p. 144) has the following description, "a very pleasant borough, producing striped textiles in great numbers, horse rugs, veils, and *natif*-sweets." Mostoufi states that it was very populated and was famous for its fruit and hazelnuts, *Nozhat ol-Qulub*, p. 91.

[55] Berzhe in his translation erroneously calculated the date as *1229*, "Karabag," 61 (1855), 260.

[56] Mirza Jamal uses the name Changiz (Chingiz). There are some discrepancies in this sentence. If one accepts the date of 1237/38 then Mirza Jamal is wrong, for Genghis Khan was long dead. "The Mongols attacked Baylaqan" would have been more correct. However, since, according to the main historian of the period, Juvaini (Joveini), the Mongols first attacked Baylaqan in 1221 (during Genghis Khan's lifetime) Mirza Jamal's narrative—not his date—is accurate, See note 57.

[57] The city was sacked by the Mongols in spring 1221, see 'Ata-malik Juvaini,

tains of Qarabagh and Shirvan.[58] The city of Baylaqan and its large canal were thus left in ruins until Emperor Timur came from Turkestan to the *velayat* of Rum and fought and defeated the sultan and emperor Bayazid Ildirim.[59] [5] On his return, he rebuilt the city of Baylaqan, repopulated it and repaired the canal. The city flourished for a time, but was on the path of invading armies moving into Georgia and Shirvan during the era of the Safavid kings and Nader Shah, and was [then] again destroyed and its population scattered. At present, it lies in ruins.

After that it [Baylaqan] remained unharmed until the Safavids and through the time of Nader Shah, in whose reign, the city, because of the frequent movement of troops which passed through to Georgia and Shirvan, and the hostile relations with Turkey, which at that time controlled Tiflis, Ganje, Qarabagh, Erevan, and Nakhichevan, was again destroyed and did not revive again.[60]

The canal is large indeed and could be highly profitable. It could irrigate and help produce grain, rice, cotton, "silk gardens" [mulberry trees for the production of silk], and various vegetables. Whatever is planted would flourish. From every *chetvert* [61] of wheat the yield could be twenty or more *chetvert*. Rice and millet would give especially good results here, with approximately fifty or more *chetvert* from every *chetvert* planted. Farming is easy here and good results could be obtained by just using [a plow with] two oxen. A stable environment around the canal

---

Tarikh-e Jahan-gosha, translated as *The History of the World Conqueror*, by John Andrew Boyle, vol. I (Manchester, 1958) pp. 148-149. After that the city of Ganje became the main center of Arran and by the fourteenth century, the southern part of Arran became known as Qarabagh.

[58] For the history of the Mongols in Qarabagh, see Rashid al-Din, *Jame' ot-Tavarikh*, translated as *The Successors of Genghis Khan*, by John Andrew Boyle (New York, 1971), pp. 74, 124, 130, 218.

[59] Mirza Jamal uses the title of "Timur padeshah," which refers to Timur the Lame (Tamerlane), the founder of the Timurids, who ruled from 1370 to 1405. Bayezid Yildirim ("the Thunderbolt," in Turkish) or Bayazid I (1389-1402) was chosen sultan on the battlefield of Kossovo, after his father, Murad I, was killed. He won that battle and defeated the European forces in Nicopolis (1395). He laid siege to Constantinople and extended Ottoman power through most of Anatolia. On July 28, 1402, he clashed with Timur in the battle of Angora (Ankara). He was defeated, captured, and died in captivity in 1403.

[60] "Karabag," 61 (1855), 260.

[61] A Russian measure of volume approximately 210 liters for dry goods and 3 liters for liquids. The weight of a *chetvert* varied, depending on time and place, ranging from 144 to 288 pounds.

could support settlements of some five or six thousand families comfortably and provide an abundance of food.

In addition to the large canal there are a number of other canals originating from the Arax. If around each of these [canals] villages of one to two hundred families settled, they could support themselves well from the grains, rice, and cotton. Despite the fact that the city of Baylaqan has been in ruins for more than three hundred years, these canals were in use during the early rule [6] of the late Panah Khan and Ebrahim Khan, and provided income for them. The canals were called by the following names: Kurek-arkhi, Lavar-arkhi, Meimat-arkhi, Kamichi-arkhi, Sari-arkh, Ayaz-arkhi, Tashqai-arkhi, and Khan-arkhi.

The canals are: Gudek-arkhi, Yuvar-arkhi, Meimana-arkhi, Giamichi-arkhi, Giurlu-arkhi, Insurkhan-arkhi, Duramanli-arkhi, Bakarlu-arkhi, Meimena-arkhi (2nd), Yuvar-arkhi (2nd), Moqaddam-arkhi, and Taibashmaklu-arkhi. The climate of Qarabagh is favorable and healthy. The soil is fertile and multiplies the fruit of the labor of those who work on it.[62]

Chapter Two:
On the Subjects, Former Customs, and
Regulations of the *Velayat* of Qarabagh [63]

During the time of the Safavid sultans[64] of Iran, who are now in paradise,[65] the *velayat* of Qarabagh, its tribes, and the *khamse* Armenian *mahals*,[66] which are those of Dizaq, Varandeh, Khachin, Chaleberd, and

---

[62] Berzhe's translation has different pronunciations for some of the canals. More important however, are his additional canals, not listed in the manuscript used for this translation; "Karabag," 61 (1855), 260. Ahmad Beg mentions another canal called Khatun-arkh, *Karabakhskogo khanstva*, p. 73; Adigozal Beg confirms this in *Qarabagh-name*, p. 63.

[63] Berzhe's translation has no title for chapter two. This chapter, in fact, describes the population of Qarabagh. The customs and regulations are included in the additional chapters at the end of the manuscript.

[64] Since Turkish was the language of the military hierarchy of Iran, the Safavid shahs were sometimes called sultans in Persian sources. Turkish sources occasionally refer to them as sultans as well.

[65] This is the only time that former rulers are so honored by Mirza Jamal. The aura of magnificence of the Safavid period lingered for a long time and compared favorably with the chaos that followed.

[66] The five Armenian districts, located in the mountains of Qarabagh (roughly the territory of present-day Nagorno-Karabakh), were known as the *khamse* or "five" in Arabic. The continued use of the Arabic term indicates that the Arme-

Talesh,[67] were all subordinate to the *beglarbegi* of Ganje.[68] Although until the reign of the late Nader Shah there were minor [autonomous] khans

---

nians must have been in control of the mountains of Qarabagh before the Turko-Mongol domination of the region. As noted, the five mahals were ruled by hereditary lords or *meliks*, most of whom were scions of Armenian nobility who had fled the Turko-Mongol invasions and had sought refuge in the mountain valleys of Qarabagh. There were also *meliks* in Ganje, Siunik-Zangezur, Lori, Erevan, and Nakhichevan. The *meliks* of Qarabagh, however, are the best known, because they had relatively large forces, were better armed, and continually fought for their autonomy. A number of them were also involved in establishing friendly relations with Russia and hence are occasionally credited with the early stages of the Armenian national revival. The only works in English on the *meliks* are the studies by Robert H. Hewsen, "The Meliks of Eastern Armenia I, II, III, and IV: The Siunid Origin of Xac'atur Abovean," in *Revue Des Études Arméniennes* (new series), IX, X, XI, XIV (1972, 1973-74, 1975-76, 1980), pp. 285-329, 281-300, 219-243, 459-470; number V appeared as "Three Armenian Noble Families of the Russian Empire," in *Hask* [new series] (Beirut, 1981-82), pp. 389-400; and number VI as "The Meliks of Eastern Armenia VI: The House of Aghamaleanc', Meliks of Erevan," in *Pazmaveb* (Venice, Spring 1984), pp. 319-333. Additional material on the *meliks* of Qarabagh can be found in Hewsen's study "The Kingdom of Arc'ax," in T. Samuelian & M. Stone, eds. *Medieval Armenian Culture* (Chico, Ca., 1983), pp. 42-68.

[67] The Armenians referred to them as Dizak, Varanda, Khachen, Jraberd, and Golestan. Since these *mahals* were inhabited by Armenians, the Armenian pronunciation will be used throughout the text. It is interesting to note that Mirza Jamal uses the former name of the Golestan *mahal*, Talesh (not to be confused with the *velayat* of Talesh situated by the Caspian Sea). The *meliks* of Golestan originally resided in the village of Talesh (its Armenian name was Turinj). They later moved to the fortress of Golestan, sometimes called the Javanshir castle, on the upper banks of the Inja-chay, some 20 miles southeast of Ganje. This fact is confirmed by the editor of Ahmad Beg's *Karabakhskogo khanstva*, p. 100, and by the editor of Adigozal Beg's, *Qarabagh-name*, p. 55. In the eighteenth century the following families ruled in the five *mahals*: The Hasan-Jalalians were the *meliks* of Khachen, the Shahnazarians were the *meliks* of Varanda, the Beglarians were the *meliks* of Talesh/Golestan, the Avanians were the *meliks* of Dizak, and the Israelians were the *meliks* of Jraberd.

[68] A *beglarbegi* was a governor general of a large province or territory, called an *ayalat*. He was in charge of all the *velayats*, ruled by khans or sultans, under his jurisdiction. According to Chardin, the Safavids divided Iran into four *ayalats* for the purposes of taxation: 'Araq-e 'Ajam (see note 95), Fars, Azerbaijan (including Transcaucasia), and Khorasan, *Voyages du Chevalier Chardin en Perse*, V (Paris, 1811), p. 439; see also map 2. The *Tadhkirat al-Muluk*, a manual of late Safavid administration, lists seven regions with a number of sub-regions ruled by khans. Once again Azerbaijan and Transcaucasia are combined into a single unit, with

among the tribes of Javanshir, Otuz-iki, Bargoshat and others,[69] they were all under the jurisdiction of the *beglarbegi* of Ganje. After Nader Shah conquered the *velayats* of Tiflis, Ganje, Erevan, Nakhichevan and Qarabagh from the people and army of Rum [the Ottomans], the *velayat* of Qarabagh remained, for a brief period, under the jurisdiction of the *beglarbegi* of Ganje or, on occasion, of the *sardar* of Azerbaijan.[70] Among the tribes and in the [Armenian] *mahals* there were khans and *meliks* who

---

its headquarters at Tabriz. The unit was, however, subdivided into four *beglarbegis*: they were Chukhur-e Sa'd (with headquarters in Erevan), Qarabagh (with headquarters in Ganje), Shirvan (with headquarters in Shamakhi), and Azerbaijan (with headquarters in Tabriz), pp. 100-102; also see map 1.

[69] The Persian term *'il* refers both to the tribe or tribes (*'ilat*) and its domain (*mahalat*). Mirza Jamal lists the Javanshir and the Otuz-iki as two separate tribes. According to Shukiurzade, the local Qajar khans, at the beginning of the six-teenth century forcibly grouped various local Turkic tribes into a confederation in the area south of Barda'. This group was called Otuz-iki, or "thirty-two." Among this confederation, the Javanshir tribe was dominant and its head was regarded as the leader of the entire confederation. At the time of Shukiurzade's writing (1961) there existed a small village called Otuz-iki in the Imishli region of Soviet Azerbaijan, Ahmad Beg, *Karabakhskogo khanstva*, pp. 99-100. The fact is that the Qajars who had been posted to Qarabagh, as well as to Erevan and Ganje, by the Safavids, had been gradually replaced by various other tribes, who went under confederations known as Otuz-iki and Ikimi-dort ("Twenty-four"). James Reid states that the Otuz-iki was a confederacy of thirty-two tribes, which included the Shahsavan tribe in northern Azerbaijan (Moghan Steppe). One of the prominent lineages in the Otuz-iki was the Javanshir clan, see his forthcom-ing volume entitled *Studies on Persia, Anatolia, and Central Asia, 1200-1750*.

[70] Nader Shah's campaigns in Daghestan and Transcaucasia are described in great detail by his chief secretary, Mirza Mohammad, see *Tarikh-e Jahangoshay*, pp. 230-265. Adigozal Beg adds more detail to this period. He states that the governors of Ganje, who were Ziadoglu Qajars, did not view Nader as the rightful king, but deemed the Safavids as the only true monarchs of Iran. Nader was aware of this, but since the Qajars were an established power in Ganje and had numerous followers, he sought to weaken them. First, he took the tribes of Qazzaq and Borchalu and forced their khans to obey the ruler of Georgia (this action began the Georgian claims to those regions). He then ordered the Qarabaghi tribes of Javanshir, Otuz-iki, and Kebirlu to relocate to the *velayat* of Khorasan, where they were given the district of Sarakhs as their permanent residence. The five Armenian *meliks* were given the right "to throw off the yoke" of the khans of Ganje and consider themselves free from their authority, directing all their needs and petitions directly to the shah. "In this fashion, the khans of Ganje lost their rights and authority and resembled birds with broken wings," *Qarabagh-name*, pp. 47-48. Bakikhanov confirms the above, adding that the

performed services to the crown at the order of the *sardar* of Azerbaijan.[71] These practices continued until the murder of Nader Shah in the Muslim year 1160, which corresponds to the Christian year 1743 (actually 1747).

After the death of Nader Shah, Panah Khan's power grew. Taking advantage of the chaotic conditions in Persia, he succeeded in forcing the submission of the villages [population] of Qarabagh. The beglarbegis of Elizavetpol' [Ganje], being weak, could not challenge him. Many who tried to resist him became obedient through the use of force. The details of this form the subject of the third chapter.[72]

Chapter Three: On the Origins of the Late Panah Khan and His Rule in the *Velayat* of Qarabagh[73]

The late Panah Khan's lineage was of the Javanshir tribe of Dizak, of the clan[74] of Sarujlu,[75] which was a group within the Bahmanli tribe, and which in times past came from Turkestan. *They were a part of the famous Afshar tribe.*[76] His ancestors were famous, [7] wealthy, respected, and

---

Qazzaq tribe was brought by Hülegü (1256-1265, grandson of Genghis Khan, brother of the Great Khan Möngke, founder of the Ilkhanids of Iran) from Turkestan and the Bozjalu (who occupied Borchalu) were brought by Shah 'Abbas I from 'Araq-e 'Ajam, *Golestan-e Eram*, p. 173.

[71] There are clear indications that certain groups, such as the Armenians, had special arrangements with the shah, either through direct contact or through the governo general of Azerbaijan, in Tabriz. Occasionally the said governor would have his own special agreement with local chiefs, see *Qarabagh-name*, p. 48.

[72] "Karabag," 62 (1855), 263-264.

[73] Berzhe's translation reads: **Chapter Three: The Rule of Panah Khan, the Son of Ebrahim Khalil 'Ali,** "Karabag," 62 (1855), 264.

[74] The text has the term *uymaq*, from the Mongol word *oboq* meaning "a lesser elite ruling clan." The terms *ferqe*, *tayefe*, and *qabile*, sometimes translated as "clan" or "tribe," are more complex. They may refer to a specific type of group, depending on the context and period.

[75] Ahmad Beg records it as Sarujali and Adigozal Beg as Sarijalu, *Karabakhskogo khanstva*, p. 69; *Qarabagh-name*, p. 49.

[76] "Karabag," 62 (1855), 264. According to Ahmad Beg, Panah Khan descended from Argun Shah, one of the grandsons of Hülegü. One of his ancestors, Mohammad Khan, lived in Alagark, on the bank of the Arax, near the village of Bahmanli. He possessed a deed, written on deerskin parchment, stating that he had purchased all of Qarabagh, a territory of two hundred *versts* (approximately 125 miles, see note 173) by two hundred *versts*, bordered by the Kurek, Kur, Arax, and Alinja rivers and Lake Gökcha (Sevan). He willed it to his three sons during his lifetime, *Karabakhskogo khanstva*, pp. 69-70. This claim is not substantiated by

beneficent among the Javanshir tribe.[77]   When the late Nader Shah subjugated[78] the *velayats* of Qarabagh, Ganje, Tiflis, and the Shirvans,[79]

---

the seventeenth-century Persian historian, Eskandar Beg Monshi, who groups all the *amirs* of the time of Shah 'Abbas (1587-1629) into two categories. In the first category are the *amirs* of the seven major Qezelbash tribes which followed the Shi'i Safavid leaders and the *amirs* of the tribes subordinate to them, totaling seventy-three in all. The Javanshir appear in the second category, the *gholam amirs*, who had the rank of khan or sultan. Number eighty-six is listed as "Nouruz Sultan, chief of the Javanshir tribe of the Otuz-iki federation, one of the *amirs* of Qarabagh." *History of Shah 'Abbas the Great*, trans. by Roger Savory, II (Boulder Co., 1978), p. 1317. The Iranian chronicler Hedayat states that Panah Khan Javanshir was from the Sarijalu clan of the tribe of Javanshir. They were one of the tribes of Oshir Khan ibn Yaldur Khan, the fourth son of Oghur Khan, and were called Ofshar or Afshar. Hedayat adds that according to Mongol custom they were among the *amirs* "of the right hand" (*javanghar* in Mongolian) in battle formation and other ceremonies. They were said to be among the 120,000-man army of Hülegü, who came from Turkestan and settled in Anatolia. They later returned from Anatolia with Timur and were scattered and settled in Turkestan, Qandahar, Kabul, and Iran. According to Hedayat some of them, during the time of Shah 'Abbas, were in Qarabagh and Arran, *Rouzat os-Safa*, IX, pp. 296-297.

[77] Adigozal Beg has additional information about Panah Khan's lineage: His great grandfather was Panah 'Ali Beg, who for a time served the *beglarbegi* of Ganje. He was too proud and outspoken, however, and soon left Ganje and returned to the Javanshir tribe. He acquired wealth, married, and had a son named 'Ali, whose round and shining countenance earned him the nickname of "yellow" [shining] 'Ali, or Sari 'Ali. This son increased the wealth and power of the family and made it a great clan known after him as Sarijlu. His son Ebrahim Khalil Aqa, the father of Panah Khan, made the clan even more powerful, acquiring his own *yeilaq* (Turkic term for tribal summer quarters) with a residence, orchards, and other *molk* (private property) in Aghdam and in Arasbar on the bank of the Arax, *Karabakhskogo khanstva* pp. 49-50. Hedayat has the following account: The family began with Ebrahim Khalil Aqa, followed by his son Panah Aqa, followed by his son, Ebrahim Khalil Aqa II, and then by Panah Aqa II, followed by Ebrahim Khalil III, followed by his son, Panah Aqa III (Mirza Jamal's Panah Khan), who was the father of Ebrahim Khalil Aqa IV (Mirza Jamal's Ebrahim Khan), *Rouzat os-Safa*, IX, p. 297.

[78] Nader's campaign against the Ottomans (who had invaded western Transcaucasia following the fall of the Safavids and the Russian occupation of eastern Transcaucasia) began on August 21, 1734, when he crossed into Shirvan and ended on October 3, 1735, with the submission of the fortress of Erevan. At the same time Nader, by the treaties of Rasht (1732) and Ganje (1735), had ended the Russian presence in Transcaucasia and northern Iran. He appointed his brother Ebrahim as the *sardar* of Azerbaijan, with authority over Transcaucasia.

[79] The Persian text reads *Shirvanat*, or greater Shirvan, which at the time of

he summoned all from among the tribes and settlements who were brave, skillful, and intelligent and drafted them into his service, giving them income, honor, and positions.[80]   One of those conscripted was Panah Khan, who among the tribes was famous as Panah 'Ali Beg Sarujlu Javanshir. He succeeded in all his duties and surpassed his peers in battle. He demonstrated particular courage during the campaigns of the late Nader Shah against the soldiers of Rum. The [shah], therefore, kept him close by, both when traveling and at court, where he served the shah conscientiously, zealously fulfilling all tasks, attaining high office and gaining the favor of the shah.

As the years passed, Nader Shah's regard for Panah Khan increased daily and the latter surpassed his comrades-in-arms and colleagues in rank and position. As is common among the avaricious and jealous, a number of wicked men at the shah's court, as well as among the tribes, secretly, as well as in the presence of the late Nader Shah, began to speak evil of the late Panah Khan and succeeded in changing the late shah's disposition towards him. Realizing the situation [that he was in] and fearing for his life,[81] Panah Khan took advantage of the shah's trip to Khorasan,[82] gathered a number of his family and friends, and in 1150

---

the Safavids covered that part of the territory of the present-day Republic of Azerbaijan which lies east of the Kur river, as well as the region of southern Daghestan all the way to Darband (see map. 5). *Shirvanat* will henceforth be translated as "the Shirvans."

[80] Ahmad Beg has a different version: He states that Nader could not conquer Daghestan and, since some of the leaders of the nomadic tribes of Transcaucasia who did not submit to his will found refuge and support among the Lezgis and, together with them, wreaked havoc on the region, Nader was obliged to forcibly relocate all the nomadic tribes of Qarabagh to Sarakhs, a district in the *ayalat* of Khorasan, *Karabakhskogo khanstva* p. 68. Bakikhanov also confirms that Nader forcibly removed the Qarabaghi tribes to Khorasan, *Golestan-e Eram*, p. 173. Iranian chroniclers agree that Nader forcibly removed some of the tribes of the region and sent them to Khorasan. Mirza Jamal does not mention the forced emigration here, but later he records the return of some of these tribes to Qarabagh. See also note 70.

[81] Ahmad Beg states that one ill-fated day, Nader, for some reason, became angry with him. Panah 'Ali feared the same fate that befell his brother, Behbud 'Ali Beg, who was beheaded by Nader because the shah did not like the way he had looked at him, *Karabakhskogo khanstva*, p. 69.

[82] This must have occurred during or after the campaigns in the Qandahar and Kabul regions. Nader had the habit of taking his hostages along, so that they would not escape or cause intrigue in his absence. His Georgian hostages (who included King Teimuraz, the father of Erekle), for example, were present at the

(1737/38) fled to the *velayat* of Qarabagh.[83]

When the shah learned of his escape, he sent couriers to overtake them, but to no avail. The shah dispatched urgent orders [8] to the *sardar* of Azerbaijan and the governors[84] of Ganje, Tiflis, and Shirvan, with instructions to seize Panah Khan wherever he might be and send him back.[85] Even though the shah ordered his [Panah's][immediate] family, members of his household, relatives, and friends to be persecuted and fined, these measures were fruitless. Once inside the boundaries of Qarabagh, the late Panah Khan, with his close associates, took refuge at times in the mountains of Qarabagh and at other times in the Qabala[86] *mahal* of the *velayat* of Shakki.

…at the house of the sultan of Qabala, where he was accorded great hospitality, which, later, Panah Khan repaid by sheltering some thirty Qabala and Shakki begs and their families, who had sought refuge with him from Mohammad Khan of Shakki.[87]

---

siege of the fortress of Qandahar, see *Tarikh-e Jahangoshay*, pp. 286-300; *Alamara-ye Naderi*, II, 495.

[83] Adigozal Beg has a different account and names another brother: When Nader Shah began gathering able tribesmen to serve him in various positions, he took the eldest son of Ebrahim, Fazl 'Ali Beg, to act as his *na'eb* (lieutenant or deputy) and *eshik-aqasi* (chamberlain). The young man was killed and his younger brother, Panah 'Ali Beg, was given fine robes and his brother's position of *eshik-aqasi*. He performed his duties well, but after a short time, Nader's bad temper (Nader Shah was indeed known to be cruel and erratic) and his own feeling that the position was beneath him, led him to escape, *Qarabagh-name*, p. 50.

[84] The Persian term is *hokam*, from the singular, *hakem*. It can be translated as "governor," "magistrate," and occasionally as "*de facto* ruler" of a city or province. The position was held by khans. At the time of the Safavids, these khans were generally appointed or hereditary governors, answerable to the central administration. After the fall of the Safavids and especially during the periods when Iran did not have a single ruler, these governors became the *de facto* rulers of their *velayats*. *Hakem* will, therefore, be translated variably as "governor" or "ruler," depending on the period.

[85] According to Ahmad Beg, Panah 'Ali and six of his kinsmen, who were also in Nader's service, fled the camp. Nader looked for them everywhere, but could not find them. Only after two months did he hear of their presence in Qarabagh, *Karabakhskogo khanstva*, p. 69.

[86] Qabala is a city in Shakki, southeast of Nukha, see map 3.

[87] "Karabag," 62 (1855), 264. The episode referred to here is discussed below in the Berzhe translation and not in the manuscript used for this translation. This

A while later his eldest son, the late Ebrahim Khalil Khan, who was almost fifteen years old, and who had lived in their family home in Khorasan, *in the district of Sarakhs,*[88] followed his esteemed father to Qarabagh, where he remained steadfastly at his honorable father's side.

Two or three years passed in this fashion until Nader Shah was killed, as stated previously, in the year 1160 (1747).[89]

Panah Khan now came out of hiding and from among the remaining people of Qarabagh[90] gathered around him capable young men and began to plunder[91] the regions of Ganje, Nakhichevan, and others.[92] The young men, especially those close to him, [thus] gained [respectable] attire, horses, goods, and positions. *He married the sister of Sahl 'Ali beg, the chief of the Kebirlu tribe.*[93]

At this time news arrived that the Javanshir and other tribes which the shah had removed to Khorasan, had decided to return to their homelands.[94] Panah Khan took his armed men and went to the borders

---

once again demonstrates that Berzhe must have had an earlier or different copy of Mirza Jamal's history. Ahmad Beg's version differs as well. According to him, Panah Khan sought refuge with the Lezgis in Jaro-Belokani (Jar and Belakan or Jaro-Belakan) from where (see map 3) he conducted raids and became popular among the people as a good and just leader, *Karabakhskogo khanstva*, p. 69.

[88] "Karabag," 62 (1855), 264.

[89] This information makes it possible to determine the approximate birthdate of Ebrahim Khalil Aqa (later Ebrahim Khan). The text reads that "two or three years passed," which would place his arrival at approximately 1745. Since he was almost fifteen at that date, he was probably born around 1730. Ahmad Beg confirms this as well, *Karabakhskogo khanstva*, p. 69.

[90] This passage is the first instance in which Mirza Jamal hints at an earlier emigration. In the next paragraph he mentions the forced migrations. Another Persian chronicle states that after the death of Nader, the Javanshir tribe went to Ghurian and defeated the Hezareh tribe. Ahmad Shah Abdali Afghan then moved them to Kabul where they remained until Panah Khan moved them to Qarabagh, *Rouzat os-Safa*, IX, p. 297.

[91] The Persian term used is *gharat*, whose possible translations include plunder, pillage, or devastation, among others.

[92] According to Ahmad Beg, after the death of Nader Shah, Panah 'Ali, with some 200 of his followers, arrived in Qarabagh and declared himself the independent khan of Qarabagh, *Karabakhskogo khanstva*, p. 69. Bakikhanov also confirms the raids and Panah Khan's rise to power, *Golestan-e Eram*, p. 173.

[93] "Karabag," 62 (1855), 264. Two sons resulted from this union. See p. 137.

[94] Ahmad Beg has a different interpretation. According to him the tribes did not return on their own initiative. Following the death of Nader, Hajji Chelebi of Shakki invaded Qarabagh and forced Panah Khan to flee to his acquaintance,

of 'Araq[-e 'Ajam][95] and Azerbaijan to greet the tribes of Qarabagh. The
tribesmen and his [Panah Khan's] kin, seeing him alive and well, and
observing his numerous companions and retainers, were overjoyed.
Together [9] with the late Panah Khan, they crossed into the territory of
Qarabagh and each tribal chief returned to his former domain, living
peacefully. Since the tribes had lost all of their possessions [during the
forceful migration] and had suffered greatly, their able young men
joined the late Panah Khan and began raiding the *velayats* of Shirvan,
Shakki, Ganje, Erevan[96], and Qaradagh[97] enabling the men to achieve
wealth and position. He earned the love and respect of the rest of the
population [those who were not able to participate in the raids] by
distributing livestock, horses, and *khal'at*.[98] Some of those who opposed
him were forced into submission, punished, or were killed. None of the
Javanshir, Otuz-iki, or other tribes and villages had the power to oppose
the will and command of Panah Khan.

When the rulers of Shirvan and Shakki learned of Panah Khan's
autonomous position and power over the *velayat* of Qarabagh, they
concluded that his presence was detrimental to them. They then formed
a union and joined forces to repel the late khan.

Since at this time the five Armenian *mahals* of Qarabagh had not
submitted to the khan,[99] Panah Khan considered it wise to build a

---

Kara Morteza Beg of southern Zangezur. After that episode, Panah Khan recalled
his tribe from Sarakhs to support him against the khan of Shakki, *Karabakhskogo
khanstva*, p. 70. According to Adigozal Beg, the Qarabaghi tribes, after their
return, were joined by the Damirchi-Hasanli and Jinli tribes from Georgia and
by part of the Kangarlu tribe from Nakhichevan, *Qarabagh-name*, p. 56.

[95] The Russian (*Istoriia Karabaga*, p. 67), Azeri (*Garabagh Tarikhi*, p. 15), and
Turkish (*Karabagh Tarihi*, p. 4) versions have erroneously translated the above as
"Iraq." 'Araq or 'Eraq signifies the province of 'Araq-e 'Ajam, in west-central
Iran, see map 2. The term 'Araq will henceforth be equated with 'Araq-e 'Ajam.

[96] "Erevan" is absent in the Russian translation, *Istoriia Karabaga*, p. 67, but is
included in the Azeri (*Garabagh Tarikhi*, p. 15) and Turkish (*Karabagh Tarihi*, p. 4)
translations.

[97] The Russian (*Istoriia Karabaga*, p. 67), Azeri (*Garabagh Tarikhi*, p. 15), and
Turkish (*Karabagh Tarihi*, p. 4) translations have misread this as "Qarabagh."

[98] The term *khal'at* means a robe of honor, an honorific dress with which princes
conferred dignity upon subjects. It consisted of a turban, robe, and girdle. Minor
subordinates would generally receive a lesser *khal'at*, consisting of weapons or cash.

[99] Mirza Jamal indicates that the Armenian districts in the mountains of
Qarabagh were autonomous as late as the mid-eighteenth century. Since they
controlled the highlands, Panah Khan built the Bayat fortress in the plains.

fortress in an appropriate place among the tribes, so that if the surrounding khans attacked him, he could safeguard his immediate family, relatives, his retainers, and the notables of Qarabagh. After some consultation he constructed the fortress of Bayat, which today is located in the Kebirlu district.[100] In a short time he built strong outer walls and a moat, a bazaar, a bath, and a mosque.[101] Into this fortress he gathered his entire family and retinue, relatives, notables, and the chiefs of the various tribes.[102] Many people, [including] artisans, from the surrounding regions, even from the *velayats* of Tabriz and Ardabil, who had heard of the prosperity, courtesy, and kindness of the late Panah Khan, came with their families and belongings and settled in the Bayat fortress.[103] In the Muslim year 1161, which corresponds to the Christian year 1745 (actually 1748) the construction of the Bayat fortress [10] was completed.[104]

The rulers of Shirvan and Shakki, who were experiencing major losses from Panah Khan's raids, viewed the strength of the Bayat fortress and the size of the late Panah Khan's army as a real threat. They made an alliance and, with a large force, arrived and laid siege to the fortress of Bayat, in order to repulse Panah Khan.[105] The late Panah Khan together

---

[100] Bakikhanov confirms the details of the construction of the Bayat fortress by Panah Khan, *Golestan-e Eram*, p. 160. As noted, one of the wives of Panah Khan was the daughter of the chief of the Kebirlu tribe; hence the khan had a support base at the site of the Bayat fortress.

[101] All major fortress-towns had similar plans. At the center of town was a square or *meidan*, around which were the main mosque, the bazaar, and baths (*hammam*). Some of these towns also possessed a citadel within their walls. Others, usually those built in the mountains, did not require a citadel.

[102] Although Mirza Jamal does not elaborate, the nature of the socioeconomic organization of the tribes was complex. The Otuz-iki and the Bargoshat were at first aloof and kept to their own domain. Later on, a mutual alliance was undertaken, which finally led to the building of the Bayat fortress for the protection of all the tribes.

[103] As the text indicates, the *ilat* or tribal domain of the Javanshir was more than just pastoral or migratory territory. The nerve centers of the domain were forts, which took on the character of minor cities. The khan supported many artisans and laborers in order to build and maintain the forts of Bayat, Shah-Bulaghi, and Shushi (the last two were built later, see below). As the text indicates, the artisan population came from other districts at first, but became part of the *il-e* Javanshir.

[104] The year 1161 is given by Adigozal Beg as well, *Qarabagh-name*, p. 53.

[105] Adigozal Beg writes that some of the chiefs of the Otuz-iki and Javanshir tribes envied Panah Khan's power and, together with the Armenian *meliks* wrote

with his famed cavalry, tribesmen, kinsmen and able attendants, made
sorties unexpectedly every two or three days and in the wide field which
separated the fortress from the invading army battled courageously
against the armies of Shirvan and Shakki, defeat them, and return to the
fortress.

The siege lasted more than a month, yet the khans of Shirvan and
Shakki made no progress. Every day they suffered major losses of horses,
pack animals, and men. They [soon] decamped and [returned] to their
own *velayats* dishevelled and disgraced. During their retreat, the ruler
of the *velayat* of Shakki, Hajji Chelebi [Khan], who was a worthy man of
his time, uttered the following, "Panah Khan was [but] a khan. Now that
we have come and fought with him, and have gained nothing, we are
returning, having made a shah out of him."[106]

After this event, the late Panah Khan's authority and independence
increased daily. He decided to subject [to his authority] the five Armenian *mahals*.[107] First to submit was Melik Shahnazar Beg, the heredi-

---

to Hajji Chelebi of Shakki, who at that time ruled all of the Shirvans (see note 79),
about this dangerous rival and his new fortress. Hajji Chelebi gathered all the
forces of the Shirvans, from Darband to Jaro-Belakan, and invaded Qarabagh,
Ibid., pp. 53-54. Although he had the title of khan, Chelebi's pilgrimage to Mecca
was considered more prestigious; see below.

[106] Two other versions of this quote exist: Ahmad Beg states, "Panah Khan
was a self-proclaimed ruler, but I, by my defeat, have turned him into a khan,"
Karabakhskogo khanstva, p. 70. Adigozal Beg's version differs considerably, "Up
to now Panah Khan resembled an unformed piece of silver; we came and struck
that silver into a coin, and are returning," *Qarabagh-name*, p. 54.

[107] Adigozal Beg and Robert Hewsen provide a description of the five *mahals*
and the *meliks* (see map 4). The first *mahal* was Dizak whose *meliks* were known
as the Melik Egans or Iegans. They had fled Lori (see map 5) some time before
and received the title of *melik* and the authority to rule from Nader Shah. The
meliks of Dizak descended from the Avan family and were scions of the noble
house of Loris-Melik of Lori and Somkhit'i, whose leader, Avan, arrived in Dizak
ca. 1535. Nader Shah elevated Avan's descendant, Melik Avan III (d. 1744), called
Egan, to the leadership of all the Armenians of Qarabagh, Zangezur, and
Azerbaijan. His name Egan (in Persian the "sole" or "intimate") underscored his
reputation as a friend of the shah; it was even rumored that the shah gave him
that name. Mohammad Kazem, confirms that Melik Egan of Togh, who was the
leader of all the Armenians, fought so bravely at the siege of Ganje, that Nader
made him the leader of the Armenians and presented him with gifts, *Alamara-ye
Naderi*, I, p. 410.

The second *mahal* was Varanda whose *meliks* came from the Shahnazarian
clan. They had descended from an even older family than the Avans and were

very much respected and trusted by all. They were originally from the Gökcha (Sevan) region, from where they fled to Qarabagh some time before and became the chiefs of Varanda. During the campaigns of Shah 'Abbas against the Ottomans in eastern Armenia, the Armenians of the village of Mazra', south of Lake Sevan, assisted the shah and offered him hospitality. The shah presented their leader with Varanda and the title of "beg." These begs took the Persian title of Shahnazar ("flourished by the shah's glance") and a number of them served in official posts. Eskandar Monshi mentions a Melik Shahnazar as the officer in charge of reserve troops, *History of Shah 'Abbas*, II, p. 1101.

The third *mahal* was Khachen which was the largest. The *meliks* of Khachen claimed to be from the senior branch of the royal house of Siunik. The patriarch who founded the Khachen clan was called Allah Vardi I. The *meliks* of Khachen were the descendants of the Hasan-Jalalian family, some of whom were so "drunk with glory" that they considered themselves kings and maintained power over all others. Adigozal states that Melik Mirza Khan, who lived in Khnzirestan, a village some 20 miles northwest of Shushi, submitted to Panah Khan and continued to rule this ancient domain. He struck silver coins in the name of Panah Khan. His son Melik Allah Vardi and his grandson Melik Qahraman, "elevated the *melikdom* to the skies." Hewsen states that Melik Mirza and Melik Qahraman were not related to the Hasan-Jalalians but were minor officials who were elevated by Panah Khan to the rank of *melik* (see note 127).

The fourth *mahal* was Jraberd. The *melik* of that *mahal* was Melik Allah Qoli. His ancestors were from the Haikazian-Israelian clan and arrived there from Megavuz (Mahavuz), a village in Zangezur, hence the village of Chardakhli (Chardahli) in the upper Tartar river of Qarabagh, is sometimes called Mahavuz. They settled in the region and built a fortress in an inaccessible place by the river called Jermykh or Chirmukh (Jermuk), where they took refuge and became famous. They soon built the fortress of Jraberd as well. When Nader Shah fought the Turkish general Koprulu Oglu 'Abdullah Pasha, Melik Allah Qoli demonstrated particular bravery against the Turks. Nader felt that the title of *melik* was not enough for such a man and ordered that he be called "sultan." Melik Allah Qoli's promotion is also mentioned by Ahmad Beg, *Karabakhskogo khanstva*, p. 71. For that particular campaign of Nader Shah see, *Tarikh-e Jahangoshay*, pp. 246-254. In fact, the mountains of Qarabagh and Zangezur were the only regions the Turks did not control during their ten-year rule in western Transcaucasia. The Armenians were also instrumental in helping Nader defeat the Turks in the Erevan campaign. Armenians cut off the Turkish troops at Ashtarak and Üch-Kilisa, *Ibid.*, p. 254. It is not surprising, therefore, that Nader not only visited the Edjmiadsin cathedral and granted various privileges to the Armenian clergy and *meliks*, but invited the Armenian *catholicos* (supreme patriarch) as an honored guest to his coronation, see L. Lockhart, *Nadir Shah* (London, 1938), pp. 97-98, 279. See also note 117.

The fifth *mahal* was Talesh (Golestan). Its *melik* was Melik Usub (Yusuf). His ancestors came from Shirvan. The *meliks* of Golestan belonged to the Beglarian clan, whose founder Abov, claimed to be related to Siunik royalty as well. For

tary[108] *melik* of the Varanda *mahal*, who had a dispute with and resented the [Armenian] *meliks* of Jraberd, Golestan, and Dizak.[109] He demon-

---

some time they lived in Talesh. Melik Usub then captured the fortress of Golestan and moved there. Adigozal Beg, *Qarabagh-name*, pp., 57-58, Hewsen, "The Meliks of Eastern Armenia," I, pp. 308-324 and II, pp. 288-296.

According to Hewsen most of the *meliks* had Armenian names which were used among family members and appear on their tombstones. Otherwise, they were only known by their Arab, Mongol, Persian, or Turkish titles and names. Some of the information provided by Adigozal Beg appears in slightly different versions in the works of Ahmad Beg and Mirza Jamal (Berzhe's translation), see below and notes 109, 110, 112, 127, 128, 129, 130 and 131.

[108] The word *qadim* also means ancient or old, implying in this context that his family had held the title of the *meliks* for some time.

[109] Bakikhanov confirms the same facts, *Golestan-e Eram*, p. 160. According to Ahmad Beg the dispute originated because Melik Shahnazar had killed his uncle, Melik Sein, and had usurped his position, *Karabakhskogo khanstva*, p. 70. Adigozal Beg refers to the uncle as Melik Husi or Husin (Hosein). He adds that Panah Khan fanned the enmity between the *meliks* of Golestan and Jraberd and tried to break their union. He goes on to state that at that time, Melik Shahnazar of Varanda, desiring "the silver mantle of rule," forced his father's brother, Melik Husi, from his position, and became *melik*. When news of this reached the other *meliks*, they all joined together and marched against him, for they considered such an act shameful. Before their arrival, Melik Shahnazar had fortified the Chanakhchi fortress (sources refer to it also as Chinakhchi, Chamakhchi, and other variants) and had sought refuge there. The warring *meliks* entered Varanda and looted all of it but could not take the fortress. They retreated vowing to return the next spring. Melik Shahnazar, realizing the weakness of his position, began to court Panah Khan's friendship and also showed the khan the site of Shushi, as a well-defended site for a future fortress. Adigozal concludes that Melik Shahnazar was from a very old and famous family and very wealthy. He goes on to say that Melik Shahnazar and his son Melik Jamshid enjoyed the continous respect, love, and attention of the late Panah Khan and Ebrahim Khan, especially since one of Melik Shahnazar's daughters was a wife of Ebrahim Khan, *Qarabagh-name*, pp. 55, 58-59. According to Hewsen Melik Shahnazar was Shahnazar III (ca. 1755-1791). He killed his brother or uncle (depending on the source) Melik Hosein or Husein II (Armenian name Hovsep) and, according to Armenian sources as well as Mirza Jamal, was actually responsible for Panah Khan's gaining access to the mountains of Qarabagh and starting his campaign against the other *meliks*. It seems that after the death of Shahnazar, Ebrahim Khan's actions forced his son, Jamshid, to leave Varanda. Jamshid returned after the Russians came to Qarabagh and held the title of *melik* in the territory of Varanda from 1805 to 1822, when Qarabagh was officially annexed to Russia. Jamshid may have been one of those responsible for the death of Ebrahim Khan, see note 409.

strated in every possible way his devotion and friendship for the late Panah Khan and in return the khan, who considered the obedience of such a great, wealthy, and respected person advantageous to his own authority, did not hesitate to respect and honor him daily.

Although the *melik* of Khachen[110] expressed hostility and wavered for some time, he eventually submitted and the late Panah Khan allowed him to remain *melik* of his own separate [hereditary] *mahal*, where his descendants are still today. [11] The inhabitants of Khachen thus all accepted the authority [of Panah Khan] and conscientiously carried out all that was required of them.[111] But the *meliks* of the *mahals* of Dizak and Jraberd and Golestan, for a number of years, remained enemies and fought with Panah Khan. Finally, after massacres, looting and other necessary measures, they submitted as well.[112]

---

[110] Ahmad Beg calls him Melik Ulubab of the Hasan-Jalalian family, *Karabakhskogo khanstva*, p. 70. According to Hewsen, Melik Ulubab must be Melik Allah Vardi I (1747-1755), whose family periodically ruled over Khachen and who were intermarried with the Ulubeg clan, hence "Ulubab." The family had a mountain fort above the Ballu River. The Hasan-Jalalians became the patriarchs of the See of Gandzasar, known as the catholicoses of the House of Albania. Among them is the famous Isaiah or Esai (served 1702-1728) who wrote a short history of that region. Another catholicos, Hovhannes Hasan-Jalalian (served 1763-1786), was killed by Ebrahim Khan. Also see note 107.

[111] In fact, as will be noted below, this was just a temporary truce. The resistance of some of the major families continued throughout the short history of the khanate. For example, when the next khan, Ebrahim, tried to place his own candidate (Israel of Gandzak) as the patriarch at Gandzasar, the Armenians rebelled and rejected his choice.

[112] Berzhe's translation of Mirza Jamal's history has more details on the conflict between the khan and the Armenian meliks, see below. According to Ahmad Beg, the *melik* of Dizak, Melik Egan, possessed a strong fortress (the fortress of Togh, also called Tugh, Tuk) where, together with his clan, he guarded the treasuries of the other *meliks*. After stubbornly resisting, some were slaughtered (Ahmad Beg's term) and others converted to Islam. The *melik* of Jraberd (who had a mountain fortress in Jraberd), Melik Allah Qoli Sultan, first submitted, but later was accused of treachery and executed by the order of Panah Khan. His brother, Melik Hatam, who was an ally of the fifth *melik*, Melik Usub of Golestan (who had a mountain fortress in Golestan), managed for a long time to remain independent, but after a bloody encounter near Mardakert, the two of them took refuge in Jraberd's other unassailable fortress, Jermuk, on the heights of the Tartar River, where they managed to resist for nearly a year. They finally fled with their families to Ganje, where they continued to intrigue against the Javanshir khans, *Karabakhskogo khanstva*, pp 70-71; Adigozal Beg confirms these

After residing five years in the fortress of Bayat, Panah Khan decided that since the fortress was surrounded by numerous foes, it was not prudent to remain there and to build a permanent city. Therefore it was imperative to construct a fortress in the mountains of Qarabagh, so that in time of war the tribes of Qarabagh [who lived on the plain] could protect their flocks and possessions from the enemy in those impregnable mountains.[113]

Since the population of Khachen *mahal* who lived in Tarnakut, located above Shah-Bulaghi, constantly displayed enmity[114] and fought with the late Panah Khan, he first made it a point to totally defeat them, and with his cavalry and infantry[115] waged war against them.[116]

---

facts, adding that both sides lost many men in battle, *Qarabagh-name*, p. 58. Melik Majnun, the son of Melik Hatam, who had settled in Ganje, as will be noted, later collaborated with the enemies of Ebrahim Khan). Also see notes 107 and 259.

[113] It is obvious that his rule was not as secure as he would have liked. Adigozal Beg adds that Panah Khan thought that "the population of Javanshir, Otuz-iki, and the Armenian *meliks* are against me, so I need a more secure place." According to him Panah Khan abandoned the Bayat fortress and went to Tarnakut on the Tartar River, where he built the Shah-Bulaghi fortress, *Qarabagh-name*, p. 55. The fortress, as will be noted, was actually located on a tributary of the Khachen river, see note 139. Mirza Jamal does not go into details here, but much of Panah Khan's apprehension was due to the activities of King Teimuraz of eastern Georgia and his son, Erekle II. Sensing the void which was created after the death of Nader Shah, they attacked Erevan in 1749, defeated the Qajar governor and generally took that khanate under their protection. In 1750 the Georgians defeated Panah Khan and assumed temporary control of Ganje and parts of Qarabagh as well. It seems that a number of Armenian *meliks* had asked Erekle's help against Panah Khan's encroachments. In 1751, however, Hajji Chelebi of Shakki soundly defeated Teimuraz and Erekle and deprived them of their gains in Ganje and Qarabagh. Erekle still considered Erevan his protectorate for he fought and defeated Azad Khan, who in 1752 had crossed the Arax into that khanate. For more details see, D. M. Lang, *The Last Years of the Georgian Monarchy, 1658-1832* (New York, 1957), pp. 147-149.

[114] Here it becomes clear that the prior agreement was just a temporary truce and that the *meliks* of Khachen constantly fought to keep their autonomy.

[115] Mirza Jamal frequently uses the term *qoshun*, a Turkish word which appears in Aq Quyunlu and Safavid texts, signifying "cavalry troops." Mirza Jamal, however, uses it as "cavalry" in some chapters and as "army" in other. He could have used the Persian word *lashkar* (army) to differentiate between the two, but has not.

[116] Panah Khan had to subdue them before he could start the construction of the Shah-Bulaghi fortress. The Khachen highlands overlook Shah-Bulagh (see map 4).

The inhabitants of Khachen, including some two thousand musketeers and their families, resisted from an impregnable *saqnaq* [117] in the
vicinity of Ballerqaye (Balluchay).[118] The late Panah Khan stormed their
stronghold and for three days the battle raged on, with continuous fire
pouring from both sides. On the third day the late Panah Khan captured
their stronghold. A number of the men were executed, and in order to
frighten the others and teach them a lesson, a tower of some three
hundred speared heads was made at Sartelli, at the bank of the Khachen
river.[119]

---

[117] Persian *saqnaq*, Turkish *síghínak*, Armenian *seghnakh*, signifies a fortified
shelter, place of refuge, or lair. In Qarabagh, they were built and used by the
Armenians during the Ottoman occupation (1724-1734) of western Transcaucasia (eastern Armenia). The Armenian *meliks*, realizing that they were not strong
enough to fight the Ottomans individually or in the open, sought refuge in the
mountains and began guerilla warfare under the leadership of David Beg and
Avan Yuzbashi, who was given the title of khan by the last Safavid shah,
Tahmasb II (1722-1732). For more details see L. Lockhart, *The Fall of the Safavid
Dynasty and the Afghan Occupation of Persia* (Cambridge, 1958), pp. 260, 354. A
number of settlements in Qarabagh and one in Georgia were thus named
Seghnakh.

[118] Ahmad Beg accurately calls it Ballu-chay (the Ballu River, see map 4),
Karabagskogo khanstva, p. 70.

[119] The Russian (*Istoriia Karabaga*, p. 69), Azeri (*Garabagh Tarikhi*, p. 17), and
Turkish (*Karabagh Tarihi*, p. 6) translations have dropped this sentence. Adigozal
Beg has the following version: "Despite the fact that Melik Shahnazar and his
family had good relations with the khan, his grandson Melik Ulubab turned
against the khan, gathered a mob from the various villages of Khachen, and with
this so-called army, fortified himself in Ballugay (Ballu-chay) and rebelled
against Panah Khan. Hearing this, the khan crushed them…[deleted pas-
sage]…After that the population of Khachen wore the ring of defeat on its ear
and took upon its shoulders the loyalty to the khan and ceased to be hostile,"
Qarabagh-name, pp. 58-59. Ahmad Beg states that Melik Ulubab of Khachen and
his sons were slaughtered [his term] by the khan, *Karabakhskogo khanstva*, p. 70.
There is no evidence in other sources that Melik Ulubab (Ulubeg), whose also
was known as Allah Vardi, and who ruled over Khachen, was the grandson of
Melik Shahnazar Beg, or was related to the Shahnazarians of Varanda. The
numerous marriage alliances between the *meliks*, however, makes it possible that
he was, or was rumored to be, a scion of the Shahnazarians, information which
Adigozal Beg must have obtained from the Qarabaghi Armenians.

Panah Khan at the head of the Javanshir, Sarujlu, Kebirlu, and other tribal
cavalry went against the melik of Khachen. He met them [the Armenians] in the
area between Shah-bulagh and the river Gargar. The Armenian forces of
Khachen united with some of the inhabitants of the Jraberd mahal and dealt him
a severe defeat and began to pursue Panah Khan. When Panah Khan's troops
noticed that the Armenians had left their mountains and had descended into the
plain [in their pursuit], they turned around, attacked, and routed the Arme-
nians, forcing them to flee. The Armenians took refuge in the mountain strong-
hold of Balliqaye where they bore the attacks of the khan, losing 300 men. In
memory of that victory, Panah Khan errected a monument by the Khachen
river.[120]

After this affair, in which Panah Khan succeeded in capturing such
a well-fortified place, defended by two thousand musketeers, the population of the surrounding regions and the remaining five [Armenian]
mahals became [12] very frightened and [while] at times they displayed
hostility, at others they came to terms with Panah Khan. A number of
skirmishes occurred with Melik Hatam,[121] the *melik* of Jraberd *mahal*
and Melik Usub Beg,[122] *melik* of the Golestan *mahal*. Both had been *meliks*
for some time,[123] were prosperous, and had a large number of men.
Finally, when they realized that they could not continue to maintain
their stand [against Panah Khan], they moved to impregnable passes
in the deep gorges or in the high mountains. Soon, however, realizing
that their property, animals, and farms were being pillaged, confiscated,
or destroyed by the late Panah Khan and his followers, they were forced
to leave their land, homes, orchards, and farms, abandon their homeland,[124] and flee to Ganje, where for the next seven years they lived in
the Shamkhor *mahal* in Ganje.[125] When Panah Khan vanquished his
enemies and quelled the sedition among the people of Khachen, he

---

[120] "Karabag," 62 (1855), 264.

[121] Melik Hatam (Armenian name, Adam) was the brother of Allah Qoli
Sultan, the head of the Israelian clan of Jraberd. He was the *melik* from 1761 to
1780 or 1782. Also see note 107.

[122] Melik Usub (Yusuf II, Armenian name, Hovsep) was the head of the
Beglarian clan of Golestan. Also see note 107.

[123] The Persian text implies hereditary rule in the family.

[124] Mirza Jamal uses the term of *vatan*, which demonstrates that he considered
the five *mahals* as Armenian homelands.

[125] The bitter feud between some of the Armenian *meliks* and Panah Khan
explains their cooperation with the enemies of the Javanshir khans, as well as
their welcome of the Russians to Ganje and Qarabagh, see below.

appointed another *melik* and the remaining population became obedient.[126]

*After the pacification of the Khachen mahal, Mirza Khan was appointed its
[new] melik. His descendants in the persons of Melik Qahramat (Qahraman)
Beg and his brothers are presently in that mahal.*[127] *Panah Khan then cast his
eyes on the Jraberd mahal, which in those days was ruled by Allah Qoli Sultan.*

*[Earlier] during the siege of Ganje by Nader Shah, when Sardar 'Abdullah
Pasha Korpuli Ogli*[128] *had headed out from Turkey to relieve that siege, as well
as the sieges of Erevan and Tiflis, Nader had entrusted the siege of Ganje to his
commanders, and had himself gone out to meet 'Abdullah Pasha, whom he
soundly defeated. 'Abdullah Pasha was killed by Rostam Sultan Qarachorli
Qarabaghi Mahavizlu and his head was brought to Nader, who ordered Hani
Effendi to transport the body, with full honors, to Turkey. In that campaign,
Melik Allah Qoli, together with a number of Armenians from Jraberd, had
demonstrated special bravery against the Turkish artillery, for which he had
been rewarded with the title of sultan.*

*Although Melik Allah Qoli displayed animosity towards Panah Khan, and
occasionally even gained the upper hand, he soon realized the futility of future
enmity. Accompanied by a number of notables of Jraberd, he set forth to meet
Panah Khan and to conclude a truce. Panah Khan treated them with respect,
gave them gifts and titles and, having concluded a truce they returned.*

*The peace, however, was broken by Panah Khan himself. Melik Shahnazar
Beg of Varanda, the meliks of Khachen, and even some of the notables of Jraberd
who hated Allah Qoli Sultan, invited Panah Khan to break the pact of friendship
and to kill the melik. When Allah Qoli Sultan paid Panah Khan a return visit,
Melik Shahnazar Beg, in the presence of Heidar Qoli Khan, the ruler of*

---

[126] The other *melik* was Melik Mirza (see note 127). Panah Khan could not and
did not desire to vacate the mountains of Qarabagh of its large Armenian
population. He needed their cooperation, food supplies, occasional taxes, and
especially, as will be noted, musketeers.

[127] After the death of Allah Vardi Khan or Ulubab (depending on the source),
Panah Khan appointed the headman of Khnzirestan (one of the Armenian
villages of Khachen), Mirza Khan, to administer the *mahal*. By 1775, however, the
Hasan-Jalalian clan had resumed control of most of the *mahal* under Allah Vardi
II (1775-1813). The family of Mirza Khan, however, kept control over their village
and its environs. Their descendants, Qahraman Beg and his brothers are therefore mentioned by Mirza Jamal. Also see note 107.

[128] The reference is to 'Abdullah Pasha Koprulu, who was killed fighting
Nader in 1735. Mohammad Kazem has a detailed account of that battle, *Alamara-
ye Naderi*, I, pp. 389-402. Also see note 107.

*Nakhichevan, incited Panah Khan with the following words, "It is difficult to
believe that a grand person such as this would be eternally loyal to you. At the
first opportunity he would turn against you. To lose such a great opportunity
[to kill him] is against the rules of caution observed by great men like yourself."*

*After hearing that statement, Panah Khan invited Allah Qoli to his quarters
at night [for supper] and on his [Allah Qoli's] return, he, together with two or
three of his attendants, was killed.*[129]

*The inhabitants of Jraberd, angered by Panah Khan's action, rallied in
determination and declared a decendant of Allah Qoli Sultan, Hatam Beg, as
their leader. The new melik allied himself with the melik of Golestan, Melik
Tahmuras (Teimuraz), a timid and weak person. Teimuraz, whose kinsman,
Yusuf Beg, did not have any support in Golestan and was at that time residing
with Melik Hatam, trusted the friendly overtures of Hatam and came to Jraberd.
He [Teimuraz] was seized on arrival, taken to the northern side of the bridge
over the river Tartar, at the border of the two mahals, and killed. Melik Hatam
then allied himself with Yusuf Beg*[130]*and began to plot against Panah Khan. The
khan, hearing of the union against him, decided to crush it at the outset. After
a long struggle, he laid siege to the fortress of Jermuk which was the residence
of Melik Hatam Beg by the Tartar River. It was in an impregnable location and
had a strong garrison. There was but one narrow road, suited mainly for the
passage of infantry. The cavalry forces of Qarabagh, composed of Javanshir,
Sarujlu, Kebirlu, and Otuz-iki accomplished the unthinkable and crossed the
road to the fortress. Melik Hatam's forces suffered a siege with many losses from
death and capture. Many of the notables of Jraberd mahal voluntarily submitted
to Panah Khan, but some families, including that of Melik Hatam, managed to
escape. The same year, Panah Khan marched against Yusuf Beg and, although
he had little success at first, there too he eventually achieved a brilliant victory.*

*After this defeat, both meliks with their families and close associates fled to
Ganje to Shahvardi Khan, who was not on friendly terms with Panah Khan, and*

---

[129] According to Adigozal Beg, it was the khan of Nakhichevan who tempted
Panah Khan to kill Allah Qoli Sultan, when the latter was visiting him in
Agh-Oghlan. He told the khan that a wealthy *melik*, who travels with such a
maginificent retinue, would not obey him for long, *Qarabagh-name*, p. 59.

[130] It seems that Yusuf went to Golestan and became its *melik*. He became the
junior member of the coalition led by Hatam of Jraberd. According to Hewsen
there is only one Teimuraz in the history of the *meliks* of Golestan. He was the
regent for Yusuf and was hanged by Yusuf and Melik Hatam. Yusuf became
melik and held that position until 1775. Although this information agrees with
the above narrative, Teimuraz's death, according to Hewsen, occurred much
earlier.

settled in Shamkhor and in the villages located in the mountains of Ganje. Here they remained until the events involving Fath 'Ali Khan Afshar which will be described below.[131] *[Eventually] after the conclusion of friendly relations between Panah Khan and Shahvardi Khan, those two meliks were assured of their safety by Panah Khan and returned to their lands. They continued as meliks to the end of Panah Khan's life and through the duration of the rule of Ebrahim Khan. They were treated well and were even exempt from all taxes, except for the Talesh mahal, from which Ebrahim Khan took 300 tomans*[132]*and 500 chetvert of wheat annually for his nephew Lotf 'Ali Beg. He himself received appropriate gifts, which he would in turn give as khal'at and gifts to others.*[133]

At the same time that Panah Khan was busy fighting the meliks of Khachen, Talesh, and Jraberd, he also brought the Dizak mahal, whose melik was Isai [Isaiah] Beg, into submission. It happened thus:

Prior to Isaiah Beg, the mahal was ruled by his father, Egan Beg, a wealthy man, who had great influence during the reign of Nader Shah,[134]*and to whom all the clans of Jraberd, all Armenians, as well as the small Muslim groups [on the fringes] of Dizak, paid tribute. Nader Shah had put him above all the other five meliks and occasionally permitted him to rule over them. Egan Beg in return supplied the Persian army with arms and provisions during their campaigns in Qarabagh, Shirvan, Ganje, and Daghestan. After his death, Nader Shah appointed his son, Isaiah Beg, as the melik. After Nader's death, because of his friendship with the sardar of Azerbaijan, who was appointed by 'Adel Shah, Isaiah continued to enjoy his special status.*[135] *Panah Khan's rise to power resulted in unfriendly relations between the two. Finally Panah Khan gathered his forces and together with Melik Shahnazar Beg, attacked the village of Tuk*

---

[131] These *meliks*, as will be noted below, allied with Fath 'Ali against Panah Khan. Adigozal Beg confirms all the above and adds that they stayed in Shamkhor for seven years, suffering under terrible conditions, *Qarabagh-name*, p. 60.

[132] The *toman* at that time equaled approximately one Russian ruble or one pound sterling. Three hundred *tomans* was a considerable sum, demonstrating the great wealth and economic potential of the Armenian *mahals*.

[133] The hostile actions of the Armenians and their alliance with Panah Khan's enemies must have jolted the khan. He considered it better to have a loyal Armenian population than risk another conflict. Hence he permitted the *meliks* to return and granted them some sort of autonomy, which included exemption from taxes.

[134] See note 107.

[135] The Armenians of Qarabagh had a number of fighting units at the disposal of the *sardar* of Azerbaijan. Melik Isaiah was the *melik* of Dizak from 1747 until 1781 when he, together with a large number of notables of his *mahal*, were killed by Ebrahim Khan.

(Togh), where Melik Isaiah Beg had gathered most of the population and 3000 bodyguards. The siege lasted several days, with both sides losing many men. Panah Khan himself was wounded and withdrew, allowing Melik Isaiah to plunder the villages of Varanda and other settlements belonging to Panah Khan or his allies. Next year Panah Khan set off once again to defeat Isaiah Beg. This time he came to Teru, located in the high mountains and accessible from only one direction. He was defeated again and Melik Isaiah pursued him, inflicting more casualties to Panah Khan's retreating forces. Panah Khan, for the third time, tried his luck, and fortune finally smiled on him, for he succeeed in defeating Isaiah Beg, who escaped to Togh. Realizing that no help was forthcoming, he asked for negotiations for a truce. He sent a number of people to Panah Khan and finally presented himself, accompanied by 300 attendants, to the khan, who was in Palutlu. He was greeted with full respect, but on the fifth day, he and his entire retinue were seized and deprived of all their belongings in Togh. Except for some elderly residents, who were left to oversee the orchards and houses, all the rest of the population of Togh were dispatched to the Chanakhchi fortress where they stayed for a long time. Melik Isaiah's family and the families of the notables were, after the construction of the Shushi fortress, transferred there.

After the conclusion of the aforementioned wars and the submission of the five Armenian mahals, as well as of the villages of the Ikirmi-dort, and Yulak, which, prior to that, were always under the suzerainty of the ruler of Ganje, Panah Khan undertook the conquest of Zangezur, Sisian, Chuldur, and Bargoshat (see map 4), which after two or three years became part of Qarabagh. Those of the meliks, sultans, and minbashis[136] of these mahals whom he could not trust were replaced by his own men. The territory of Qarabagh increased as well as its population, which was composed mainly of Armenians and Muslims.[137] At the same time, Panah Khan made the positions of the sultans and begs hereditary. In case one died and his children were not of age, Panah Khan would appoint several capable administrators until the heirs could manage for themselves.[138]

After that he began the construction of the fortress of Tarnakut, which today is famous as the Shah-Bulaghi ("King of Locks") fortress. [Panah

---

[136] The Safavids had established the practice of using the term *sultan* for local rulers. *Minbashi*, as noted, literally means "head of one thousand," and generally referred to tribal chiefs.

[137] The Armenians are listed first in the original text.

[138] "Karabag," 62 (1855), 264 and 63 (1855), 270. This section is the largest part not included in Mirza Jamal's manuscript of 1877/78. See introduction, also see notes 107, 109, 110, and 112.

Khan] decided to abandon the Bayat fortress and instead planned another fortress in Shah-Bulaghi, in the vicinity of its large spring.[139] There he dug and built [a fortress] on high ground, surrounded it with high walls, with a bazaar, a square, a bath, and a mosque.[140]

In the year of the Muslims 1165 [1751/52] all the tribes and their households, together with all notables, artisans and craftsmen, and administrators [of Bayat] were transferred to the Shah-Bulaghi fortress.[141]

In the meantime Hajji Chelebi, the ruler of Shakki,[142] who was known for his intelligence and bravery, demanded that Panah Khan accept his authority and not attempt to do anything without consulting him. Panah Khan, considered this request insulting and beneath him and in order to protect himself against a sudden attack from Chelebi Khan, he began to search for an ally. He eventually made an alliance with Heidar Qoli Khan of Nakhichevan, Qasem (Kazem) Khan[143] of Qaradagh, and Shahvardi Khan of Ganje.[144] They also agreed to send

---

[139] According to various maps the fortress is situated by a spring which connects to the Khachen river. The Russian (*Istoriia Karabaga*, p. 70) and Azeri (*Garabagh Tarikhi*, p. 16) editors place it on the Tartar River, which is in northern Khachen. Had Panah Khan built his fortress there, in the mountains of Qarabagh, he would have had no need for another fortress in the mountains (the later Shushi fortress). Bakikhanov calls the fortress "Tarnavut" and states that evidence of the fortress still existed in his time, *Golestan-e Eram*, p. 160; Donboli also calls it "Tarnavut," *Ma'ser-e Soltaniye*, p. 151. In some sources "Tarnakut" or "Tarnavut" replaces Shah-Bulaghi, which itself is occasionally called "Shah-Bulagh."

[140] Adigozal Beg adds that the fortress was built of stone, *Qarabagh-name*, p. 55

[141] Ahmad Beg gives the year as 1752, but states that the climate and location were not suitable and the fortress was soon abandoned, *Karabakhskogo khanstva*, p. 72. Adigozal Beg confirms the date 1165 (1751/52), *Qarabagh-name*, p. 55. The tribal domain of Panah Khan now embraced the various *ilat* and *mahalat*. The text indicates that everyone was transferred to the new fortress. The extreme insecurity of the times required the khan's allies and dependents to live within the walls of a fortress.

[142] Adigozal Beg substitutes Shirvan for Shakki, which is not farfetched, considering that Hajji Chelebi controlled most of the lands east of the Kur river, *Ibid.*, p. 65.

[143] "Qasem" is an incorrect transliteration. Ahmad Beg has "Kazem," *Karabakhskogo khanstva*, p. 72, Adigozal Beg and Bakikhanov also mention "Kazem," *Qarabagh-name*, p. 65, and *Golestan-e Eram*, p. 161. Some sources identify him as the khan of Qaraje-dagh.

[144] Shahvardi Khan was named after his great-grandfather Shahvardi Sultan Ziadoglu Qajar, who was appointed to his post in Ganje by Shah Tahmasb I

an envoy to the vali of Georgia[145] *[Erekle] to warn him of the danger from the ruler of Shakki, who at times had made alliances with the ruler of Daghestan, as well as a marriage alliance with the khan of Kazikumik (Qazi Qumuq),*[146] *and to ask him not to refuse a meeting to figure a way to halt the ambitions of the mighty Hajji Chelebi. The embassy was successful and they received a promise of aid from the lofty vali of Georgia.*[147] *A few days later, the vali invited them to a feast, where all four khans were seized. Not fearing that anyone would come to their rescue, the vali stayed on in the vicinity of Ganje. Hajji Chelebi, learning of this despicable act of the Georgian vali, despite the malevolent plans of the khans against him, decided to free them. Having collected a large force, he moved on the vali, crossed the Kur, attacked and crushed him.*[148] *He pursued him to*

Safavi (1524-1576). It seems that the Ziadogli Qajars were among the earliest Turkmen groups to obey Shah Esma'il and join the Shahsavan. Although not a major tribe, they were rewarded by the Safavids and rose to govern Ganje and Erevan as the *beglarbegis* of Qarabagh and Chukhur-e Sa'd. With the exception of the periods when the Ottomans controlled Ganje, the descendants of Shahvardi Sultan were the hereditary khans of Ganje. Even Nader Shah did not oust them from that position, although, as noted, he did reduce their holdings by separating Qarabagh, Borchalu, and Qazzaq from their jurisdiction. Shahvardi's son, Javad Khan, was the last khan of Ganje. He died defending Ganje against the Russians. One of his sons, Oghurlu Khan, and some other family members left for Iran after the Russian conquest of their khanate, see note 348.

[145] Erekle II, (1744-1762) as king of Kakhet'i, and (1762-1798) as king of the united K'art'li and Kakhet'i kingdom. Although Teimuraz II, the father of Erekle II, was a co-ruler with Erekle until 1762, Mirza Jamal and other local sources refer to Erekle as the *vali*. The title of *vali* or viceroy was given to the Georgian rulers of the Bagrationi family by the Safavids. Georgia, unlike the rest of Transcaucasia, had a special status under the Safavids. It supplied troops to the shahs and enjoyed a degree of autonomy.

[146] The khan of Kazikumik (Kumuk) refers to the khan of the Qumuq tribe of northern Daghestan.

[147] Adigozal Beg adds that they met north of Ganje in a small village called Qezel-Qay. The editor of the Russian translation also adds that the date, according to the anonymous Georgian Chronicle, was 1752, *Qarabagh-name*, p. 66.

[148] Shukiurzade gives the location near the mausoleum of Nezami, *Karabakhskogo khanstva*, p. 100. Adigozal Beg adds that an attendant of Panah Khan's rode a swift horse to Hajji Chelebi, who was preparing for war against the khans, to inform him of what had occurred, whereby Chelebi made a grand gesture to free the khans. The two forces met near the mausoleum of Sheikh Nezami. Erekle panicked, for he had faced the Hajji before, when he and his father Teimuraz were defeated by Chelebi in 1751. Erekle was defeated this time as well. The Shirvani forces pursued the Georgians until three *aghach* (the same as *farsakh*, equal to seven *versts*) before the Broken Bridge. Hajji Chelebi almost

the Akstafa River and freed the khans and brought them back to Ganje.[149]

Panah Khan could not forget this kindness and constantly sought an opportunity to repay it. The opportunity presented itself soon, although unfortunately after Hajji Chelebi's death [1758]. The khan of Shakki was related to the ruler of Kazikumik in Daghestan, for the daughter of the latter was the wife of the son of Hajji Chelebi, Aqa Kishi Beg, a worthy and brave young man, as ingenious as his father. Mohammad Khan Surkhai, the ruler of Kazikumik, invited his son-in-law with his wife and upon his arrival, ignoring kinship, tortured and killed him. The next day he marched into Nukha (capital of Shakki) where he took possession of the property of the dead beg. Hosein, the son of Aqa Kishi Beg, from another wife, escaped to the Sultan of Qabala, and with his help gathered a small force from the inhabitants of Qabala, Kutkashin, Khachmaza,[150] *and the surrounding regions of Shirvan. He also requested help from Panah Khan, who, having heard of the presence of Daghestanis in Nukha, had prepared his army, just in case Mohammad Khan decided to enter Qarabagh. Panah Khan's army was by the bank of the Kur and was composed of warriors from the five Armenian mahals, Jevanshirs, Kebirlu, Otuz-iki, Demurchi, Hasanli, Kolani, Qarachorli Kurds, and Persians.*[151] *Here he heard of the murder committed by Mohammad Khan Surkhai. He gathered his troops around and gave a rousing speech reminding them of Hajji Chelebi's deed and the need to avenge and to wash away the blood of the unlucky Aqa Kishi Beg. They all agreed to do so and to follow Panah Khan. He immediately crossed the Kur and entered the road to Nukha. The inhabitants of the districts of Shakki, hearing this, joined his forces. Hosein Khan, who had come out of Qabala, joined him by the village of Dakhpalu [Dahpalu]. Surkhai heard the news and*

---

[149] reached Tiflis, a distance of only five *aghach*. On their retreat through Shamkhor, Shams od-Din, and Qazzaq, the Georgian soldiers suffered many losses. Hajji Chelebi ordered trenches and fortifications to be built in the area of Baidar and named his son, Aqa Kishi Beg, the ruler of the Muslims of the region up to Tiflis. Aqa Kishi ruled for three years, until Erekle gathered some of his men, and together with the forces of Imeret'i (a small kingdom in western Georgia) and the Circassians forced Aqa Kishi to flee to Shakki. Some of Aqa Kishi's men were captured. Erekle's army reached the Khoda-afarin Bridge and on their way plundered many villages in Ganje and Qarabagh.

[149] Bakikhanov confirms the above, except he adds Hosein 'Ali Khan of Erevan to the coalition of khans, *Golestan-e Eram*, p. 161. Ahmad Beg describes the same coalition but against Erekle, *Karabagskogo khanstva*, p. 72, an alliance which had occurred earlier. Adigozal Beg follows the Berzhe translation, *Qarabagh-name*, p. 65.

[150] Villages in Shakki.

[151] The Armenian forces are listed first in the source.

prepared his own troops to meet Panah Khan. The two armies met in Nukha, in whose streets a massacre took place. Surkhai lost everything and fled to Kazikumik, leaving all the loot he had gathered from Aqa Kishi Beg's property to [Aqa Kishi Beg's] son, Hosein [Khan]. Panah Khan confirmed Hosein Khan as the ruler of Shakki and returned to Qarabagh.[152]

[13] Three or four years later, the late Panah Khan's fully independent reign in Shah-Bulaghi, his authority, and the size of his force, increased his fame daily and spread it into nearby regions. The khans of Shirvan, Shakki, Ganje, Erevan, Nakhichevan, Tabriz, and Qaradagh sent letters and messengers to the late Panah Khan expressing their friendship and solidarity. He became related to a number of these khans. [In the meantime], he took control of the *mahals* of Zangezur from Nakhichevan; the Qapans[153] from Tabriz; and Chuldur, Meghri, and Gunay from Qaradagh which were [respectively] under the rulers of Nakhichevan, Tabriz, and Qaradagh, and attached them to Qarabagh, appointing his own *meliks* and sultans.[154] They all obeyed the late Panah Khan's rule. These [borders and officials] are in effect to this day.[155]

---

[152] "Karabag," 63 (1855), 270. According to some Russian sources Hosein Khan was not the son of Aqa Kishi but his nephew, see *Akty*, V, p. 1120.

[153] The Persian text reads "Qapanat," which refers to the town of Qapan or Ghapan and its surrounding region.

[154] These lands were given as *toyul*. According to Bakikhanov, it was only after the construction of the Shushi fortress that Panah Khan's power increased. He controlled all the territory from the Khoda-afarin bridge to the Kurek River and Bargoshat, as well as the *mahals* of Meghri and Gunay, which belonged to Qaradagh; Tatev and Sisian, which belonged to Nakhichevan; Terter-Kolani which was under the control of Erevan; and Zangezur and Qapan which belonged to Tabriz. He also occasionally held power over other surrounding regions, like Ardabil. Bakikhanov, unlike Mirza Jamal, does not exaggerate the power of Panah Khan, *Golestan-e Eram*, p. 160. Adigozal Beg's version is basically the same, with some additions. According to him, the *minbashis* of the Kangarlu tribe of Nakhichevan, the Damirchi-Hasanli and Jinli tribes on the borders of Georgia, also accepted his authority. The khan, in return, was very much involved in their welfare. According to Adigozal Beg the native Javanshir, Otuz-iki and Kebirlu tribes who had arrived with the Turks or Mongols were split. The Kebirlu were faithful and devoted to the khan, but the other two acted in a fashion that made them suspect, *Qarabagh-name*, p. 56. Iranian chroniclers do not ascribe such power to Panah Khan. For example, Mohammad Hashem states that Panah Khan, even later, was the master of Shushi, but that the rest of Qarabagh was not under his permanent control, *Rostam ot-Tavarikh*, p. 351.

[155] Not all of these regions remained part of Qarabagh after the Russian

Chapter Four:
On the Issuing of the Decree Which Named
Him Khan of Qarabagh and the Rule of
the Late Panah Khan[156]

After the murder of the late Nader Shah, his brother's[157] son, 'Ali Qoli Khan, gave himself the title of 'Adel Shah[158] and ascended the late shah's throne. Amir Aslan Khan Sardar, who had been appointed by 'Adel Shah as the *sardar* of Azerbaijan, and who was stationed in Tabriz, heard of the independent rule and fame of Panah Khan in Qarabagh, and on his own initiative sent him a horse, sword, and *khal'at*.[159] He urged and encouraged him to recognize and submit to 'Adel Shah.[160]

The late Panah Khan showed kindness and respect to the messengers

---

conquest. Mirza Jamal exaggerates, for by the time of his writing Iran had control over the lands south of the Arax and Russia had incorporated all the rest into her empire and had divided it into new administrative units (see introduction). The main reason for Mirza Jamal's statement is not political, but economic. The titles and prerogatives of *meliks*, begs, and sultans survived under the Russians into the first half of the nineteenth century. By the second half of the century, most local dignitaries had to produce documents to support their claims to lands and titles. Some of the claims were disputed and Armenian and Turkic feudal chiefs were challenged not only by the Russians, but by their own upstarts. Mirza Jamal's history, although objective by contemporary standards, naturally favors his own clan.

[156] Berzhe's translation reads, **Chapter Four: Continuation of the Rule of Panah Khan Following the Death of Nader Shah,** "Karabag," 65 (1855), 278.

[157] Adigozal Beg identifies Nader's brother as Ebrahim, *Qarabagh-name*, p. 52.

[158] Bakikhanov calls him 'Ali Shah, *Golestan-e Eram*, p. 156. Iranian sources refer to him both as 'Ali Shah and 'Adel Shah.

[159] Amir Aslan Khan Afshar was the nephew of Nader Shah and one of his able commanders. He was appointed as the beglarbegi of Azerbaijan and Transcaucasia by Nader, a post in which he remained until 1161 (1748). Ahmad Beg claims that Panah Khan, surrounded by unfriendly neighboring khans and by the Armenian *meliks*, who did not appreciate his rise to power at their expense, made the first overture and sent an embassy. This is the more probable account, *Karabakhskogo khanstva*, p. 72.

[160] Adigozal Beg records that Amir Aslan Khan came to meet Panah Khan and immediately gave him the title of sultan. The next day he made him khan and asked him to submit, which Panah Khan did, *Qarabagh-name*, p. 52.

of Amir Aslan Khan Sardar and dispatched with them a number of noted *kadkhodas* (village headmen) of the tribes [of Qarabagh], who were respected [14] and known for their acumen, for it was not the time to foster enmity and war with so powerful and exhalted person as the *sardar*. This was especially so, since some of the khans of the surrounding *velayats*, although appearing friendly and loyal, in reality were against him. Therefore, he [Panah Khan] acted humble and sent gifts and letters in which he declared his obedience to the rule of 'Adel Shah.

Amir Aslan Khan Sardar considered such obedience and the coming of [such] messengers of great assistance to the rule of 'Adel Shah, and he, [therefore], wrote to the shah [about it]. In the year of the Muslims 1161, corresponding to the Christian year 1745 (actually 1748), a trusted messenger of Amir Aslan Khan Sardar aarived in the fortress of Bayat with 'Adel Shah's *farman* (decree) granting him [Panah Khan] the title of khan and appointing him [Panah Khan] the governor of Qarabagh.[161] [In addition, the shah] sent a costly *khal'at*, a horse with a gold-inlaid saddle, and a jeweled sword. At the same time, Amir Aslan Sardar sent his own gifts to the late Panah Khan, while the elders [messengers] who had come from Panah Khan were accorded all manner of respect, and [also] returned with gifts.[162]

In this fashion, the [official] title of khan and the authority to rule was, for the first time, granted to the late Panah Khan by 'Adel Shah, son of the late Nader Shah's brother. It was not long after that, that the late Panah Khan heard that Shahrokh Mirza, the son[163] of the late Nader Shah, had killed 'Ali Qoli Khan, who was called 'Adel Shah, [15] and had ascended the royal throne in Khorasan, and that this action had prompted unrest in the territories of 'Araq, Azerbaijan, and Fars.[164]

---

[161] In order to set the stage for the official appointment of Panah Khan and the creation of the khanate of Qarabagh, Mirza Jamal moves the narrative back from 1756 to 1748.

[162] This was customary, to demonstrate that the *sardar* was the overlord of Panah Khan. Ahmad Beg adds that Amir Aslan Khan and Panah Khan then forced the Ganje, Shirvan, and Shakki khanates to recognize 'Adel Shah, *Karabakhskogo khanstva*, p. 71.

[163] Actually his grandson; Ahmad Beg correctly identifies him as the grandson, *Ibid.*, p. 71.

[164] The events were as follows: 'Adel Shah was overthrown in 1748 by his brother Ebrahim, who himself was overthrown by Shahrokh in the same year. Shahrokh, was deposed and blinded by one of his officers. According to Adigozal Beg, the events brought new forces into the region, resulting in the arrest of Amir Aslan Khan by Kazem Khan of Qaraje-dagh, who appointed someone else to

During these troubled times, the late Panah Khan decided to seize the *velayats* of Ganje, Erevan, Nakhichevan, and, in particular Ardabil, and to force the khans of those regions to obey him. Within a short period of time, he made them obedient, some by force, others through envoys or through marriage alliances. In the city of Ardabil, in particular, he appointed Dargah Qoli Beg Sarujlu as governor.[165] He would appoint governors from among the progeny of the khans of Ganje, [appointing] those who humbly requested it and removing them at will.[166] He brought a number of the sons of the khans of the aforementioned *velayats* to the Shah-Bulaghi fortress as hostages.[167]

---

govern Tabriz, *Qarabagh-name*, p. 52. Ahmad Beg writes that Amir Aslan Khan was killed by Kazem whom he identifies as Khan of Qaradagh, *Karabakhskogo khanstva*, p. 71. Iranian sources state that Amir Aslan allied himself with Ebrahim Shah and together they overthrew 'Adel Shah. Amir Aslan's power, however, frightened Ebrahim, and he soon arrived with an army. Amir Aslan met him in battle, was defeated, and sought refuge with Kazem Khan of Qaraje-dagh. Soon after, Kazem betrayed him and handed him to Ebrahim Shah, who killed him, *Bamdad*, I, pp. 166-167. Mirza Jamal and other Qarabaghi chroniclers do not mention the details of what occured in this period, much of which took place in Azerbaijan and Georgia. The main players were Azad Khan and Erekle. In 1750/51, Azad marched on the governor of Tabriz, who was supported by Kazem Khan of Qaraje-dagh, Panah Khan, as well as the Shaqaqi Kurd, 'Ali Khan. Azad Khan Afghan defeated the coalition, took Tabriz and then looked beyond the Arax, where Teimuraz and his son Erekle, taking advantage of the chaos, were enjoying their own success in expanding Georgian hegemony in Transcaucasia, especially at the expense of Erevan. Azad laid siege to Erevan, but was repulsed by Erekle with heavy losses. Erekle went on to Tabriz but had to retreat when a group of Transcaucasian khans, led by Mohammad Hasan Khan Qajar, forced him to retire to Tiflis. Azad then made an arrangement to marry a sister of Erekle, and by 1752 had become the supreme power in Azerbaijan and even controlled Nakhichevan. *Mojmal ot-Tavarikh*, 183-188.

[165] Ahmad Beg places this action later, during Mohammad Hasan Khan's invasion of Qarabagh, *Karabakhskogo khanstva*, p. 73 (see note 179). Adigozal Beg has "Sarijalu" and does not include Erevan in the list of *velayats*, *Qarabagh-name*, p.61

[166] Berzhe's translation reads, *He appointed a khan from the Ziadoglu Qajar family to rule in Ganje*, "Karabag," 65 (1855), 278.

[167] Berzhe's translation adds, *They stayed until the rise to power of Mohammad Khan*, "Karabagh," 65 (1855), 278. He does not mention which Mohammad Khan, but the context makes it certain that he means Mohammad Hasan Khan Qajar, see below.

When it became apparent that Mohammad Hasan Khan Qajar[168] had assumed power as the independent ruler of Mazandaran, 'Araq and Azerbaijan, the late Panah Khan's experienced advisors, who were ever mindful of the affairs of state, assembled by his order and advised him as follows:

"Upon the death of the late Nader Shah we had an alliance and friendly relations with 'Ali Qoli Khan ['Adel Shah] and Amir Aslan Sardar. It is possible, however, that we will not have such friendly relations with Mohammad Hasan Khan; nor are we sure of our neighboring khans. It is very possible that they would incite [Mohammad Hasan Khan], and that together they would defeat us. In that case the tribes and militia of Qarabagh would be trampled by the Qezelbash[169]

---

[168] The Qajars were a minor Turkmen tribe which had arrived with other major tribes in Iran sometime between the eleventh and thirteenth centuries. Their later claims of Oghuz, Mongol, or Timurid ancestry have not been substantiated. By the fifteenth century, they were in Anatolia and Azerbaijan, from where a number of them entered the regions of Erevan, Ganje, and Qarabagh. They fell under the influence of Shi'ism and were one of the original seven Turkmen tribes (referred to as the Qezelbash) who supported the Safavids. The early Safavids awarded them most of eastern Armenia. It is probable that during this period the division between the two rival branches of the Yukhari-bash and Ashaqa-bash took shape. Each branch was further subdivided into the clans of Qoyunlu or Qavanlu, Develu or Davalu, Izzadinlu, and Ziadlu or Ziadoglu. The Qavanlu of the Ashaqa-bash later started the Qajar dynasty of Iran, while the Davalu from the Yukhari-bash provided many of the functionaries and military commanders of Iran. Shah 'Abbas I, mistrusting the growing power of Turkmen tribes, divided the Qajars, sending some to Khorasan as a buffer against the Uzbeks, others to Astarabad in Mazandaran, as a buffer against the Turkmen (see map 2). The rest remained in Erevan, Ganje, and Qarabagh, where they were soon replaced or absorbed by other tribes. After the fall of Esfahan to the Afghans, Fath 'Ali Khan Qavanlu of the Astarabad Qajars tried to extend his influence by supporting Shah Tahmasb II. He became a close companion of the shah but soon clashed with a new favorite, Tahmasb Qoli Khan Afshar (later Nader Shah). Fath 'Ali was murdered in 1726 (the Qavanlu later blamed the murder on the Davalu and Nader). His son, Mohammad Hasan spent his youth as a fugitive from the Afshars and the Davalu Qajars. By 1744, however, together with his supporters, he took Astarabad. For the next fifteen years he fought various contenders for the Safavid throne, such as Karim Khan Zand and Azad Khan Afghan, among others.

[169] It is interesting that Mirza Jamal refers to the Iranian army or any force south of the Arax as the Qezelbash. This term was also used by the Russians, which may be one reason that Mirza Jamal uses it. The other reason, as noted, was the aura of the Safavids, which lingered on until the end of the eighteenth century.

army, for the fortress of Shah-Bulaghi would not withstand such a powerful foe and [especially if allied with] the neighboring khans. We would surely all perish. Therefore [we have to] devise a solution before these events occur. [You should] build a fortress inside the mountains, [16] one which would remain forever; strong, impregnable, and unassailable, so that even the mightiest foe could not besiege or penetrate it. The fortress should be permanently accessible on one side to the inhabitants of the mountains; nor should it be cut off from the *mahals* [of Qarabagh]."

This advice was shared with Melik Shahnazar Beg, who had always wished [the khan] well, and with the help and supervision of that *melik*, the decision to construct the Shushi fortress was made.[170] In the meantime, the khan also sent a number of other experts and trusted people in his service to look over the location and the environs of the future fortress. It was discovered that there was no running water at the site of the fortress, except for two or three small springs, which would not be sufficient for such a [large] army and residents. They began digging wells at sites where they thought they could strike water. Most of their excavations struck water. News of all this was sent to the late Panah Khan, who was very pleased and with a number of close associates, visited the site and approved the construction of the fortress.[171]

In the Muslim year 1170, corresponding to the Christian year 1754 (actually 1756/57), all the *ra'iyat* (peasants) of the Shah-Bulaghi fortress, along with the noble families and persons, *meliks*, attendants, tribal elders, and the inhabitants of some villages were sent to reside in the new fortress.[172] Prior to this, no one had lived at that site. It had

---

[170] The Armenians had been building fortesses in the region for some two thousand years, while the nomadic Turkmen had no experience. The fortress, as shall be seen, truly withstood many an enemy.

[171] Bakikhanov implies that there was a small fort already there which belonged to Melik Shahnazar Beg of Varanda and at the request of the *melik*, Panah Khan repaired and enlarged it, from where he forced the other Armenian *meliks* to submit to him, *Golestan-e Eram*, p. 160.

[172] The date of 1170 (inaccurately calculated as 1754 by Ahmad Beg as well) has been cited both by Adigozal Beg and Ahmad Beg, *Qarabagh-name*, p. 62, *Karabakhskogo khanstva*, p. 72. The Iranian chroniclers agree with Mirza Jamal. Hedayat has 1171 as the arrival of Mohammad Hasan Khan Qajar to Shushi, which according to Mirza Jamal was a year after the fortress was completed, *Rouzat os-Safa*, IX, p. 37. Mohammad Hasan E'temad os-Saltane states that a group of Afghans from Azad Khan's forces appeared before the fortress in late 1170 (1757), *Montazam-e Naseri*, II, p. 1156. The Azeri editors of Ahmad Beg's and

occasionally been used as a pasture by the villagers of Shoshi, who lived some six *versts*[173] east of the fortress.[174] After seeing to the needs of the population, the khan designated the living area [for them], and especially, the site of his home and personal quarters. He then had skilled masters and able and alert supervisors errect the walls of the fortress.[175] These walls and fortifications, which were built by the late Panah Khan, are currently in ruins, except for a few places where there is still evidence of them.

A year after the construction of [17] the fortress, Mohammad Hasan Khan Qajar, who was the father of Aqa Mohammad Shah, came with the armies of 'Araq and Azerbaijan to capture the fortress of Shushi and to force the late Panah Khan to bow to his will.[176] He crossed the Arax and

---

Adigozal Beg's chronicles are skeptical. Shukiurzade points out that the exact date is unknown. According to him it is possible that the fortress rose around 1751, for a coin bearing its name was struck at that date, *Karabakhskogo khanstva*, p. 101. The editor of Adigozal suggests that the fortress was built earlier, in 1750-51. He sites the fact that the fortress existed during the Chelebi-Erekle conflict, which, according to the anonymous Georgian chronicle, took place in 1752, *Qarabagh-name*, pp. 62-63. It is possible that the foundations were laid sometime in 1751 and the final move into the completed fortress took place at a later date. The text indicates that some villages moved to the fortress (these were settled groups who now farmed in the vicinity of the fortress and could seek refuge there if necessary). It also states that tribal chiefs also moved into the fortress, but not the tribes, who probably continued to live in a dispersed condition as pastoralists. The social hierarchy of Qarabagh is also apparent here. After the Javanshir family came the nobles, the Armenian *meliks*, the attendants, the tribal headmen, and finally the peasants.

[173] *Verst* is a Russian measure of length equalling 3500 feet or two-thirds of a mile.

[174] There was an Armenian village called Shosh or Shush-kend in the vicinity. The fortress had a mint and was originally called Panahabad ("built by Panah"), *Karabakhskogo khanstva*, p. 72, *Rouzat os-Safa*, IX, p. 297, and Bakikhanov, *Golestan-e Eram*, p. 160. Panah Khan's silver coins bearing the incription of "There is one God, His name is Allah, and Mohammad was His Prophet," on the obverse side and "minted in Panahabad," on the reverse side, were still found in Iran at the beginning of the twentieth century. The coins weighed one *mesqal* (4.4 grams) and were valued up to ten *shahis*, *Bamdad*, V, p. 41.

[175] Ahmad Beg mentions that artisans and other skilled people came from other places and settled there, *Karabakhskogo khanstva*, p. 73.

[176] Hedayat gives 1171 as the date of his arrival, *Rouzat os-Safa*, IX, p. 37. Ahmad Beg seems to imply that Panah Khan had earlier accepted the leadership of Mohammad Hasan Khan, for, during the struggle for the Afshar throne, after the

camped four *farsakhs* from the fortress.[177] He remained there for an entire month trying everything he could think of and using various schemes to bring the late Panah Khan into obedience and to take control of the Shushi fortress. However, despite his extremely large army, he could not even manage to come close to the fortress. In the meantime, the bold Qarabaghis[178] openly and covertly grabbed horses, mules, and other four-legged beasts from the troops, inflicting damage upon the army of Mohammad Hasan Khan.[179]

At this time word came to Mohammad Hasan Khan that Karim Khan Zand had gathered a large army in the city of Shiraz, in the realm[180] of Fars and was planning to take 'Araq and Mazandaran. [Mohammad Hasan Khan] then abandoned the idea of capturing the [Shushi] fortress, as well as of taking control of the Shirvans, Ganje and other *velayats*, and with great speed he moved towards 'Araq, Fars, and Mazandaran.[181]

---

death of Nader, Azad Khan Afghan (whom he incorrectly indentified as Aziz Khan Uzbek), came with a large army to Iran from Turkestan and took Tabriz in 1750/51. Azad Khan, as noted, soon moved on Erevan, but Erekle came to the aid of the Khan of Erevan and repulsed him (see note 164). Azad's heavy taxes, brutality, and plans to move eastward led to an alliance of Shi'i khans, under the leadership of Mohammad Hasan Khan Qajar. An army of 18,000 men, 3000 of whom were Qarabaghi cavalry under the command of Mehr 'Ali Khan, a son of Panah Khan, attacked Azad Khan and forced him to flee to Kurdistan, *Karabakhskogo khanstva*, p. 72. Azad planned an alliance with and sought asylum with Erekle, who kept him as a well-treated prisoner. Erekle surrendered him later to Karim Khan Zand who took him to Shiraz, where he died in 1196 (1781/82).

[177] Adigozal Beg states that Mohammad Hasan Khan Qajar gathered his forces from Astarabad, Mazandaran, and Gilan and came to Shushi, camping near the Khatun-arkh settlement not far from the fortress, p. 63.

[178] The Persian word is *qoldor*, which can be translated as "ruffians." The Russian translator has chosen the word "brave," which may have been the intention of Mirza Jamal.

[179] Ahmad Beg states that the two forces met thirty *versts* from Shushi, near the canal of Khatun-arkh. After a bloody battle, Mohammad Hasan Khan was defeated. Not only did his cannons fell into the hands of Panah Khan (later to be used against the Iranians) but he was pursued across the Arax, where Panah Khan took Ardabil and installed Dargah Qoli Beg as its ruler, *Karabakhskogo khanstva*, p. 73. Mirza Jamal describes the taking of Ardabil and the installation of Dargah Qoli as taking place earlier (see p. 69 in text).

[180] The Persian term is *mamlekat*.

[181] This is confirmed by Hedayat, who adds that this occured in the year 1171 (1758/59), *Rouzat os-Safa*, IX, p. 39. Adigozal Beg states that he left in such a hurry that his cannons were left in Khatun-arkh and that they were used against the

Karim Khan Zand, prior to the arrival of Mohammad Hasan Khan, had taken control of the entire *velayat* of Fars, parts of 'Araq, and other *velayats*, and prepared to do battle with Mohammad Hasan Khan, who had gathered a large force from Azerbaijan, the Gilans,[182] and other *velayats* and had proceeded to Fars to repulse Karim Khan. But fortune and prosperity are gifts of the benevolent God, hence, some of the close companions of Mohammad Hasan Khan decided to betray him. They killed him, and hoping to obtain high positions and financial rewards, took his head to Karim Khan.[183]

But since defending the honor of *sardars* and noblemen against such base actions is the duty of [other] *sardars*, he [Karim Khan] refused to reward the murderers of Mohammad Hasan Khan in any fashion, but rather punished them publicly,[184] so that others would not be tempted to betray their benefactors.

Qezelbash during the Russo-Iranian war, *Qarabagh-name*, p. 64. Nami states that having no success in taking Shushi, Mohammad Hasan gathered Fath 'Ali Khan Afshar, Shahbaz Khan Donboli and other chiefs of Azerbaijan and went to Shiraz in 1171, *Tarikh-e Giti-gosha*, pp. 60-61. Following the death of Nader Shah, Mohammad Hasan Khan fought a number of battles and almost succeeded in becoming the sole ruler of Iran. His son Aqa Mohammad Khan finally succeeded in making the Qajars the rulers of Iran.

[182] The text reads "Gilanat," which signifies Gilan and its surrounding regions along the Caspian Sea.

[183] This version does not correspond to the Iranian primary sources which mention that Mohammad Hasan Khan died a year later, on 12th or 14th February 1759. After retreating from the Zands, he entered Mazandaran where due to the treachery of his Davalu followers he was forced to flee. His horse was stuck in mud and he was struck down by Sabz 'Ali Kurd or, according to some sources, Mohammad Khan of Savadkuh. Mohammad 'Ali Aqa Davalu then severed Mohammad Hasan's head, which was sent to Karim Khan in Tehran. Karim Khan was extremely distressed, and had it buried with honors. Mohammad Hasan's body was buried with full honors in Astarabad by Sheikh 'Ali Khan, a commander of Karim Khan's, see *Tarikh-e Giti-gosha*, pp. 45-47; *Golshan-e Morad*, pp. 107-109, *Rouzat os-Safa*, IX, pp. 64-71. Fasa'i, and Hedayat also add that Mohammad Hasan Khan's slayer (Sabz 'Ali) was not rewarded; but, rather, upon his arrival in Tehran was himself put to death by the order of Karim Khan, *Farsname-ye Naseri*, I, 212; *Rouzat os-Safa*, IX, p. 70. Mirza Jamal incorrectly places Mohammad Hasan Khan's death immediately after his attack on Shiraz; in fact, it occurred much later. It is obvious that Mirza Jamal was more concerned with the details of events in Qarabagh and condensed other extraneous material.

[184] The Persian term *siyasat* has a number of meanings, among which is "public punishment."

After the episode concerning Mohammad Hasan Khan, Fath 'Ali Khan Afshar Urumi[185] of the *velayat* of Urumiye (Urmiye),[186] who was one of the [18] *sardars* of Nader Shah, aspired to rule and had gained control over all of Azerbaijan.[187] No matter how many eloquent messengers he sent to persuade the late Panah Khan to submit and to ally with him, he [Panah Khan] rightfully considered submission to such a *sardar* shameful and beneath him, and thus returned the envoys with harsh replies.

After the return of his envoys, Fath 'Ali Khan gathered a large army from among the inhabitants of Azerbaijan, Urmiye, and other *velayats* and, determined to capture the fortress, gain control of Qarabagh, and defeat Panah Khan, came to Shushi and set up camp one *farsakh* from the fortress.[188] The [Armenian] *meliks* of Jraberd and Talesh, who secretly harbored enmity towards the late Panah Khan, joined Fath 'Ali Khan.[189] For six months they remained close by the fortress and there were battles and skirmishes every few days between the late Panah Khan

---

[185] Ahmad Beg incorrectly refers to him as Fath 'Ali Khan Rumeli, *Karabakhskogo khanstva*, p. 73.

[186] Urmiye is the region west of Lake Urmiye in northwestern Iran, see map 2.

[187] Fath 'Ali Khan was one of Nader Shah's most trusted commanders and had participated in the Indian campaign. After Nader's death he joined Ebrahim Shah and was appointed the governor of Fars. After the death of Ebrahim, in 1163 (1749/50) he was appointed as the military commander of Chukhur-e Sa'd, Ganje, and Qarabagh by the Safavid prince Soleiman II (1749-1750), one of the nominal rulers in Iran. He soon joined Azad Khan and became one of his main allies. Mirza Mohammad Khalil Mar'ashi states that Soleiman gave Fath 'Ali *khal'at*, a sword and dagger, five horses, and an enameled saddle, *Majma' ot-Tavarikh* (Tehran, 1983), p. 120. Fath 'Ali Khan probably felt that he had the right to ask the Transcaucasian khans to submit to his authority.

[188] Ahmad Beg describes a 30,000-man army which arrived just before winter, *Karabakhskogo khanstva*, p. 73. Adigozal Beg states that after seven failed attempts to rush the fortress they then trenches and settled in for the winter. The evidence of their trenches, he adds, was still there in his day, *Qarabagh-name*, p. 68.

[189] As noted, these Armenian *meliks* had good reason to go against Panah Khan. The passage also demonstrates that Panah Khan had no firm control over the Armenian *mahals* even after the flight of the *meliks*, as there was no Muslim administrative apparatus in place there. It also reaffirms the fact that the *meliks* still had armed forces which they could muster for or against Panah Khan. Adigozal Beg identifies these *meliks* as Melik Hatam and Melik Usub. According to him there was, at his time, still evidence of their trenches as well, *Qarabagh-name*, p. 69.

and the army of Fath 'Ali Khan.[190] The troops of the late Panah Khan were always victorious over the Qezelbash army. During this time Fath 'Ali Khan could not do anything but witness his daily defeats with distress.

Finally one day, with all his cavalry and infantry, as well as the troops of the aforementioned *meliks*, he [Fath 'Ali Khan] stormed the fortress. Crossing the Shushi river,[191] he approached the fortress and came within half a *verst* of it.[192] The late Panah Khan, with skilled young warriors and the famed sharp-shooting musketeers from the tribes and from the districts of Varanda and Khachen[193] counter-attacked from one side, while from the other side the tribal cavalry and the brave kinsmen of the late Panah Khan also went on the offensive. The forces of Fath 'Ali Khan suffered a major defeat and were captured or killed in the deep valleys and narrow passes [of the region]. The killing and capturing continued and ceased [only] in the vicinity of Fath 'Ali Khan's camp. The storming [of the fortress] left the army of Fath 'Ali Khan with approximately two thousand dead or captured cavalrymen and infantrymen. [19] [The rest], dishevelled and penitent, returned to their camp, while the late Panah Khan, accompanied by trophies of war and prisoners, made a victorious and triumphant entry into the fortress [of Shushi].[194]

Fath 'Ali Khan Afshar, seeing such a defeat, as well as the approach of [another] winter, took on a peaceful and agreeable tone.[195] He dis-

---

[190] The six months were in addition to the winter spent there, see *Ibid.*, p. 69.

[191] Mirza Jamal means the river which runs by Shushi, the Gargar.

[192] Ahmad Beg states that they crossed the Gargar river and approached the fortress from an undefended and deserted side where they were ambushed, *Karabakhskogo khanstva*, p. 73.

[193] This passage perfectly illustrates the fact that the Armenian *meliks* were divided, some working with the khans of Qarabagh, others not.

[194] Ahmad Beg states that having lost the siege of Shushi, Fath 'Ali gathered those who did not like Panah Khan, including the Armenian *meliks* and neighboring khans, and set up camp in Khojalu 17 *versts* from Shushi. A guerilla warfare ensued, in which Kara Morteza Beg and other associates of Panah Khan took full advantage against the enemy, some of whom were unfamiliar with the terrain. *Karabakhskogo khanstva*, p. 73

[195] Adigozal Beg states that Fath 'Ali Khan and Panah Khan finally agreed to a truce. Their envoys met at the Aqa Bridge (close to Shushi) and peace was concluded. Then Fath 'Ali Khan invited Ebrahim to his camp with safe conduct for a feast. There is no mention of a wedding, prisoners, or an exchange of hostages, *Qarabagh-name*, p. 70.

patched skilled envoys, who delivered the following sworn promise: "If Panah Khan releases the prisoners of war and agrees to union and friendship, I, with a truthful countenance, promise to give my daughter to his eldest son Ebrahim Khalil Aqa, and we will become eternal kinsmen and friends. [This will be] on the condition that he [Panah Khan] will send Ebrahim Khalil Aqa to me to eat sweets[196] in my camp, to participate in the ceremony of marriage and to return after two or three days." In order that the late Panah Khan would be assured [of the return of his son], he sent three of his own sons and kinsmen to remain Panah Khan's hostages until the safe return of Ebrahim Khalil Aqa.

Trusting the firm vows of Fath 'Ali Khan and seeing the sending of [Fath 'Ali's] sons and kinsmen [as a sign of good faith], the late Panah Khan dispatched Ebrahim Khalil Aqa with two or three elders to the camp of Fath 'Ali Khan. Fath 'Ali Khan, upon hearing the news, became glad and sent a number of his sons to greet Ebrahim Khalil Aqa and to escort him with great honor and music to the camp.

Being given the pretext that the omens were not favorable [for the wedding], Ebrahim Khalil Aqa was kept waiting for two days in the camp and was entertained with music and banquets. During the same two days, Fath 'Ali Khan continously dispatched trusted men to the fortress with wedding sweets for Panah Khan, following all the necessary customs and using all the proper salutations. Thus he succeeded in his insidious plan and fooled [Panah Khan] into releasing his prisoners [of war] and the hostages.

On the third day Ebrahim Khalil Aqa, with the elders [who had accompanied him], was [20] imprisoned, and [the invading army] decamped and rushed to the fortress of Urmiye without stopping anywhere.[197]

The late Panah Khan and the nobles of Qarabagh were full of sorrow,

---

[196] A traditional Iranian wedding custom.

[197] Ahmad Beg states that he left with his hostage, announcing that Panah Khan was his vassal, *Karabakhskogo khanstva*, p. 73. Bakikhanov does not mention the trick, but states that Ebrahim was given as a hostage to Fath 'Ali Khan. The event, according to him, took place in 1175 (1761/62), *Golestan-e Eram*, p. 162. Adigozal Beg states that Ebrahim, after a few days, realized that he could not leave the camp, and that he was always observed or was in the company of *amirs*. He wrote to his father to send him his swift red horse to escape, but before the horse arrived he was bound and taken across the border, *Qarabagh-name*, pp. 70-71

confusion, and despair. But realizing that in the end nothing would come from being dejected and grief-stricken they began to devise ways to release [Panah Khan's] son and to defeat Fath 'Ali Khan.

Since the Creator of the universe and the Maker of mankind's body and soul, in every moment of time, is the patron and friend of upright, just, and sincere people, and grants success and victory especially to those who remain steadfast and firm in their pledges, agreements, and treaties and who avoid the slyness and perfidy which result in regret and downfall, the God of the universe gave full power and independence of action to Karim Khan Zand, who, by taking over 'Araq and Fars, had laid claim to the throne.

He [Karim Khan] incited a conflict with Fath 'Ali Khan, appointing one of his [Karim Khan's] relatives to subdue him.[198] He was dispatched with the army of 'Araq and Fars to Azerbaijan. Hearing this, Fath 'Ali Khan, prior to the arrival of the invaders, immediately gathered his own army from Azerbaijan and the surrounding regions, and went to meet the force sent by Karim Khan. The two armies clashed in the *velayat* of Esfahan.[199] Karim Khan's army suffered a defeat and the member of his family who was the commander of the army was killed. Fath 'Ali Khan returned victorious, along the way annexing a number of districts of

---

[198] Adigozal Beg identifies him as Karim's brother, but calls him Eskandar Khan during this episode and Eskandar Beg later on, *Qarabagh-name*, pp. 71, 73. Golestane also identifies him as Karim's brother, *Mojmal ot-Tavarikh*, p. 212. In fact, Eskandar was Karim Khan's half-brother.

[199] Esfahan, the capital of the Safavids, is located in southwestern Iran (see map 2). Nami states that the two met some nine *farsakhs* outside Esfahan in a place called Qomshe. His account and those of other Iranian chroniclers differ considerably from Mirza Jamal's and those of other local historians. According to Nami, the enemies of Karim Khan were led by Azad Khan, with Fath 'Ali Khan being one of his allies. He adds that Azad Khan and his forces were defeated and on the run, when Eskandar Khan followed them and was killed by bullets in an ambush, *Tarikh-e Giti-gosha*, pp. 38-39. Golestane also cites Azad Khan as the main enemy, but adds that Karim Khan was present at the battle. The forces of Azad Khan and his allies were so large, that Eskandar Khan decided to ride out and kill Azad Khan before the battle. He rode into the ranks of the enemy, who, assuming that he had a message and afraid of his bold manner, let him pass. He came close to the group of commanders, but not knowing who Azad was, killed the man standing next to him. He was then shot, rode back wounded and with his dying breath exclaimed to Karim, "I have killed either Azad or someone else; if the first is true you have won the day, otherwise, retreat immediately," *Mojmal ot-Tavarikh*, pp. 287-289.

'Araq. Following this event, Karim Khan Zand sought revenge and with his entire large army moved from the *velayat* of Fars to Azerbaijan to defeat Fath 'Ali Khan. Prior to entering the territory of Azerbaijan, he dispatched a trusted person to the late Panah Khan conveying his [Karim Khan's] friendship, honored him with his favor, and expressed his desire for an alliance. The letter sent by him contained the following message: "Fath 'Ali Khan has become not only our enemy, [21] but is a murderer. To you he did that which should not have been done—he broke his word and oath and took your son with cunning and insidiousness and has imprisoned him. We expect your total support, so that our revenge and the release of your son will bring you happiness and bring us the fulfillment of our desired goal."[200]

Taking advantage of these fortuitous events to crush his crafty and conniving enemy, Panah Khan, with his troops and famed Qarabaghi horsemen went to join Karim Khan in Azerbaijan.[201]

He entrusted the governing of Qarabagh to his younger son, Mehr 'Ali Beg and his nephew, Esma'il Beg.[202] Karim Khan met him with great fanfare, respect, and gifts, and together they went to the *velayat* of Urmiye to crush Fath 'Ali Khan.[203]

Fath 'Ali Khan had gathered a large army from the regions under his domain and rose to meet them. Both sides entered into battle, which

---

[200] Adigozal Beg adds: "He daily attacks one *amir* or another...and I have therefore decided to go against him. I ask you as a friend to join me without delay. I need your aid and from the bottom of my heart, I promise to avenge my brother and free your son," *Qarabagh-name*, p. 72.

[201] Ghaffari states that Karim Khan's order arrived when Panah Khan was on the way to fight with Kazem Khan of Qaraje-dagh, *Golshan-e Morad*, p. 175. His version presents it as an order and not a request.

[202] "Karabag," 65 (1855), 278. This passage is the only source that confirms Ahmad Beg's claim that his great grandfather was appointed as khan of Qarabagh. See introduction and note 206. The text, however, divides the power between two inexperienced youths, clearly anticipating his own and Ebrahim's return.

[203] Nami gives the names of the other khans who joined Karim Khan: Kazem Khan of Qaraje-dagh, Shahbaz Khan Donboli and his brother Ahmad Beg, and Panah Khan Javanshir. He adds that Panah Khan was a major chief and had numerous tribes under his control, including the Javanshir, Qazzaq, Borchalu, with over 20,000 families in total. He possessed the famous fortress of Shushi as well, which was atop a high mountain and, up to that time, had never been surrendered to anyone, *Tarikh-e Giti-gosha*, p. 105.

ended with the defeat of Fath 'Ali Khan and his retreat into the Urmiye fortress.

After a few days, having no other recourse, except submission and hope for clemency from Karim Khan,[204] he [Fath 'Ali Khan] surrendered and the Urmiye fortress was taken by Karim Khan, who became a [more powerful] independent ruler.[205]

Karim Khan called himself *vakil* (regent) of the Shah of Iran, stating that: "Since Iran [at the present] does not have a sovereign shah, I shall act as the representative of the shah until one appears and ascends the throne." That is why they called Karim Khan, the *vakil*.

Karim Khan freed Ebrahim Khalil Aqa, who was imprisoned in Urmiye, and had him brought to him. A horse, sword, *khal'at* as well as the title of khan, and the authority to rule Qarabagh was granted to him and he was sent with gifts and a retinue to Qarabagh.[206] Having a

---

[204] Adigozal Beg states that Karim Khan promised to spare his life, *Qarabagh-name*, p. 72. Nami confirms this clemency, *Tarikh-e Giti-gosha*, p. 122.

[205] Bakikhanov cites the date as 1176 (1762/63), *Golestan-e Eram*, p. 162. Ghaffari puts it at the end of 1175 (1762), *Golshan-e Morad*, p. 196. Although Mirza Jamal claims that Fath 'Ali surrendered the fortress after a few days, Iranian sources mention a long siege of seven months (24 July 1762 to 20 February 1763), see *Mojmal ot-Tavarikh*, p. 457; *Golshan-e Morad*, pp. 192-197.

[206] Bakikhanov and Adigozal Beg confirm that Ebrahim was sent to Qarabagh, *Golestan-e Eram*, p. 162, *Qarabagh-name*, p. 72. Ahmad Beg has a very different version. He states that Ebrahim Khan was also taken to Shiraz and that the governorship was entrusted to Mehr 'Ali Khan, the younger son of Panah Khan. Ebrahim Khan soon returned (1761) and hence the people usually referred to Mehr 'Ali as "beg" and not "khan." Ebrahim brought the remains of his father. He clashed with Mehr 'Ali over the rule of Qarabagh and was not firmly established until he married the sister of 'Umma Khan of the Avars. Mehr 'Ali then fled to Karim Khan, who ordered Hedayat Khan, the ruler of Ardabil, to replace Ebrahim Khan, but he was unable to do so. When Karim Khan died in 1779, Mehr 'Ali fled to Fath 'Ali Khan of Qobbe and was later killed (1783/84) by Aghasi Khan of Shirvan and his son, who were dispossessed of their seat of government by Fath 'Ali Khan, *Karabakhskogo khanstva*, pp. 74-75. Ahmad Beg's date of the return of Ebrahim Khan, as will be noted, is totally inaccurate. Bakikhanov has a different version of the death of Mehr 'Ali. He states that when Fath 'Ali Khan of Qobbe was fighting Aghasi Khan of Shirvan and his ally Mohammad Hasan Khan, Mehr 'Ali beg, who was fleeing his brother, Ebrahim Khan of Qarabagh, joined him. One night, on his way to Shirvan, Mehr 'Ali was killed by Ahmad Khan, the eldest son of Aghasi Khan. His body was sent with great honors to Qarabagh. This action brought Ebrahim and Fath 'Ali into a short-lived alliance, *Golestan-e Eram*, p. 168.

special affection for Panah Khan, [22] he (Karim Khan), out of kindness, graciousness, and generosity requested the following: "In order for me to repay your loyalty and trust, you must spend some time with me." He thus took [Panah Khan] with him to the *velayat* of Shiraz.[207] *Fearing that after his return, he would raise arms against him, he [Karim Khan] demanded that Panah Khan stay with him.*[208]

The late Ebrahim Khalil Khan entered Qarabagh as an independent khan and governor and did not take orders from anyone, but rather forced the submission of all of Qarabagh and other *velayats*.[209]

The late Panah Khan spent a short time in the city of Shiraz, the capital of Karim Khan. Finally his time came and he died in Shiraz. His body was brought with great respect to Qarabagh and was committed to earth in his legal and private estate,[210] in the area known today as Aghdam. May Allah have mercy on him.[211]

---

[207] Other primary sources unanimously state that Panah Khan was taken as a hostage. Golestane states that Karim Khan demanded that Erekle send Azad Khan Afghan, who was in Tiflis, to him and that after his arrival he decamped and with all of his baggage set out for 'Araq. He also took with him Fath 'Ali Khan Afshar; Panah Khan Javanshir; Kazem Khan Qaraje-daghi; Shahbaz Khan and Najaf Qoli Khan Donboli; Hasan 'Ali Khan Qajar of Erevan; Hajji Khan Kangarlu, the ruler of Nakhichevan; Reza Qoli Khan, the brother of Shahvardi Khan Ziadoglu, the beglarbegi of Ganje; and Hajji Mohammad Qoli Khan, the ruler of Maraghe. After some time in 'Araq he continued his journey and in 1179 (1765/66) entered Shiraz, *Mojmal ot-tavarikh*, P. 457; Ghaffari confirms the above, *Golshan-e Morad*, 212; Hedayat also confirms Panah Khan's fate, *Rouzat os-Safa*, IX, p. 74; Mohammad Hashem confirms the above as well, *Rostam ol-Tavarikh*, p. 334. Nami's version does not mention the khan of Erevan but lists his nephews instead, as well as Amir Gunay Khan and many other elders of the Shaqaqi, Afshar, and Shahsavan tribal chiefs and others among the hostages, *Tarikh-e Giti-gosha*, p. 114.

[208] "Karabag," 65 (1855), 278. The version of Mirza Jamal's history that was in Berzhe's possession was, as noted, different from manuscript C (see intoduction). Berzhe's version obviously agrees with the primary sources cited above.

[209] This paragraph once more illustrates that Qarabagh, contrary to Mirza Jamal's earlier statements, had not totally submitted to Panah Khan. The Armenian *meliks* and a number of tribes had resisted and at the first opportunity sought to re-establish their own autonomy. In fact, Ebrahim Khan acted with more force and brutality than his father and transformed the khanate of Qarabagh into a major power.

[210] The text has *molk hallal va zarkharid* ("private property legally purchased in cash"), which illustrates a very important custom among those powerful leaders who had usurped property: In order for their body and soul to lie in peace, they had to be buried in a plot that they had purchased legally and for cash.

[211] The date of the death of Panah Khan is debated. Shukiurzade is sure it was

As is evident from his work and from events which have passed, victories, success, fortune, and wealth *and the love of the people [of Qarabagh]*,[212] were always with the late Panah Khan during the entire twelve-year period of his rule, following the death of the late Nader Shah. Most of the *velayats* of Azerbaijan were under his rule or obeyed him.

Karim Khan took Fath 'Ali Khan with him to the outskirts of Isfahan and executed him on the same spot on which his kinsman was killed during the war with Fath 'Ali Khan's troops, and thus he took his revenge.[213] Because he [Fath 'Ali Khan) had broken his word to the late Panah Khan and had sworn falsely and used tricks and cunning, the Lord of the universe rewarded him only with regret and death.[214]

---

in 1172 (1758-1759). He bases this on calculating the *abjad* value (the arrangement of the Arabic alphabet, according to the numerical value of the letters from one to a thousand) of the letters of the last line of a Persian poem on the grave of Panah Khan at a site called the 'Amarat, in Aghdam. He also feels that by 1759 Panah Khan was in Shushi where he died in July or August. He bases this on a document in Edjmiadsin monastery, which states that at the end of June 1759, Hosein 'Ali Khan of Erevan was planning to visit Panah Khan in Shushi and had demanded 100 *tomans* from the Armenian priests for his travel expenses. He settled for fifty *tomans* after they told him they did not possess such a large sum, *Karabakhskogo khanstva*, p. 102. Shukiurzade is mistaken, for all primary Iranian sources of the time, as well as Bakikhanov, confirm that Panah Khan died in Shiraz, that Karim Khan came and took Urmiye in 1176 (1762/63), and that on October 16, 1763, Panah Khan, together with the other hostages, set out from Ardabil. After staying in other parts of Iran, he returned to Shiraz with his hostages in 1179 (1765/66), *Mojmalot-tavarikh* p. 457; *Golshan-e Morad*, p. 222-223; *Tarikh-e Giti-gosha*, pp. 113-114; *Golestan-e Eram*, p. 162. Soon after his arrival in Shiraz, probably in 1180 (1766/67), Panah Khan died. As for the Armenian document, it is correct. The trip of Hosein 'Ali Khan of Erevan was in 1759, which was even before Fath 'Ali Khan's campaign in Qarabagh, at which time Panah Khan was still in Shushi.

[212] "Karabag," 65 (1855), 278.

[213] According to Bakikhanov, Panah Khan incited Karim Khan to kill Fath 'Ali Khan, *Golestan-e Eram*, p. 162. Nami states that Karim Khan was incited by a number of khans who despised the bold attitude of Fath 'Ali Khan and could not bear his insults, *Tarikh-e Giti-gosha* p. 122.

[214] Adigozal Beg states that although Karim Khan's mother had repeatedly asked him to kill Fath 'Ali for the murder of his brother, Karim Khan wanted to keep his promise of clemency. When they arrived at the spot, he asked Fath 'Ali if he knew what that place was, to which he boldly replied, "where the sun set on Eskandar Beg." Karim Khan was so angry that he killed him on the spot,

The Lord of the universe forbids his slaves insidiousness, guile, false oaths, and the breaking of promises. [23] Experience demonstrates that he who lies to his friends, his patron, or his master, and tricks or betrays him, falls from the protection and generosity of his master, for the Lord has named him the master, and he will not gain anything but regret and death. "Allah deals out rewards and retribution, he rewards good deeds and punishes evil deeds."[215]

Chapter Five:
On the Rule of the Late Ebrahim Khan and
the Conditions and Events of That Time[216]

The late Ebrahim Khan commenced his rule as the independent ruler of Qarabagh in the Muslim year 1174,[217] which corresponds to the Christian year 1756 (actually 1760/61). His rule was terminated in the year 1221, which corresponds to the Christian year 1806. He did not acknowledge either Iran's or Rum's [Ottoman] suzerainty.[218] *In the meantime, in Persia, Karim Khan died. His death ushered in a power struggle between his sons and the khans of 'Araq, who tried to destroy each other. The governors of the Shirvans, who had been appointed by Iran, also fought each other, and asked for Ebrahim Khan's protection and aid. He helped one side or the other, as it suited his plans or was profitable for him. The exception [to this] was Fath 'Ali Khan, the ruler of Darband, Qobbe, and Baku, a strong and enterprising man, who was related to the tribes of Akoshe (Akhusha)*[219] *and the*

Qarabagh-name, p. 73. Ghaffari gives a similar account without the name of Eskandar being mentioned. He also dates the event in 1177 (1763/64), *Golshan-e Morad*, p. 236.

[215] Berzhe has the same passage in the conclusion of his fifth chapter, "Karabag," 67 (1855), 290. The sentence loosely echoes sentiments expressed in Surah X of the Qur'an.

[216] Berzhe's translation has no chapter number, it reads, **The Rule of Ebrahim Khan 1173-1221 Hijri (1756-1806 A.D.)**. He also combined chapters five and six of Mirza Jamal's history, "Karabag," 67 (1855), 290. Since chapter five is very brief, it is possible that the copy used by Berzhe had these two chapters combined.

[217] Actually 1176. Berzhe's translation has *1173*, "Karabag," 67 (1855), 290. Adigozal Beg's history has the date 1173 (1759/60) as well, *Qarabagh-name*, p. 74.

[218] Adigozal Beg adds, "or other states," *Ibid.*, p. 74.

[219] Fath 'Ali Khan of Qobbe should not be confused with Fath 'Ali Khan Afshar mentioned in the previous chapter. Akhusha was a Lezgian tribe in Daghestan.

Shamkhal of Tarkov (Tarqu),[220] *to whom he also paid an annual subsidy for an alliance. Planning to conquer all of Azerbaijan, Fath 'Ali Khan encountered a strong foe in Ebrahim Khan, who forced him to retreat a number of times. When Fath 'Ali Khan died, his son Ahmad Khan immediately concluded a treaty of friendship with Ebrahim Khan.*[221] Ebrahim's decrees and wishes were carried out in the *velayats* of Shirvan, Shakki, Ganje, Erevan, Nakhichevan, Khoi, Qaradagh, Tabriz, and Ardabil, including even Maraghe and Qaplan-kuh, which is the border between Azerbaijan and 'Araq.[222] The dismissal or appointment of the khans of these *velayats* had to have the approval of the late Ebrahim Khan. He was also related to the *vali* of the *velayats* of Avar and Dagehstan, 'Umma Khan, son of Nousal Khan.[223] He was married to the honorable sister of 'Umma Khan.[224] *In order to secure his position and to have, in case it was needed, a trusted ally, his first act was to become related by marriage to 'Umma Khan, son of Nousal Khan, the ruler of the Avars, whose sister he took to wife.*[225] In times of need he would ask for the armies of the *velayat* of Daghestan and the Lezgis,[226] whom he would bring, with 'Umma Khan and other

---

[220] Tarqe or Tarqu was a tribe that lived north of Darband on the Caspian coast. The title of their leader was *shamkhal*.

[221] "Karabag," 67 (1855), 290.

[222] Ahmad Beg adds Rasht to the above list and states that Ebrahim's nephew, Asadollah Beg, was the governor of Tabriz and that in the region of Qaplan-kuh Ebrahim stationed a unit of 600 cavalry troops to keep control over the tribes of the region, *Karabakhskogo khanstva*, p. 75. Although Ebrahim had strong influence over Qaradagh, Ardabil, Nakhichevan, and Ganje, he had little control over the khans of Shakki, Shirvan, Tabriz, Khoi, Maraghe, and Erevan. Erevan, in fact, would at times submit to Erekle, who was enjoying his own expansion, in the meantime, against Qazzaq, Borchalu, Sham od-Din, and occasionally even Ganje (see map 3). Mirza Jamal's account is, therefore, exaggerated, for although Ebrahim Khan did actually achieve great power and influence, he did not truly control all these regions.

[223] Adigozal Beg also calls him 'Umma Khan, son of Nousal Khan, *Qarabagh-name*, p. 74. The line, "son of Nousal Khan," was not translated in the Russian translation, *Istoriia Karabaga*, p. 78, but appears in both the Azeri and Turkish translations. Bakikhanov identifies him as 'Om Khan, *Golestan-e Eram*, p. 169. Russian and Georgian sources call him 'Omar Khan, son of Nursal Beg of the Avars, D. M. Lang, *The Last Years of the Georgian Monarchy, 1658-1832* (New York, 1957), p. 175; Ahmad Beg, *Karabakhskogo khanstva*, p. 104.

[224] Adigozal Beg identifies her as Bikia (Bike) Aqa, *Qarabagh-name*, p. 74.

[225] "Karabag," 67 (1855), 290.

[226] A tribe in southern Daghestan who raided Georgia and other settled communities for plunder and slaves.

military leaders, to Qarabagh. Together with his own troops and commanders, he would dispatch them to wherever it was necessary, in order to punish or to bring into submission [those who disobeyed him].[227]

[24] In addition, he was also related to the khans of the *velayats* of Shahsavan, Qaradagh, Khoi, and Ganje and all of them, either through force or through kinship, accepted with body and soul the authority of Ebrahim Khalil Khan.[228] He even presented certain *mahals*, from the *velayats* of Tabriz and Qaradagh, upon some of his famed warriors. Although Ebrahim Khan did not have the title of shah, he possessed the same stature as Iranian kings and many of the sons and relatives of the aforementioned khans lived as his hostages in the Shushi fortress.

Such was the situation, when even before Aqa Mohammad Shah took over Fars, 'Araq, and Azerbaijan, in the small town of Aq-Dagirman, lying four farsakhs from Shushi in the Varanda mahal, there came to Ebrahim Khan the son of Ahmad Khan, the ruler of Khoi; the son of Najaf Qoli Khan, the beglarbegi of Tabriz; Mostafa Khan, the ruler of Qaraje-dagh; Sadeq Khan and Mohammad Reza Khan Shaqaqi; Naser Khan, ruler of Ardabil and Shahsavan; and Shokrollah Khan, who stated the following: "We are all Azerbaijani khans who have accepted your authority and are here at your disposal. The rulers of Shirvan, Shakki, and Ganje are likewise under your command. The Avar Khan is also at your disposal. What is preventing you from declaring yourself shah? The situation in 'Araq, Fars, and Kerman is extremely critical. All you have to do for their rulers to accept your authority is to appear at the borders of these velayats." To these words, to which Ebrahim Khan listened quietly and care-

---

[227] Adigozal Beg adds that at one time, with the help of the Daghestanis, Ebrahim defeated the Qaradaghis and destroyed their Ghayurdasht (Kurdasht) district, evidence of its ruins still being there. The population fled to Ahar in Azerbaijan, while the governor Mostafa Khan was taken prisoner, *Qarabagh-name*, p. 75.

[228] The velayat of Qobbe is not included in the list. Under Fath 'Ali Khan, this khanate itself laid claims to large areas in Transcaucasia and Azerbaijan, and according to Bakikhanov, the only one who was spared its influence and remained a foe, was Ebrahim Khan of Qarabagh, whose mountains kept him secure, *Golestan-e Eram*, p. 169. Mohammad Fathollah states that Hosein Khan Donboli, the ruler of Khoi, was related to Ebrahim Khan. He later became the ruler of Tabriz, but the extent of Ebrahim's influence over him is not mentioned, *Tarikh-e Mohammadi*, p. 194. Bamdad also mentions the fact that a daughter of Ebrahim Khan was married to Hosein Khan Donboli. She was sent as a hostage to Qazvin at the request of Aqa Mohammad Khan. Hosein Qoli Khan was killed in 1213 (1798/99), *Bamdad*, I, 448.

fully, he replied, "I regard the older of you, my brothers, and the younger ones, my sons. I do not seek anything more than having you unanimously accept me as your leader. Do not remind me of the royal crown. I have never looked for this honor, of which I deem myself unworthy. I, therefore, at the present time, reject your offer."[229]

This situation continued until Aqa Mohammad Khan, the son of Mohammad Hasan Khan Qajar, who was a hostage in the city of Shiraz, escaped, following the death of Karim Khan, and set claim to the throne [of Iran].[230] After several years of struggle, he managed to gain control over 'Araq and Fars and made the city of Tehran his royal residence.[231] In the Muslim year 1107 [1207][232] [1792-1793], he [Aqa Mohammad Khan] came to the *velayat* of Azerbaijan and conquered all the *velayats*

---

[229] "Karabag," 67 (1855), 290. Ahmad Beg repeats this, *Karabakhskogo khanstva*, p. 75.

[230] Karim Khan died in February 1779. According to Fasa'i, Aqa Mohammad Khan was born on March 14, 1742. His father was hiding from the Afshars and had left his family in Astarabad. His enemies betrayed the family and had the young Aqa Mohammad brought to 'Adel Shah Afshar, who at first wanted to kill him, but at the intercession of a friend, ordered his castration. After 'Adel's death, Aqa Mohammad went back to his father. After the murder of his father, he was sent to Shiraz by the Davalu Qajars, who did not favor a leader of the Qavanlu among them. He was raised at the court of Karim, who treated him like a son. Upon the death of Karim Khan, he went on to kill the Afshar and Zand chiefs, and a number of Davalu Qajars, and established his rule in Iran proper, before venturing across the Arax. He was an extremely cruel man. His enemies made a pun of his title. During his father's lifetime, he was the eldest son, hence he was called *aqa*. After his father's death, he became the head of his tribe and family, hence again the title of *aqa*. When he became powerful they called him *agha*, or lord, commander, and great chief. The title of *agha*, however, also applies to the chief eunuch of the harem. Since Aqa Mohammad was castrated in his youth, his enemies jokingly called him the *agha*. For details see, *Farsname-ye Naseri*, I, pp. 228-240. For a biographical account of Aqa Mohammad Khan, see E. Pakravan, *Agha Mohammad Khan* Qajar (Tehran, 1969).

[231] Since Aqa Mohammad was not shah yet, Mirza Jamal's reference to Tehran as the royal residence is premature. After the death of Karim Khan in 1779, Aqa Mohammad Khan fled to Mazandaran, where, with the help of his clan, he gained control of a large part of Iran by 1789. He spent the next five years warring against the Afshars, whom he blamed for the murder of his grandfather, and the Zands, whom he blamed for the murder of his father. He blamed both for his castration, as well, and destroyed their chiefs with particular vehemence.

[232] An obvious scribal error, it should read 1207. The interesting fact is that Adigozal Beg's text also has an error, for it reads 1176 (1762/63), *Qarabagh-name*, p. 76.

south of the Arax, with the exception of the *velayats* of Erevan and Talesh.[233] Prior to that he had sent the late Ebrahim Khan a sword, and a horse with a gold-inlaid saddle and bridle, and *khal'at*,[234] and he now solicited his submission. [Ebrahim Khan] pretended to do so through verbal and outward formalities, as well as an exchange of messengers. Ebrahim Khan, in addition, dispatched his cousin 'Abd os-Samad Beg[235] with Mirza Vali Baharlu, who was an experienced and eloquent man, as hostages, whom the shah[236] kept by his side as well-treated [25] and respected guests.[237]

---

[233] Mirza Jamal must have known that Erevan was north of the Arax. This is probably another scribal error.

[234] Aqa Mohammad Khan had asked Ebrahim to come to Tehran and to submit in 1793, but the latter had made excuses and sent impressive gifts instead. It is unclear whether or not he had sent family members as hostages at that time. Adigozal Beg records that Aqa Mohammad was forced to leave the north to quell revolts in Fars, *Qarabagh-name*, p. 76. Iranian chroniclers state that Aqa Mohammad Khan did not come to the region but sent a *sardar* to watch over it, *Nasekh ot-Tavarikh*, I, pp. 56-61.

[235] Ahmad Beg has his name as 'Abu-Samad, *Karabakhskogo khanstva*, p. 75. 'Abd os-Samad was the son of Panah Khan's brother. Some sources refer to him as Ebrahim's nephew.

[236] Aqa Mohammad was not shah at this time. Mirza Jamal follows most chroniclers of the Qajars who honor him with the title of shah before his official coronation.

[237] Mohammad Fathollah states that Aqa Mohammad Khan left his cousin, Soleiman Khan Qavanlu Qajar, as the ruler of Tabriz to watch over the Trans-caucasian khans. Sadeq Khan Shaqaqi, Nasir Khan Shahsavan, Kalb 'Ali Khan of Nakhichevan, Mohammad Khan of Erevan, Javad Khan of Ganje, and even Eshaq Pasha, the governor of Bayazid, all came to Tabriz and submitted. Ebrahim Khan sent a number of notables to Tabriz to assess the situation. He had many enemies and feared that they had already given a bad impression of him to the *beglarbegi*. Soleiman Khan assured them of Aqa Mohammad's friendship and so upon their return, Ebrahim sent his uncle's son, 'Abd os-Samad, as a hostage, together with expensive gifts to Tabriz, from where he was sent to Tehran by Soleiman Khan, *Tarikh-e Mohammadi*, pp. 241-242; confirmed by E'temad os-Salt-ane, *Montazam-e Naseri*, III, 1421. Hedayat confirms the above, but adds Mohammad Qoli Khan of Urmiye to those who submitted and states that Ebrahim Khan submitted right away, *Rouzat os-Safa*, IX, p. 253. Soleiman Khan continued to serve in his post until the coronation of Fath 'Ali Shah. Later on he returned to Tabriz as the *atabeg* (advisor and tutor) of 'Abbas Mirza, who at age eleven, had been appointed the crown prince and the governor of Azerbaijan. For more details see *Bamdad*, II, pp. 118-124.

When Aqa Mohammad Khan overcame the young, brave, and generous Lotf 'Ali Khan Zand,[238] who was in Kerman and who was his
enemy, and proceeded to massacre the population of Kerman,[239] there
occurred a number of incidents which fractured the relationship between Ebrahim Khalil Khan and Aqa Mohammad Shah.[240] 'Abd os-
Samad Beg, together with Mirza Vali Baharlu and a number of retainers,
escaped from Kerman [during the above events]. Couriers sped night
and day and preceeded them, where they told the inhabitants of the
village of Sarjam to stop the escapees. Thus, troops composed of cavalry
and infantry awaited [the escapees] near the Qezel-Uzun river and
blocked all roads of escape. In the ensuing struggle 'Abd os-Samad Beg
received a bullet wound in the knee. He and his companions, including
Mirza Vali, were arrested. 'Abd os-Samad Beg died there from his bullet
wound, while the others, together with Mirza Vali, were taken to the
shah and imprisoned in the city of Tehran.[241]   [Later] while Aqa

---

[238] Lotf 'Ali Khan, the great grandson of Karim Khan's half brother, Zaki,
was the last of the Zands. He tried to revive the dynasty of Karim Khan. He
fought Aqa Mohammad Khan and although he was popular and achieved a
number of victories, he was eventually captured, tortured, and killed by Aqa
Mohammad in 1209 (1794).

[239] This occurred at the start of 1209 (1794). Some 8000 women and children
were distributed as slaves, and all the men were either killed or blinded. The
destruction was so terrible that Kerman never revived, and a new smaller town
was eventually built outside the old town, *Farsname-ye Naseri*, I, 238.

[240] Although Mirza Jamal generally refers to him as shah, Ahmad Beg,
following the Russian historians, refuses to call him shah and uses the title of
khan throughout. Mirza Jamal does not describe these various incidents, but
Ebrahim's refusal to appear before the khan and his haughty attitude angered
Aqa Mohammad, who considered himself the ruler of all former Safavid do-
mains.

[241] Mohammad Fathollah's account is the most detailed. He states that taking
advantage of Aqa Mohammad's campaign in Kerman, the hostages, who had
accompanied him, escaped. Orders were sent to stop them. When they reached
the Shahsavan tribe, 'Abd os-Samad was recognized and they rushed to capture
him. He fought back and tried to escape. Since Aqa Mohammad's orders were
to capture the hostages alive, the troops fired at the horse. One bullet struck 'Abd
os-Samad in the leg, and exiting, entered his other leg. Horse and man fell and
died. His severed head was sent to Aqa Mohammad Khan, *Tarikh-e Mohammadi*,
p. 257. The location of their capture is unclear. Mirza Jamal mentions the village
of Sarjam, which is in the vicinity of Mashhad in Khorasan. Mohammad Hasan
E'temad os-Saltane states that they were overtaken near Tehran, *Montazam-e
Naseri*, III, p. 1426; Sepehr claims they were taken in Azerbaijan, Nasekh ot-

Mohammad Shah was besieging the fortress of Shushi, the late Ebrahim Khan's envoys periodically arrived [to negotiate]. Aqa Mohammad Shah was angered by one of the late Ebrahim Khan's offers and sent instructions to Tehran to have Mirza Vali tied to the mouth of a cannon there and blown apart. None of the rest of the prisoners, ten in all, survived either; they were all executed. May Allah have mercy on them.

Thus perished these unlucky and innocent victims, whose blood was washed [clean] with the blood of many Persian khans, who perished under the walls of Shushi. The Almighty repays good with good and evil with evil. [242]

Chapter Six:
On Other Events and the End of
Aqa Mohammad Shah [243]

Since relations between Ebrahim Khan and Aqa Mohammad Shah had deteriorated, in the year 1209 (1794/95), Aqa Mohammad Shah, *after quelling the sudden revolts in Fars, once again*,[244] came to Azerbaijan with a large army to conquer the *velayats* of Tiflis, [26] Erevan, Qarabagh, and Talesh.[245] He first sent 'Ali Qoli Khan Shahsavan,[246] who was the principal commander of Aqa Mohammad Shah's army, together with a number of other khans to [take] the fortress of Erevan. He himself, with the entire army of 'Araq, Fars, Azerbaijan, and Khorasan, marched on

---

Tavarikh, I, p. 70; Hedayat has the Zanjan region as the location, *Rouzat os-Safa*, IX, p. 261. Ahmad Beg claims that after the death of 'Abd os-Samad Beg, another hostage was demanded, to which Ebrahim sarcastically replied that he could not honor another person with such a duty, *Karabakhskogo khanstva*, p. 75.

[242] "Karabag," 67 (1855), 290. The same quote appears in chapter four of the Persian text, referring to Fath 'Ali Khan's death.

[243] Berzhe's translation has this chapter included in his chapter five.

[244] "Karabag," 67 (1855), 290.

[245] The year is confirmed by Bakikhanov, who goes on to say that Aqa Mohammad repaired the Khoda-afarin bridge, which had been destroyed by Ebrahim Khan to forestall his crossing the Arax, and came to the Shushi fortress, *Golestan-e Eram*, p. 174. Fasa'i, has the exact date as 12 May, 1795, *Farsname-ye Naseri*, I, 240. Sepehr and Hedayat confirm the above events and the repairing of the bridge, *Nasekh ot-Tavarikh*, I, 71; Hedayat, *Rouzat os-Safa*, IX, p. 262.

[246] Berzhe has *his brother 'Ali Qoli Khan*,"Karabag," 67 (1855), 290. Adigozal Beg also states that he was not a Shahsavan khan, but Aqa Mohammad's brother, *Qarabagh-name*, p. 76.

the fortress of Shushi and struck camp at the station of Qavakhan, one *farsakh* [247] from the fortress.[248]

The *vali* of Tiflis, the lofty Erekle Khan; the governor of Erevan, Mohammad Khan; and the governor of Talesh, Mir Mostafa Khan, had all sworn with the late Ebrahim Khan not to accept Aqa Mohammad Shah's suzerainty, but to remain united and assist each other.[249]

Hence a part of the tribal [cavalry] forces of Qarabagh were sent to Tiflis, and another part to Shirvan, where Mostafa Khan had been installed as the governor of the *velayat* of Shirvan by Ebrahim Khan. The remainder of the tribal forces, and the [infantry] troops, who were listed in the military rolls,[250] were placed by Ebrahim Khan in the mountains of Qarabagh and inside the fortress [of Shushi]. He gathered a large number of infantry and cavalry from the tribes and from the *mahals* of Qarabagh for the defense of the fortress. He assembled large and small cannons and was ready to do battle against the shah.[251]

---

[247] Adigozal Beg uses the Turkish term, *aghach*, which is the same distance as a *farsakh*, *Qarabagh-name*, p. 76.

[248] Hedayat and 'Etemad os-Saltane state that some of the Armenians of Qarabagh took refuge in a *saqnaq* and fought Aqa Mohammad's forces, but eventually gave up against superior forces and fled to Shushi, *Rouzat os-Safa*, IX, pp. 263-64; *Montazam-e Naseri*, III, 1249.

[249] Mohammad Fathollah states that it was Ebrahim Khan who asked the vali of Georgia not to submit to Aqa Mohammad, *Tarikh-e Mohammadi*, p. 273. Hedayat states that Ebrahim Khan, after the arrival of Aqa Mohammad Khan, asked all the khans of Transcaucasia to help him repel the invader, *Rouzat os-Safa*, IX, 263.

[250] Unlike the cavalry, which were composed of tribal forces and who received income from villages assigned to them as *toyul*, the infantry was composed of peasants, who were listed on special rolls. They received tax exemptions and income for the duration of the campaign (see below).

[251] Ahmad Beg states that he had 15,000 troops altogether and expected aid from Russia as well, *Karabakhskogo khanstva*, p. 76. Shukiurzade has passed on a couplet which the shah sent to Ebrahim Khan stating that Ebrahim has foolishly taken refuge in a glass fortress (a pun on Persian word *shishe*) which would be crushed by a rain of stones (cannonballs). Ebrahim's vazir, Molla Panah, known as Vaqef (the well-known Azeri poet, Vagif), answered immediately with another couplet which replied that the glass which protected him was hewed into rock, *Ibid.*, pp. 102-103. The same account, with more embellishment, can be found in Adigozal Beg, who adds that prior to the sending of the poem (the author of which he identifies as Seyyed Mohammad Shirazi, known as Urfi), Aqa Mohammad sent numerous messages requesting Ebrahim's submission. Vaqef's response so infuriated Aqa Mohammad Khan that he ordered the cannons to bombard Shushi relentlessly, *Qarabagh-name*, pp. 77-78.

Aqa Mohammad Shah spent thirty-three days[252] in the vicinity of the fortress, but he could not, despite his large army, cross the river which ran some five *versts* from the fortress in order to get closer to it. The infantry and cavalry forces of Qarabagh, together with the tribal and village leaders and the *meliks* of Varanda, Dizak, and Khachen *mahals*,[253] would hide in the thickets, roadways, and passes attacking and pillaging the Qezelbash army, and stealing hordes of horses, mules, and camels daily. [27] They also grabbed and looted caravans, which brought grain from the *velayats* to the encampment and would bring the captured men, animals, and provisions to the late Ebrahim Khan. The situation became such that one mule, in the money of those times, sold for [only] four rubles,[254] a camel for [only] six rubles, and a good horse for [only] ten rubles.[255]

Fearing a night raid by the forces of Qarabagh on their encampment, they [Aqa Mohammad Khan's troops] erected a number of strong and well-constructed towers. [Nonetheless], one night, a group of soldiers from Varanda *mahal*[256] captured a large tower which housed Aqa Mohammad Shah's private musketeer guard and in one hour killed all of them, except for two or three, who at dawn were brought to the late Ebrahim Khan.[257] There was no peace or rest, day or night, for the

---

[252] Berzhe's translation reads *thirty-two days*, "Karabag," 67 (1855), 290. Official Georgian records have it as more than a month, A. Tsagareli, ed., *Gramoty i drugie istoricheskie dokumenti*, II (pt. 2), no. 73, p. 93; Fasa'i has 8 July to 9 August, 1795, *Farsname-ye Naseri*, I, 240; Adigozal Beg has 33 days, *Qarabagh-name*, p. 77; as does Mohammad Fathollah, *Tarikh-e Mohammadi*, p. 271.

[253] Once again the Armenian *meliks* felt threatened and hoping to gain favor decided to cooperate with Ebrahim Khan.

[254] Mirza Jamal uses *manat*, a Russian term for a silver ruble, taken from the Italian *moneta*. The term eventually slipped into Persian and Azeri as well.

[255] According to Ahmad Beg the setbacks angered Aqa Mohammad so much that he at one point took 100 Qarabaghi captives, tied them up, laid them on the ground and had horses with sharp nails attached to their horseshoes trample over them until they became a mass of bloody flesh, *Karabakhskogo khanstva*, p. 76.

[256] These were part of the Armenian musketeer units.

[257] Ahmad Beg states that in response to Aqa Mohammad's cruelty (see note 255), the Armenian leader Melik 'Abbas (the great grandson of Melik Egan of Dizak) of Togh and Mohammad Beg, a nephew of the khan (more will be said of him later), on that same night, in two separate raids, captured 100 Persian prisoners, who were tied and shown off (probably killed as well), in the main square of Shushi, *Karabakhskogo khanstva*, pp. 76-77.

Qezelbash army. The shah himself tried three of four times to cross the river with his entire army and approach the fortress, but the swift infantry and brave horsemen [of Qarabagh], led by their commanders, met him, and, after manly exchanges of blows, defeated him and threw him back [across the river].[258]

Finally, Javad Khan, the ruler of Ganje, and Melik Majnun, the *melik* of Jraberd,[259] who had turned away from the late Ebrahim Khan, and who had chosen to reside in the *velayat* of Ganje with Javad Khan, came to Aqa Mohammad Shah. Acting upon their advice, he decided to give up the siege of the [Shushi] fortress, which had led to numerous defeats and great anxiety, and moved in the direction of Tiflis, with the aim of conquering Georgia.[260]

The late Ebrahim Khan, prior to the shah's move [into Georgia], sent the following message to the lofty *vali* of Georgia, "Aqa Mohammad Shah has given up the attempt to take the fortress [of Shushi] and has

---

[258] The Persian chroniclers state that the shah's forces caused havoc in Qarabagh and defeated the Qarabaghis in the field many times, *Tarikh-e Mohammadi*, pp. 269-270, *Rouzat os-Safa*, IX, 265-267.

[259] Melik Majnun was the son of Melik Hatam of Jraberd, who was forced by Panah Khan to abandon his land and settle in Ganje (see note 112). The family had thus become fierce enemies of the Javanshir khans.

[260] Iranian chronicles have a very different version of the siege of Shushi. According to Fasa'i, Ebrahim Khan was defeated so many times that he sent a number of Javanshir notables to Aqa Mohammad and offered to pay taxes and subsidies (*baj va kharaj*) and to send hostages (*gerogan*). The shah forgave his "sin" and accepted his offer, *Farsname-ye Naseri*, I, p. 240. Mohammad Fathollah states that after some of his family members, who were hiding outside the fortress, were captured, Ebrahim Khan, who was not having any success against the troops of Aqa Mohammad and who was tired of the bombardments, submitted by giving one of his sons as a hostage together with money and presents. He asked Aqa Mohammad "to forgive an old man," *Tarikh-e Mohammadi*, p. 270. Hedayat and E'temad os-Saltane both mention that his nephews Mohammad Beg and Assadollah Beg and their wives were hiding outside the fortress. Their capture by Aqa Mohammad forced Ebrahim to come to terms, promising to appear in person soon after, *Rouzat os-Safa*, IX, 267-68; *Montazam-e Naseri*, III, 1428-1429. The reality is somewhere in between. Ebrahim did not surrender the fortress and waited to see the result of the Georgian campaign. He seems to have given presents and hostages to get rid of Aqa Mohammad; each side thus saved face. On his return from Georgia, Aqa Mohammad continued to harass and loot Qarabagh, but before Ebrahim could act, Aqa Mohammad Khan left for Tehran. On his return, Ebrahim, as will be seen, fled the fortress and the population, tired of the plunder, opened the doors to the shah.

suffered large losses of men and animals. He now wants to make up his losses [save face] by taking Tiflis and pillaging the settlements of Georgia. Prepare yourselves to repulse his encroachment."[261]

Aqa Mohammad Shah, in order to give respite to his cavalry and troops, which in fact were [themselves] under siege, set up camp near Aghdam and rested there for a month [28] or more.[262] From there he set out to conquer the *velayat* of Georgia and the city of Tiflis. Javad Khan and Melik Majnun constantly rode in front of the troops, acting as guides to the shah.[263]

Once they approached Tiflis, they took the city in a short time.[264] The population of the city and villages in its environs were pillaged, prisoners were taken, and the city burned.[265] He then moved back to

---

[261] Adigozal Beg adds that the *vali*, after receiving the message, immediately informed the *vali* of Imeret'i, who was his grandson, Solomon Khan, and with his sons and grandsons, to whom he had willed various parts of Georgia, prepared to do battle at age seventy, *Qarabagh-name*, pp. 79-80.

[262] Fasa'i says he encamped in the region of Ganje, *Farsname-ye Naseri*, I p. 240. Mohammad Fathollah gives an exact period of 27 days, *Tarikh-e Mohammadi*, p. 271.

[263] Mohammad Fathollah states that, after observing the terrible fate of Qarabagh, Mohammad Khan of Erevan, came bearing great gifts; Javad Khan of Ganje arrived with 1000 troops, attendants, and many gifts; Melik Majnun, Melik Qoli, and Melik Esma'il, who were the leaders of the Armenians, arrived with presents and 600 troops, and that they all joined Aqa Mohammad Khan. At the same time Sheikh 'Ali, son of Fath 'Ali Khan of Qobbe, sent 5000 *tomans* with a relative, Hosein Khan of Baku dispatched 'Ali Beg, his uncle (from his mother's side) and his brother Mahdi Qoli Khan, with money and gifts. Even the governor of Baghdad, Suleiman Pasha, sent horses, *Tarikh-e Mohammadi*, pp. 270-271. Hedayat states that after the sack of Tiflis, Mohammad Khan of Erevan and Javad Khan of Ganje came with gifts and were reinstated as governors, *Rouzat os-Safa*, IX, 271. Sources indicate that the submission of Ebrahim Khan and the campaign against Georgia was a signal that the Qajars were finally reestablishing the Safavid realm.

[264] The date was 12 September, 1795.

[265] Adigozal Beg has more details on Aqa Mohammad's campaign in Georgia, *Qarabagh-name*, pp. 80-82. The number of prisoners, according to various Russian and Georgian sources, ranges from 3,000 to 30,000, see *Karabakhskogo khanstva*, p. 103. Fasa'i has 15,000 women and children taken as slaves, *Farsname-ye Naseri*, I, p. 240. Mohammad Fathollah has great details of the Georgian campaign, *Tarikh-e Mohammadi*, pp. 272-277. Hedayat describes this event, the death of Armenian and Georgian priests, looting, and the taking of 15,000 prisoners as slaves, *Rouzat os-Safa*, IX, 269-271. The famous Armenian bard (*gusan*) Sayat Nova was one of those who was killed.

Azerbaijan, keeping to the banks of the Kur until he reached the conflu-
ence of the Arax River near the settlement of Javad. Here, in the plain of
Moghan, Aqa Mohammad and his army set their winter quarters.[266] In
the spring, with the fortress and *velayat* of Erevan still not taken,[267] a
rebellion once again broke out in Fars, as well as major uprisings in
Kerman and other [places], forcing [the shah] to go to Fars.[268] During
that spring while the shah was in Fars, the late Ebrahim Khan, having
convinced the *vali* of Georgia [to join him], brought an army from
Daghestan and together they laid siege to the city of Ganje, whose ruler
[Javad Khan] they blamed for the destruction of Tiflis.[269]

Within a short time Javad Khan submitted and swore eternal obedience and an unbreakable alliance with the late Ebrahim Khan. He also
gave his son and sister to the late Ebrahim Khan as hostages.[270] During
that siege Melik Majnun was killed.

---

[266] The Turkic term *qeshlaq* used by Mirza Jamal refers to winter quarters.

[267] Mirza Jamal has made an error, for the khan of Erevan and most others
had already submitted and were generally confirmed or replaced with loyal
commanders, *Farsname-ye Naseri*, I, p. 240. In Erevan, Aqa Mohammad Khan's
brother, 'Ali Qoli Khan, stayed on for a while to ensure the obedience of
Erevan's khan. The khan of Nakhichevan, Kalb 'Ali, was blinded, and a garrison
obedient to 'Ali Qoli was stationed there as well, for more details, see Bournoutian,
Erevan, p. 9

[268] Mirza Jamal does not mention the coronation of Aqa Mohammad Shah
which followed in Tehran immediately after his return there. The exact date of
the coronation is debated but according to Fasa'i and other sources it was in the
spring of 1796, *Farsname-ye Naseri*, I, 241. Bakikhanov is the only local historian,
who, in passing, states that Aqa Mohammad was crowned in Tehran, *Golestan-e
Eram*, p. 180.

[269] A lame excuse to attack, since Javad was not responsible for the sack of
Tiflis. Aqa Mohammad had written Erekle to submit long before that, see
Gramoty, II (pt 2), pp. 82-83, 85-89. Bakikhanov states that during the shah's
absence, his sardar in Tabriz, Mostafa Khan Davalu Qajar, fought various khans
and kept them under control and obedient to Aqa Mohammad Shah. He gave
his sister to Ebrahim Khan and married Ebrahim's daughter, *Golestan-e Eram*, p.
175. It thus seems that once Ebrahim realized that the Qajars were there to stay,
a truce was reached, for the moment.

[270] Berzhe's version has *nephew*, "Karabag," 68 (1855), 294. Adigozal Beg
writes "son and daughter," *Qarabagh-name*, p. 84.

In the meantime, when Aqa Mohammad Shah was still in the region of Fars and Khorasan, the supreme *sardar*, *general en-chef*[271] Count Valerian Zubov,[272] by the order of the great empress Catherine, entered the region of Darband with a great force and unlimited equipment and took its fortress. [He then] arrived at the outskirts of the city of Shamakhi and struck camp there.[273]

The late Ebrahim Khan voluntarily sent his son, Abo'l Fath Khan, accompanied by a number of the sons of the begs of Qarabagh, to the supreme *sardar* Zubov with thoroughbred horses and other gifts and offered, from the bottom of his heart, his submission, loyalty and friendship to the Exalted Russian State.[274] [The young men] also carried a letter petitioning the empress' protection and expressing his [Ebrahim Khan's] devotion.[275]

[29] Showing great respect to Abo'l Fath Khan and the sons of the begs of Qarabagh, the supreme *sardar* forwarded the petition of the late Ebrahim Khan to her majesty the empress, through a trusted adjutant, who went via the Darband and Qezlar [Kizliar] route. A prince was sent

---

[271] Mirza Jamal uses this term, which appears in some Russian and Georgian sources as well. The exact definition is unclear, but it probably signifies a very high-ranking general, or commander in chief.

[272] Valerian Aleksandrovich Zubov (1771-1804), the brother of Platon Zubov, a favorite of Catherine II, participated in the Russian action against the Polish uprising of 1749. He was wounded and lost one leg. In 1796 he was dispatched by Catherine II to conquer Transcaucasia and to rid the khans of the Qajar threat and bring them into the Russian sphere, for details, see Atkin, *Russia and Iran*, pp. 39-42 Ahmad Beg refers to him as *Qezel Ayagh* (Qiz'il Ayaq or "golden leg" in the local Turkic dialect), *Karabakhskogo khanstva*, p.77. Fasa'i also calls him by that name and explains that it was because his false leg was made of gold, *Farsname-ye Naseri*, I, p. 242. Hedayat calls him by the same name, *Rouzat os-Safa*, IX, 291. Qezel has a number of meanings in Azeri, such as "gold," "red," and "expensive," among others.

[273] Adigozal Beg states that he reached the borders of Qarabagh and camped at Selian, *Qarabagh-name*, p. 83.

[274] Bakikhanov confirm the above, *Golestan-e Eram*, p. 179. Abo'l Fath Khan was one of the younger sons of Ebrahim Khan, who later turned against his father (see below).

[275] Ebrahim Khan was eager to have the Russians as the protectors of Qarabagh. The same agreement had been made with Georgia earlier. Although the Russians had violated that agreement, Ebrahim never had any intention of surrendering his authority or the khanate.

with expensive gifts to the late Ebrahim Khan, assuring him of the eternal friendship of her majesty the empress.[276]

When the neighboring khans discovered that Ebrahim Khan had sent his son to the supreme *sardar*, all of them, that is: Mir Mostafa Khan of Talesh, Mostafa Khan of Shirvan, and Javad Khan of Ganje, and even the khans of Erevan, Nakhichevan, Khoi, and Qaradagh, dispatched envoys to the late Ebrahim Khan and declared, "We do not want to go against your decision.[277] Since you have decided to submit to the Russian government, all of us will agree to submit to the benevolent king of Russia."[278] The late Ebrahim Khan forwarded all these letters and messages to the supreme *sardar* Zubov.

Although the *vali* of Georgia surpassed the khans of Shirvan, Khoi, Erevan, and others in power and majesty, as he was of a very old dynasty[279] and possessed a vast and wealthy territory, he, nevertheless, consulted in all matters with the late Ebrahim Khan. This was due to the fact that the late 'Umma Khan,[280] the ruler of the Avars and Daghestan, and other elders of those regions, because of kinship ties, were obedient to and always in agreement with the late Ebrahim Khan. Should there have been a sudden falling out between the *vali* of Georgia and the late Ebrahim Khan, 'Umma Khan and the other khans of Daghestan, at a sign from Ebrahim Khan, would have raided [30] Georgia with a large army and caused major devastation.[281] [Such an attack indeed occurred] in the year 1199 (1784/85), when there was a falling out between the *vali* and the late Ebrahim Khan. 'Umma Khan, the ruler of Avars, attacked Georgia with a large force. He took the fortress, *saqnaq*, and *kumesh-*

---

[276] Adigozal Beg adds that Molla Panah was sent a staff with precious stones, *Qarabagh-name*, p. 83.

[277] Khoi is not included in Adigozal Beg's list, *Qarabagh-name*, p. 83.

[278] The word used here is *padeshah*. The irony is that the ancient Persian word applies only to a king, while the "king" in question was Catherine. A woman ruler had caused amazement earlier, when Anna was on the throne of Russia. Nader Shah had even proposed to the Russian envoy that Anna become one of his wives, see *Alamara-ye Naderi*, I, pp. 410-411. Bakikhanov has Salim Khan of Shakki as the only one sending a message, *Golestan-e Eram*, p. 179.

[279] Erekle was of the Georgian Bagrationi (Bagratuni) family, a branch of the Armenian Bagratids, whose nobility was established in the classical period and who ruled Armenia and parts of Georgia as kings during the medieval period.

[280] Ahmad Beg has Ummay Khan, *Karabakhskogo khanstva*, p. 93,

[281] Adigozal Beg's editor has an ellipsis here, probably because what follows has little to do with the flow of the text, *Qarabagh-name*, p. 84.

khane,[282] killed many people, and imprisoned the remaining women and children of the place.[283] After looting many of the surrounding villages, he ['Umma] went to Akhesghe (Akhaltsikhe) and wintered with Suleiman Pasha.[284] He received *khal'at* and many gifts from the sultan of Rum. In spring, on his way [back] to Daghestan, again through Georgia, he besieged the fortress of Vakhan (Vakhun) on the border. This was a strong fortress where Prince Abashirza (Abashidze) and his family resided.[285] After surrounding it, he ['Umma Khan] took the fortress, killed many of its inhabitants and imprisoned the women and children, taking their money and belongings. He sent one of the daughters of the prince, along with some of the plunder, as gifts to the late Ebrahim Khan. Ebrahim Khan married her, and from this same daughter of Prince Abashidze were born a boy and a girl. 'Umma Khan himself married the other daughter of Prince Abashidze, who remained in his harem.[286]

Given all of this, the *vali* greatly desired [the goodwill] of the late Ebrahim Khan, especially since the khans of Shirvan, Shakki, Ganje, Erevan, Khoi, Qaradagh, Nakhichevan, Talesh, [31] Tabriz, and the khans of Shahsavan and Shaqaqi [tribes] obeyed[287] the late Ebrahim

---

[282] The exact meaning of this word is difficult to ascertain. Bakikhanov also mentions it, *Golestan-e Eram*, p. 185, but none of the translators or editors have been able to define it. *Kumesh* or *kumish* is a well-digger; *kumesh-khane* would imply the house of the well-digger, which does not apply in this case. It could mean the well-head or water-supply, which was necessary for any fortress or *saqnaq* to withstand a long siege. If the word was spelled *kamsh*, it would mean provisions, which would also apply.

[283] The Persian texts do not identify what city or settlement in Georgia was attacked. Georgian texts refer to Tiflis and its environs.

[284] Suleiman Pasha, the Pasha of Akhaltsikhe, would also periodically raid Georgia. Erekle had merged his house with that of Imeret'i, in western Georgia. The rise of Georgia and its close ties to Russia made the Ottomans, and especially the neighboring pashas, nervous, hence, with the approval and support of the Ottoman sultan, the pashas and Daghestani tribes would raid the region.

[285] The Abashidze were of one the main feudal families of western Georgia. They had constantly fought to remain autonomous and had even refused to accept the authority of Nader Shah. It is probable that the prince in question was the son of Levan Abashidze, one of the great lords of Imeret'i.

[286] Bakikhanov calls him 'Om Khan and mentions his looting and destruction in Georgia, which forced Erekle to pay him an annual subsidy of 5000 *manat* to keep him out of his domain. He would raid and plunder Ganje and one time, when Ebrahim Khan, his ally, gave him safe passage, 'Umma Khan even raided Nakhichevan, *Golestan-e Eram*, p. 185.

[287] Once again Mirza Jamal exaggerates the extent of Ebrahim's influence.

Khan and would not go against him. Being cautious, the *vali* of Tiflis
expediently submitted to the Exalted State of Russia, as well, sending
envoys and petitions [there].[288] Thus, everyone was ready to accept
Russian suzerainty, when suddenly the great empress died.[289] The
supreme *sardar* Zubov gave leave to Abo'l Fath Khan and the sons of the
begs and elders of Qarabagh and sent them with respectful greetings and
gifts to the late Ebrahim Khan, informing him of his departure to Russia
at the order of the late emperor Paul.[290]

This news distressed everyone,[291] and also unleashed the animosity
of Aqa Mohammad Shah, who had hoped to gain the late Ebrahim
Khan's submission with kindness and without much effort. The action
of the late Ebrahim Khan, who without any struggle or resistance had
offered his loyalty and friendship to the eternal Russian State, while
cutting himself off from the Islamic ruler of Iran, greatly enraged him.
He decided to crush the late Ebrahim Khan [once and for all] and in the
spring [1797], moved with a huge army toward Azerbaijan.[292]

The *velayat* of Qarabagh was suffering from a three-year drought sent
by God. No wheat or vegetables grew, and there was major famine. The

---

[288] Mirza Jamal does not seem to recall that Erekle had already a treaty with
Catherine, the Georgievsk agreement of 1783.

[289] November 6, 1796.

[290] It seems that the Qarabaghi notables had served as hostages of sorts.
Bakikhanov states that Javad Khan of Ganje now realized that Russia had
decided to annex his khanate to Georgia, and thus began to look towards Iran.
Erekle, Ebrahim Khan, and Salim Khan of Shakki then came to Ganje, deposed
Javad and installed 'Ali Sultan Shams od-Dinlu, as the *na'eb* (deputy) of the khan.
Javad Khan was planning to flee, but his wife went to the young commander
and reminded him of a kindness she once had done for him, after which 'Ali
Sultan gave up the keys to the fortress to Javad and remained at his side,
Golestan-e Eram, pp. 179-180. Adigozal Beg places the first siege of Ganje by
Ebrahim and Erekle here, with a different sequence of events. He also adds that
after the affairs of Ganje were settled, the vali did not return to Tiflis, but went
on to Kakhet'i, where after two years, he died in Telavi on January 11, 1798. His
eldest son, Georgii, took over the reign. Adigozal then goes on to describe the
family arguments in Georgia and how Prince Alexander ended up a refugee in
Qarabagh, *Qarabagh-name*, pp. 84-85.

[291] Particularly in Transcaucasia, which now had to deal with Aqa
Mohammad Khan, who viewed their past actions as treason.

[292] Fasa'i places it in late May or early June 1797, *Farsname-ye Naseri*, I, p. 242.
This passage sounds like a mild rebuke by Mirza Jamal for those who do not
back their co-religionists. There is some evidence that Ebrahim Khan once again

price of grain had increased so, that one *chetvert* of wheat was difficult to obtain even at 45 rubles at the price of that time. The situation was unbearable and thus when the Qezelbash army and Aqa Mohammad Shah reached the Arax River, it would have been difficult, in the face of the famine and the difficulties of the previous few years, to resist such a strong foe and remain in the fortress of Shushi.[293]

Therefore, having no other alternative, [Ebrahim Khan], together with his family, relatives, the families of the important begs, and his loyal attendants [32] left the fortress for Jar and Tale,[294] to wait and see if any help would be forthcoming from Daghestan, Georgia, and other *velayats* in the preparation of a counteroffensive.[295] At worst, he could go from there to Daghestan, to his relative, 'Umma Khan, the ruler of the Avars, where he would be safe from Aqa Mohammad Shah's punishment.

Among the khans who accompanied him and refused to be parted with him were Nasir Khan, the khan's son-in-law; 'Ata Khan Shahsavan; and Salim Khan, the ruler of Shakki, who was also the khan's son-in-law; and the begs of the *velayats* of Shakki and Shahsavan and their families.[296]

Upon hearing about Ebrahim Khan's flight from the fortress, Aqa Mohammad Shah, who was at the Arax [river], dispatched some two thousand horsemen with commanders so they could perhaps intercept him on the road to Ganje or by the Kur river. This force caught up with

---

tried to damage the Khoda-afarin Bridge and either succeeded in doing so or was stopped by Soleiman Khan of Tabriz, who had stationed a garrison near the bridge. Ebrahim then opened a number of irrigation canals and flooded parts of Qarabagh to halt the shah's advance, *Bamdad*, I, 12.

[293] Ahmad Beg describes the horrible conditions in Qarabagh at that time. His account is based on oral history gathered from those who survived the famine. Apparently there was no bread, and wheat was not even sown. Animals were slaughtered, and people consumed carrion, roots and acorns. Cases of cannibalism were reported as well. Thousands died and many emigrated to other lands, *Karabakhskogo khanstva*, p. 78.

[294] Ahmad Beg has Jaro-Belakan, *Karabakhskogo khanstva*, p. 78.

[295] Bakikhanov, confirms the above, *Golestan-e Eram*, p. 180. Hedayat also confirms the flight of Ebrahim Khan, *Rouzat os-Safa*, IX, 297.

[296] Fasa'i's account is different and interesting. Since Ebrahim Khan had not submitted as had the others (that is he had not allowed Aqa Mohammad to enter Shushi) the shah decided to settle the affair once and for all. Seeing the shah, the citizens of Shushi claimed that they were planning to rebel and arrest Ebrahim for going against the shah, but that he and his family had escaped to Daghestan, *Farsname-ye Naseri*, I, p. 242. Ahmad Beg also mentions that the citizens were happy to see the shah and welcomed him with songs, *Karabakhskogo khanstva*, p. 78.

the baggage carts of the retreating group accompanying the late Ebrahim Khan, near a bridge by the Tartar River. They attacked but did not harm the servants and other people. They did, however, loot some of the baggage on the carts and returned.[297]

The late Ebrahim Khan crossed the Kur, went through the *velayat* of Shakki, and entered the region of Belkan and Jar (Jaro-Belakan).[298] Aqa Mohammad Shah [gave] orders to all the elders and leaders of Jar and Tale[299] to detain the late Ebrahim Khan and the other khans and not to allow them to proceed to Daghestan. Despite this, the inhabitants of Jar, Belakan, and Ilisu[300] showed the necessary respect and hospitality, because they had enjoyed the kindness and gifts of Ebrahim Khan for a long time and were always ready to selflessly carry out all of his wishes.

They had stayed [no more than] twenty days in the land of Belakan when the news of the murder of Aqa Mohammad Shah within the fortress of Shushi [33] reached the late Ebrahim Khan. The details of the murder of Aqa Mohammad Shah are as follows:

After Ebrahim Khan's departure from the fortress of Shushi for Belakan, Aqa Mohammad Shah entered the fortress without any resistance.[301] After a week's stay there, he condemned to severe punishment two of his close attendants, Safar 'Ali Beg and 'Abbas Beg, because of something they had done one night which had greatly displeased and angered him.[302] Knowing that he [the shah] never changed his mind and fearing for their lives, they [the two] decided to kill him before daybreak. At dawn, while the shah was asleep, they entered [the bedroom] with sharp daggers and murdered him.[303] They shut the doors and took his

---

[297] Berzhe's translation states that *all their belongings were taken*, "Karabag," 68 (1855), 294.

[298] Jar and Belakan were settlements located northwest of Shakki on the border of Daghestan, see map 3.

[299] Tale is south of Jar, see map 3.

[300] Ilisu or Elisu was a town and territory by the banks of the Alazani River. This small state was established by the Tsakhur tribe; its leader bore the title of sultan; see map 3.

[301] Ahmad Beg gives great details on the reaction of the population, and their welcoming of the shah into Qarabagh. He also details all of the conversations and events involving Mohammad Beg, Molla Panah and others, that led to the fateful, final night, *Karabakhskogo khanstva*, pp. 79-84.

[302] Severe punishment or *siyasat-e 'azim*, was equal to capital punishment.

[303] According to Hasan Fasa'i it was the night of June 16-17, 1797. He also has a slightly different account. There is no Safar 'Ali Beg in his version. Three days

armband, crown, and his jewel-encrusted cordon[304] and went to Sadeq Khan Shaqaqi and told him the truth of what had transpired.[305] Sadeq Khan was terribly fearful of the shah and did not trust him; [therefore], he did not believe them.[306] Being in constant fear of his life, he thought this story to be a trick of the shah [to trap him into betrayal]. Finally after receiving numerous oaths, he gathered up his nerve, and still greatly fearful, entered the apartments of the shah, which were in the house of the late Major-General Mohammad Hasan Aqa,[307] the eldest son of Ebrahim Khan, where Aqa Mohammad Shah had been residing. Still following all the appropriate protocol, he slowly approached the shah's bedroom, pulled the curtain that was across the door and peeked in. Then he very slowly entered the room and approached the bed. No matter how much Safar 'Ali Beg assured him, he was still afraid. Safar 'Ali Beg then stepped forward and lifted the quilt which covered the shah and showed him the corpse of the shah bloodied with [34] dagger slashes.

---

after his arrival in Shushi, the shah's Georgian servant, named Sadeq, and his valet, Khodadad Esfahani, had a row and raised their voices. The shah got angry and ordered their execution. Sadeq Khan Shaqaqi tried to intercede but to no avail. Since it was Friday (the Muslim Sabbath), the shah postponed their execution until Saturday and allowed them to go on serving in the royal apartments. Knowing the shah always kept his word, they, together with another valet, 'Abbas Mazandarani, murdered the shah, *Farsname-ye Naseri*, I, p. 242. This version is also confirmed by Hedayat, *Rouzat os-Safa*, IX, 298.

[304] Hasan Fasa'i describes the jewels worn by the shah at his coronation: The armbands were studded with the "Ocean of Light" and the "Crown of the Moon" diamonds, and the cordon hanging on his neck was composed a string of pearls, each one as big as a sparrow's egg and as white as camphor, *Farsname-ye Naseri*, I, p. 241.

[305] Ahmad Beg states that Mohammad Beg, the nephew of Ebrahim Khan, was present when the assassins brought the jewels, *Karabakhskogo khanstva*, pp. 81-82. Donboli states that they also took a box of precious jewels and brought it to Sadeq Khan, *Ma'ser-e Soltaniye*, p. 25. Nader Shah during his Indian campaign had taken the treasury of the Mughals. A number of famous stones, such as the *Kuh-e Nur*, *Darya-ye Nur* and *Taj-e Mah*, among others, as well as the great peacock throne, were among the loot, see *Alamara-ye Naderi*, II, 739.

[306] In 1205 (1790) Sadeq Khan had fought Aqa Mohammad's forces, was defeated, and sought refuge with Ebrahim Khan in Shushi. He later apologized and joined Aqa Mohammad, but was always fearful for his life, *Montazam-e Naseri*, III, 1413.

[307] This title was given to Mohammad Hasan Aqa by the Russians at a later date. Berzhe's version reads *Mohammad Hasan 'Ali*, "Karabag," 68 (1855), 294.

Sadeq Khan was not able to tolerate the scene. He took the armbands, crown, and cordon [from the two killers] and rushed to his apartments, where he announced that the shah had ordered him to depart for Ganje and Georgia. He left the fortress with all his followers and the Shaqaqi army (Kurds), taking one of the shah's murderers, 'Abbas [Beg], with him. Safar 'Ali Beg remained in the fortress.[308] Barely two hours after the departure of Sadeq Khan, the news of the shah's murder had spread all over the fortress. The confused Qezelbash khans gathered whatever followers were close by and, group after group, escaped from the fortress. The population of the city surrounded those [remaining] inside the fortress and whomever they caught they stripped of everything.[309] They rushed into the apartments [of the shah] and started looting carpets, furniture and other household goods, gold and silver objects, and jewels belonging to the shah.[310]

When Mohammad Beg, the son of the brother of Ebrahim Khan, and a youth famed for his bravery, heard of this, he, together with a number of servants, stood by the door and took back the jewels and gold coins, silver and gold utensils, carpets, and other items which were left, from those who had not already absconded.[311] He transferred all of these items from the apartments of Mohammad Hasan Aqa to his household and began to govern and administer the fortress. He sent the head of Aqa Mohammad Shah, which had been cut off, together with a letter, with an old trusted retainer to the late Ebrahim Khan in Belakan.[312] Once the head of the shah reached Ebrahim Khan, it became clear to everyone that the shah had really been killed. The head of the shah was washed with

---

[308] Ahmad Beg states that Mohammad Beg and Sadeq Khan felt that one was to go after the throne of Iran and the other to take over Shushi, *Karabakhskogo khanstva*, p. 85

[309] This confirms the famine and poverty, as well as the hatred of the population for Aqa Mohammad Khan's army and the devastation they had inflicted on Qarabagh for a number of years.

[310] Bakikhanov confirms the general events but not in the same detail, *Golestan-e Eram*, p. 180.

[311] Ahmad Beg states that he organized his followers into units, arrested those commanders of Aqa Mohammad who had remained, released the prisoners, including Molla Panah, the vazir of Qarabagh and began to rule the region, *Karabakhskogo khanstva*, pp. 85-86.

[312] Adigozal mentions that Mohammad Beg sent the head with Mohammad Rafi' Beg Qarabaghi to Ebrahim in Belakan who sent it to Erekle, *Qarabagh-name*, p. 88.

great honor, wrapped in a shroud, and sent with esteemed mollas who knew the obligatory rituals, to Jar where it was buried in the cemetery of great nobles.[313]

[35] For three months [Ebrahim Khan], due to several obstacles, delayed his return to Qarabagh and stayed in Belakan.[314] He received gifts and messages of loyalty and friendship from everyone, especially the *vali* of Georgia, Javad Khan, the governor of Ganje, and Mostafa Khan of Shirvan. Since the shah, who had been a powerful enemy, was dead, all the khans of Azerbaijan and other [regions], who had always been aware of the power, greatness, and authority of the late Ebrahim Khan, wanted, primarily for their own benefit and security, to gain his attention and establish a strong friendship with him. Until the arrival of the late Ebrahim Khan, Mohammad Beg continued to manage the affairs of Qarabagh.[315]

A month after the arrival of the late Ebrahim Khan at Belakan, 'Umma Khan, the ruler of the Avars, and other leaders of Daghestan, arrived with a large army and provisions of food and clothing, all evidence of the kindness, kinship, and hospitality due such a grand *amir* (Ebrahim).[316] This treatment was not limited only to the late khan [Ebrahim], his renowned sons, and the begs of Qarabagh, but extended even to the Shahsavan khans and the offspring of their begs, who were granted all their food and expenses.

Two months after the arrival of 'Umma Khan, [Ebrahim Khan] accompanied by the army of Daghestan, some of the Qarabaghi people, and the leaders of the Shahsavan, left Belakan for Qarabagh.[317] Prior to his

---

[313] His body was buried in Shushi.

[314] Ahmad Beg states that Ebrahim did not trust Mohammad Beg's assurances of his return to Shushi, *Karabakhskogo khanstva*, p. 88.

[315] Ahmad Beg states that Sadeq Khan had advised him to take over Qarabagh and to declare himself independent. Javad Khan of Ganje offered him a marriage alliance, and offered to kill the family of Ebrahim who had remained in Shushi. Ebrahim's brother, Taleb Khan, had already been killed by the tribesmen of Jaro-Belakan who hoped to satisfy Aqa Mohammad Khan's wrath. The notables of Shushi also encouraged him to take the reins of government stating that Ebrahim was already too old. But his reply was that he would not go against his uncle and commit a shameful act, *Karabakhskogo khanstva*, p. 87.

[316] It is interesting to note that this sudden hospitality occurred only after the murder of the shah. Prior to that Ebrahim Khan, despite Mirza Jamal's account, was not assured of his safety.

[317] Ahmad Beg states that Ebrahim Khan, in order to gain the favor of Fath 'Ali Shah, at his request, returned Safar 'Ali, one of the assassins of Aqa Mohammad Shah, *Karabakhskogo khanstva*, p. 88. Iranian chronicles do not men-

departure the late Ebrahim Khan sent Mahdi Qoli Khan, who in those days was called Mahdi Qoli Aqa,[318] together with the sons of some of the begs of Qarabagh, ahead of him to warn the population against any [possible] opposition and to force them to abandon any thought of disobedience after the arrival of his excellency. In addition, they were to inform Mohammad Beg, who was full of youthful pride and energy, and moreover, [36] was [due to the circumstances] in control of some of the wealth and instruments of kingship, not to be tempted by Satan and not to dare to go against [Ebrahim Khan] and claim supreme authority.[319]

Mahdi Qoli Khan, together with the sons of the begs, entered Qarabagh. Mohammad Beg, although outwardly expressing his devotion, and boasting of his friendship, stating that he would never cease to obey the late khan [Ebrahim]; inwardly, however, wished to rule [in Qarabagh]. He gathered around himself a group of traitors, liars, and ruffians and planned a takeover. Mahdi Qoli khan, out of necessity, treated him [with respect]; to denounce him outright would not have been prudent. He carefully observed the situation inside the fortress as well as in the surrounding region, accurately reported conditions to the late khan [Ebrahim], and awaited his [decision]. Receiving the report while on the banks of the Kur, the late Ebrahim Khan immediately dispatched his eldest[320] son the late Mohammad Hasan Aqa with five hundred Lezgi warriors and leaders of Qarabagh [to the fortress]. Mohammad Beg, hearing of the arrival of the late khan [and his cavalry], decided to [forcibly] transfer the tribes of Qarabagh to the Arax and stopped by the river to foment dissent.[321] When the late Mohammad Hasan Aqa reached the vicinity of Mount Kers,[322] three *farsakhs*[323] from

---

tion any demands for the assassins. According to them the killers were all in Iran, see note 333.

[318] Mahdi Qoli, in fact, succeeded Ebrahim as the last (nominal) khan of Qarabagh (1806-1822).

[319] Ebrahim Khan did not feel secure. Some of the Armenian *meliks*, tribal chiefs, Erekle, Javad Khan, as well as the Qajars, were still major threats. The economic conditions were also not favorable.

[320] The Persian text emphasizes that he was the eldest; in this context it means he was also the most capable.

[321] Ahmad Beg puts the place at 40 *versts* from Shushi, by the Togh settlement, *Karabakhskogo khanstva*, p. 91.

[322] The present-day Bolshoi or Büyük Kers, located in the southern part of the Qarabagh range.

[323] Berzhe's translation from this point on transforms all *farsakhs* to Russian

the fortress, where the supporters and troops of Mohammad Beg were located, the people of Qarabagh, seeing the late aqa and his soldiers, came out in droves, appeared before him and kissed his hand. The tribal forces gathered [by Mohammad Beg] were [forced into] the steppes and thickets. [Mohammad Hasan Aqa] sent a messenger calling Mohammad Beg to appear before him. At first Mohammad Beg was afraid, but he was eventually assured [37] and came to the late Mohammad Hasan Aqa, kissed his hand, and remained trustfully at his side.[324] A number of criminals, who during [Mohammad] Beg's control had committed outrages, were executed by [Mohammad Hasan Aqa] in the presence of Mohammad Beg. In the meantime, Mahdi Qoli Khan, who was in the fortress and heard the news of the arrival of the Aqa [his brother] and his approach with troops, arrested the appointees of his [paternal] cousin, Mohammad Beg.

The late Mohammad Hasan Aqa calmed and assured the tribes of Qarabagh and wrote to all the *mahals* to resume their work and trades. After that, Ebrahim Khan, accompanied by troops and the retinue of Nasir Khan and 'Ata Khan Shahsavan, arrived and entered Qarabagh.

Chapter Seven:
On a Number of Events Which Occurred after the Death of Aqa Mohammad Shah and the Return of Ebrahim Khan from Belakan to Qarabagh[325]

After the late [Ebrahim] Khan reached Qarabagh and took up the reins of government, the population of the *velayat* [continued to] suffer from famine, hardships, and the unsettled conditions. Many [members] of tribes and [people of] villages were forced to go into the *velayats* of Georgia, Ganje, Erevan, and the Shirvans, and even to the *velayats* of Rum. Their belongings and wealth were all plundered. Although the

---

measures of *versts*. Each *farsakh* is seven *versts*; the changes will not otherwise be noted, "Karabag," 68 (1855), 294.

[324] Ahmad Beg states that Mohammad Hasan Aqa, even prior to that, was the main protector of Mohammad Beg against Ebrahim Khan's suspicions and against his being sent to Fath 'Ali Shah. According to Ahmad Beg, the shah blamed Mohammad Beg for the murder of his uncle, Aqa Mohammad Shah, for a detailed account, see *Karabakhskogo khanstva*, pp. 88-91.

[325] Berzhe's translation reads **Chapter Six**, with no title. It is, as noted, a very condensed version of the manuscript used in this translation, "Karabag," 69 (1855), 297.

neighboring khans outwardly spouted words of obedience and friendship [to Ebrahim], inwardly they desired private gain. Among them [for example, was] Mostafa Khan of Shirvan. During the absence of Ebrahim Khan in Belakan, he brought over Mohammad Hasan Khan, the elder brother of Salim Khan [of Shakki], and assisted in appointing him as the ruler [of Shakki]; so that Salim Khan, the son-in-law of the late Ebrahim Khan may not [one day] sit in Shakki and endanger his own rule. [At the same time], Mohammad Beg, [38] after being reassured [of his safety] by the late Mohammad Hasan Aqa, like the other sons of the khans of the late Panah Khan's clan, did not fear for his life. But being youthful and arrogant, he went to the bank of the Kur [River] and made friends with Mohammad Hasan Khan of Shakki.[326] Mohammad Hasan Khan deceived him, [saying], "I am a blind man and I can no longer tolerate Mostafa Khan's rule [over me].[327] Come join me and I will wed you to my daughter and you will [eventually] rise to [become] the ruler of Shakki." Mohammad Beg was fooled by such words and turned away from his famed kinsman and esteemed uncle [Ebrahim] and went to Mohammad Hasan Khan. Upon arrival [in Shakki], Mohammad Hasan Khan captured and imprisoned Mohammad Beg and took all the jewels, money, and goods which were in his possession.

Mostafa Khan, who for many years had been the mortal enemy of Mohammad Beg, as he had killed Mostafa's father and brother to avenge his own father's death, sent a agent to Mohammad Hasan Khan, to take Mohammad Beg [to Shirvan], and executed him.[328] Having killed the son of the late Ebrahim Khan's brother, he [Mostafa] became even more of an enemy of the khan, and, out of fear, commenced hostile activity

---

[326] He was the son of Hosein Khan and grandson of Hajji Chelebi. Ahmad Beg's version is different. He states that once Ebrahim Khan entered Shushi, Mohammad Aqa, instead of going to Ganje or Russia, fled to Shakki, *Karabakhskogo khanstva*, p. 91. Bakikhanov states that Mohammad Aqa was the son of Mehr 'Ali Beg, son of Ebrahim Khan (he was Ebrahim's nephew), who for a short time claimed to rule Qarabagh, but upon the arrival of Ebrahim Khan fled to Shakki, *Golestan-e Eram*, p. 181.

[327] The khan of Shakki's blindness is confirmed by Ahmad Beg, who calls him *Kör* or *Kur* (blind) Mohammad, *Karabakhskogo khanstva*, p. 91.

[328] Events confirmed by Bakikhanov, *Golestan-e Eram*, p. 181. Ahmad Beg claims that folk songs were composed about the brave deeds of Mohammad Beg. He adds that Safar 'Ali Beg, one of the assassins of the late shah, who had accompanied Mohammad Beg, was handed over to Fath 'Ali Shah by the khan of Shakki, a fact not confirmed by Iranian chroniclers, *Karabakhskogo khanstva*, p. 92, see note 333.

against Qarabagh. On another side, Mohammad Hasan Khan [of Shakki] also became an enemy [of Ebrahim Khan's], and Javad Khan, the ruler of Ganje, joined them.[329]

At that time news arrived that Fath 'Ali Shah, who was called Baba Khan Sardar, and who had been appointed the *vali* of the *velayat* of Fars in Shiraz by Aqa Mohammad Shah, had heard the news of the shah's murder, moved from Shiraz, and had entered Tehran.[330] He had taken over the treasury and other royal property and had ascended the throne.[331] At the same time, the above-mentioned Sadeq Khan Shaqaqi, who had fled the fortress of Shushi, found Azerbaijan without a governor and claimed the throne. [39] He gathered a large army and moved towards 'Araq to capture Tehran and release his kin, who were hostages there.[332]

Fath 'Ali Shah met and defeated him, and forced him to flee. After that he [Fath 'Ali] sent an envoy to the late Ebrahim Khan with utmost respects. He asked for the body of Aqa Mohammad Shah and expressed his sincere desire for Ebrahim khan's obedience.[333] [Economic] Condi-

---

[329] This and other similar passages clearly demonstrate that just as among the Armenian *meliks*, there was no feeling of unity among the Turkic groups. Personal gain and clan allegiance came first.

[330] Baba Khan was the nephew of Aqa Mohammad Shah. Since Aqa Mohammad was castrated at youth, the Qajar dynasty was continued by Baba Khan, who took the title of Fath 'Ali Shah (1797/8-1834). Fath 'Ali Shah made up for his uncle's childlessness. His large harem gave him over one hundred princes and princesses.

[331] Mirza Jamal, following the Qajar chroniclers, once again jumps ahead and gives Fath 'Ali the title of shah, before the fact. Fath 'Ali Shah, was not crowned until the defeat of Sadeq Khan and a few other pretenders and his gaining control of central Iran. His coronation occurred in 1798 after the body of Aqa Mohammad was recovered, see *Rouzat os-Safa*, IX, 320 and *Ma'ser-e Soltaniye*, pp. 30-31. Fasa'i has March 11, 1798 as the auspicious day, *Farsname-ye Naseri*, I, 244.

[332] Aqa Mohammad, like previous Iranian rulers, had kept hostages, usually sons, to assure the obedience of the khans of the various provinces.

[333] The messenger, Hosein Qoli Khan, actually came from the new governor of Tabriz, Ja'far Qoli Khan Donboli, who was rewarded by the new shah for his loyalty to the Qajars. E'temad os-Saltane adds that Hosein Qoli escorted the body back to Tehran, *Montazam-e Naseri*, III, 1442. Hedayat and Mirza Jamal mention that Ebrahim's son, Abo'l Fath Khan, escorted the body, *Rouzat os-Safa*, IX, pp. 314-315. Donboli states that Ebrahim was ordered by the new *sardar* to exhume the body and to return it with proper dignity to Tehran, *Ma'ser-e Soltaniye*, p. 31. Ahmad Beg states that the Persian party in Qarabagh led by Mirza 'Ali Beg, Fazel Beg, and others urged Ebrahim to follow the example of Shakki and acknowledge

tions of the Qarabagh *velayat* were destitute and it was surrounded by enemies; [therefore], the late Ebrahim Khan deemed conciliation prudent, and with great honors, sent the corpse of Aqa Mohammad Shah to Tehran. Fath 'Ali Shah interpreted this action of the late Ebrahim Khan's as a good sign. He generously rewarded the envoys who had brought the body, and sent them back with *khal'at*, swords, and gave the governorship of Qaradagh[334] with all its income to Ebrahim Khan, and expressed his wish to become related to him. He stated: "For the peace of both our parties, consider your beloved daughter Aqa Begum Aqa, worthy of our harem, [to] become the lady[335] of our harem."

After some consultation, it was considered appropriate. The shah made huge preparations, dispatching noted khans [to fetch] Aqa Begum Aqa with great honor, and married her. She became his respected wife and the head of his harem.[336] The son of the late Ebrahim Khan, Abo'l

---

Fath 'Ali Shah, *Karabakhskogo khanstva*, pp. 92-93. Silver coins (*saheb qeran*) bearing the name of the shah were struck in Shushi. Fasa'i states that Fath 'Ali Shah ordered by royal *farman* that Ebrahim put the corpse on a litter and arrange its transfer with all the respect due a shah. Fasa'i states that the three murderers of the shah were also executed at this time, suffering horrible deaths, *Farsname-ye Naseri*, I, 244. Donboli states that they were executed earlier, *Ma'ser-e Soltaniye*, p. 30. Two of the assassins were caught in Qazvin, after the defeat of Sadeq Khan. They were hacked to death. The third one was caught in Kermanshah and burnt to death in Tehran.

[334] Ebrahim Khan became the governor of Qarabagh and Qaradagh. The Turkish translation erroneously has "Qarabagh," *Karabagh Tarihi*, p. 22.

[335] The term *banu* implies the main wife.

[336] Hedayat and Donboli do not mention the marriage, *Ma'ser-e Soltaniye*, p. 31; *Rouzat os-Safa*, IX, 314-315. Since the marriage did occur, it may have occurred either earlier or later. E'temad os-Saltane has the marriage earlier in 1214 (1799), *Montazam-e Naseri*, III, 1453. There is more evidence that the legal affair occured later. This can be explained by the fact that Fath 'Ali Shah, at that time, had four legal wives. He therefore took Aqa Begum as a *sighe* (temporary wife). Upon the death of Asiye Khanum, the daughter of Mohammad Khan Qajar Qavanlu, he married Aga Begum, who became his wife, *Bamdad*, I, p. 12. Aqa Begum, whose mother was Tuti Begum, the daughter of the khan of Ganje, became a very powerful women. According to some sources, after the death of Fath 'Ali Shah, she became a recluse in a mosque in Qom and died there. She apparently wrote poetry in Persian and Turkish. She was extremely anti-Russian, due to the fact that the Russians had killed her family in Ganje (see below), Shukiurzade in *Karabakhskogo khanstva*, p. 104. Fasa'i confirms Mirza Jamal's account and states that she was the primary lady of the harem. In fact she was the same lady to whom Sir Gore Ouseley presented, through his own wife, who had received the

Fath Khan, who was then called Abo'l Fath Aqa, was sent to the shah, where he was treated as one of the grand khans. [The shah] made him a close confidant and always showed him great respect.[337] Every year Fath 'Ali Shah would send *khal'at*, a sword, a horse with golden-inlaid saddle and bridle, and other ceremonial items to the late Ebrahim Khan and the late Mohammad Hasan Aqa.[338] This continued until the Supreme Emperor of the Exalted and Mighty Russian State sent a *sardar*, who entered Georgia with an army and who settled in Tiflis as its independent [governor].[339] Since [40] even before the heads of Russian State had contemplated the conquest of the *velayats* of Erevan, Ganje, the Shirvans, and Qarabagh, the late Ebrahim Khan had freely expressed his feelings of devotion and loyalty to the late ruler of the everlasting state of Russia, Catherine, and had especially shown friendliness at the time of the arrival of *general en-chef* Zubov, with the approval of the *vali* of Georgia—he and the *vali* of Georgia had a friendly relationship and

---

special privilege of visiting the harem, with an expensive gift from the wife of George III of England in late 1811, *Farsname-ye Naseri*, I, p. 261. Bamdad's account differs. He states that she was known as Agha Baji, the 129th wife of Fath 'Ali Shah. He adds that either because of Ebrahim Khan's behavior, or for other reasons, the shah, from the very first day, did not like her. He refused to sleep with her, but did not divorce her. She lived a life of luxury in Qom and died there just prior to Fath 'Ali Shah in 1833, *Bamdad*, I. p. 12.

[337] It seems that he started as a hostage but was soon persuaded by Fath 'Ali Shah to serve him, with hopes of becoming the next khan. Abo'l Fath Khan, realizing that there was no chance of him ever becoming the khan of Qarabagh, threw his lot with the Iranians and was rewarded with various posts. His son, 'Abbas Qoli Khan Javanshir, known as Mo'tamed od-Doule, held a number of governorships under Mohammad Shah, and became the minister of justice under Naser od-Din Shah, *Bamdad*, I, 44.

[338] Mohammad Hasan Aqa was the heir of Ebrahim Khan and hence was accorded special honors as well.

[339] Mirza Jamal does not mention who this *sardar* was. The commander of the Caucasian Line was Lieutenant General Karl Fedorovich Knorring, but he did not come to Tiflis at that time or assume the position of governor. It is probable that Mirza Jamal refers to Major General Ivan Petrovich Lazarev (a member of the wealthy and influential Russian Armenian Lararev [Lazarian] family), who in 1799 was the commander of the Russian regiment in Tiflis. On 3 August, 1800 Lazarev, by imperial decree, became the official representative of Russia at the Georgian court. Upon the death of Giorgi XII, Lazarev temporarily assumed the control of Tiflis. Lazarev was stabbed to death on April 18, 1803 by the queen dowager of Georgia.

watched for each other's well being——the envoy of the late Ebrahim Khan, together with the envoy of the *vali* of Georgia, were sent to Count Gudovich,[340] who was the *sardar* of the Mozdok Line, expressing their devotion and obedience to the eternal Russian State. Meanwhile, he wrote a letter, [with the intention of] renewing this old friendship, and sent it with an envoy to the *sardar*, who, representing the Exalted Russian State, had entered Tiflis.

After that *sardar* took his leave, General Kovalenskii[341] was appointed *sardar*. Another envoy bearing gifts was sent to Kovalenskii, expressing his [the khan's] friendship. Indeed, Kovalenskii treated the envoys [of the khan] with great respect. He sent the late Ebrahim Khan grand and special gifts, expressing particular kindness to him.

Finally, the supreme *sardar*, Prince Tsitsianov,[342] arrived in Georgia. Since His Excellency was a bold and brave *sardar*, he did not tolerate certain actions of the Lezgi of Jar and Tale, and of Javad Khan, the

---

[340] General, Field Marshal, and Count Ivan Vasil'evich Gudovich (1741-1820) fought the Ottomans in the Russo-Turkish war of 1768-1774 under the command of General P. A. Rumiantsev. He served as a commander of a unit under General G. A. Potemkin in the Russo-Turkish war of 1787-1792. In 1791 he was appointed as the commander of the Russian forces on the Caucasian Line (see map 5). After Aqa Mohammad's sack of Tiflis, he began preparing a campaign against Iran, but Catherine appointed Zubov, a favorite. Gudovich resigned in anger and Catherine gave him the title of *general en-chef* as a consolation. After Catherine's death, Paul removed Zubov and others of her favorites, and Gudovich was reinstated as the commander-in-chief of the Caucasian forces. Alexander I soon replaced him with Tsitsianov. After the death of Tsitsianov, Gudovich led the Russian command on the eastern front of the Russo-Turkish war (1806-1812) and fought the Iranians in the First Russo-Iranian war (1804-1813). He was a tyrannical and reckless commander. In 1809 he was replaced by General Alexander Tormasov and left for Russia, where he was appointed state counselor and senator. He retired in 1812.

[341] Peter Ivanovich Kovalenskii was Tsar Paul's emissary to Tiflis. He arrived in 1799.

[342] Tsitsianov arrived in February 1803. He was a Russified Georgian nobleman. Extremely arrogant and ambitious, he considered the Muslims of Transcaucasia contemptible and treated the khans accordingly. His plan was not to have alliances with the local rulers, but to annex their territory outright. A number of times he went against the wishes of his superiors. One of his titles was Inspector of the Caucasian Line. The word inspector was pronounced *ishpokhdor*, which in the local Turkic dialect meant "his work is dirt." Persian sources call him the one who shed blood and other derogatory names, see Hedayat, *Rouzat os-Safa*, IX, 389.

governor of Ganje, as had the previous *sardars*.[343] He decided that for the peace of mind of the population of Georgia, the Lezgi of Jar and Tale and Javad Khan had to be punished.[344]

At the end of the Christian year 1803 he laid siege to the fortress of Ganje. The siege lasted one month, [during which time] he sent a number of messengers to Javad Khan and urged him to submit to the great emperor and surrender the fortress, [41] but to no avail.[345] Finally on the last day of the month of Ramazan (Ramadhan) on the night before the 'Aid-e Fetr, the fortress was stormed and taken.[346] Javad Khan and one of his sons, Hosein Qoli Aqa, were killed in the massacre [that ensued].[347] The rest of the family of the khan were taken prisoner. Some of the inhabitants of the city were killed, but the rest survived.[348]

---

[343] Tsitsianov was indeed different. He exiled most of the Georgian royal family and began the formal annexation of that kingdom. Two Georgian princes, one of them the famed Alexander, fled to Daghestan and Iran and for some years fought the Russians to reclaim their throne, see *Ma'ser-e Soltaniye*, pp. 108-109.

[344] The real reason was Tsitsianov's plan to annex the khanate of Ganje. On the pretext that it was part of Georgia, he attacked without any real provocation. Javad Khan, however, realizing that the Russians had decided to make his khanate part of Georgia, had begun correspondance with the Iranians. There was no threat from Ganje or its allies at that time, for Ahmad Beg clearly states that General Lazarev had defeated 'Omar ('Umma) Khan and thus the threat from the Avars had subsided, *Karabakhskogo khanstva*, pp. 93-94. Russian primary sources also record that the Avar and Lezgi tribesmen and their Georgian allies under the command of Prince Alexander of Georgia and 'Omar Khan were routed by Lazarev on November 7, 1800. In fact 'Omar died a few weeks after, *Akty*, II, pp. 111, 170-175. Some time later (April 1803) Tsitsianov sent troops to Belakan under the command of Guliakov, *Ibid.*, II, p. 685. Adigozal Beg has details on the Russian campaigns in Georgia and Daghestan. He adds that the Russian and Ganjavi armies met in the Kulu-Kobe (Qulu-Qobbe?) field where Javad Khan was defeated and retreated into the citadel in Ganje, *Qarabagh-name*, pp. 95-98.

[345] See letters from Tsitsianov to Javad Khan (November 29 through December 29, 1803) in *Akty*, II, pp. 588-591. As stated, Javad Khan did not want to give up his khanate to Georgia and hoped for an Iranian relief force.

[346] Dawn of January 3, 1804.

[347] E'temad os-Saltane states that the massacre continued for three days, *Montazam-e Naseri*, III, 1469. Hedayat has a more accurate time of three hours, *Rouzat os-Safa*, IX, p. 390. Adigozal Beg states that Javad fought bravely but was finally shot by Major Lisanevich, *Qarabagh-name*, p. 98.

[348] Donboli blames the Armenian population and Nasib Beg Shams od-Dinlu for the fall of the fortress and the death of many people, *Ma'ser-e Soltaniye*, pp.

[Tsitsianov] dispatched Major Lisanevich[349] from the fortress of Ganje to the late Ebrahim Khan and urged him to submit to the ever-gracious ruler of Russia. The late Ebrahim Khan gave the major a favorable answer and treated him with great respect and sent him back with a letter in which he expressed his deference [to Tsitsianov].[350]

In the spring of 1804, the governor of Erevan, Mohammad Khan, who feared Fath 'Ali Shah, and Kalb 'Ali Khan, the governor of Nakhichevan, who had fled from Fath 'Ali Shah and who had taken refuge in Erevan, sent an envoy to *sardar* Tsitsianov, seeking his help. They stated, "Fath 'Ali Shah has ordered his son, crown prince 'Abbas Mirza,[351] to take Erevan. If the *sardar* would honor us with his visit and gives us [military] aid, we will surrender the fortress to him and will accept the suzerainty of the Exalted Russian State."[352]

Therefore, Sardar Tsitsianov moved towards Erevan. From the Qezelbash State [Iran][353] the army of the crown prince ['Abbas Mirza]

109-110. Adigozal Beg's account, as noted in the introduction, is extremely pro-Russian. He blames Javad Khan for not heeding the peaceful overtures of Tsitsianov and does not mention the massacre, *Qarabagh-name*, p. 98. The wives, daughters and grandchildren of Javad Khan sought refuge in a mosque and years later (1812) were given permission to go to Iran via Baku. His younger son, Oghurlu or Oghuzlu, survived, went to Iran and later fought against the Russians when the Iranians attacked Ganje in the Second Russo-Iranian war.

[349] Major D. T. Lisanevich was appointed as the commandant of Shusha. He served in the Caucasus until 1825, when he was murdered by a Chechen he had insulted (see introduction).

[350] Confirmed by Donboli, *Ma'ser-e Soltaniye*, p. 110. Although Ebrahim had made contacts with the Russians before this, the bloody encounter in Ganje frightened many other khanates into submitting to Tsitsianov. Some Iranian sources claim that the massacre was carried out specifically to scare the remaining khans into submission, *Bamdad*, I, p. 288.

[351] The Persian term *nayeb ol-saltane* can be translated as "heir to the throne," "heir-apparent," "vice-regent," or "crown prince." 'Abbas Mirza was not the first son of Fath 'Ali Shah, but since he was born from a Qajar princess, he was named the heir. He was a believer in Western military superiority and tried to set up modern infantry and artillery units under his command. Although he died a year before Fath 'Ali Shah (1833), his son Mohammad Shah (1834-1848) continued the Qajar dynasty.

[352] Donboli points out that the khan's abusive rule had forced many to emigrate and that he occasionally did not obey the central government. He had flirted with the Russians and Fath 'Ali Shah in 1804 was on his way to punish him and bring him into submission, *Ma'ser-e Soltaniye*, pp. 95-96

[353] As noted, the aura of magnificence of the Safavids lingered on, hence the

made its appearance. The two forces clashed and the Qezelbash were defeated.[354] Hearing the news, Fath 'Ali Shah himself arrived in the field to crush Prince Tsitsianov and to prevent the fortress of Erevan from being turned over to the Russian State. He entered Erevan with a large force. From one side, Fath 'Ali Shah, from another, the army of the crown prince, and from the third, Mohammad Khan and Kalb 'Ali Khan, who had broken their pact with the *sardar* and had not surrendered the fortress, surrounded the Russian army from all sides.[355] They would not even let provisions reach the Russian force. But despite many attempts they did not succeed in gaining a victory over the Russians. Both sides suffered heavy losses and [42] finally Sardar Tsitsianov decided to return to Tiflis. Fath 'Ali Shah also returned to Azerbaijan and then Tehran.[356]

Since Fath 'Ali Shah had been informed of the missions of the late Ebrahim Khan's envoys to the Russian commanders, on his return from Erevan, he sent Abo'l Fath Khan [Ebrahim's son] to Qarabagh with five thousand troops, to assure the late khan of [royal] protection and assistance.[357] He asked that [Ebrahim] send Mohammad Hasan Aqa and a number of begs of Qarabagh to the shah.[358] He also instructed Abo'l Fath Khan, whom he invested with the authority of acting on behalf of [the khan], to remain permanently at the side of the late Ebrahim Khan for as long as he lived and make sure that no decision was made without his [Abo'l Fath's] advice or approval.

Qajar army and the Iranians are occasionally referred to as the *Qezelbash* by local as well as Russian chroniclers.

[354] June 19 or 20, 1804 near Edjmiadsin, but this was just a skirmish; there were other battles which the Russians lost.

[355] The attack began on July 2, 1804. Donboli states that Mohammad Khan of Erevan, after the siege of Erevan by the crown prince, realizing the size of the Iranian forces, changed his allegiance, sent his son as a hostage to 'Abbas Mirza and begged forgiveness, *Ma'ser-e Soltaniye*, p. 114.

[356] Donboli has more details of this campaign as seen from the Iranian point of view, *Ma'ser Soltaniye* pp. 110-120.

[357] Abo'l Fath Khan had accompanied the shah on his campaign in Erevan. Ahmad Beg states that the shah dispatched him from his camp prior to his departure for Iran, *Karabakhskogo khanstva*, p. 94.

[358] This was a polite way of asking for hostages. Ahmad Beg states that Mohammad Hasan Aqa represented the Russian party in Shushi, *Karabakhskogo khanstva*, p. 94. This explains why the shah wanted him in Tehran, why he was later decorated by the Russians, and why the Russians agreed that in the event of his death, his son would succeed as khan of Qarabagh.

Fath 'Ali Shah's instructions insulted the late Ebrahim Khan. He wrote a harsh reply to Abo'l Fath Khan, demanding that he return [to the shah] and not set foot in the territory of Qarabagh. Abo'l Fath Khan did not obey the order of [his] esteemed father and entered [crossed the Arax] with his Qezelbash army.[359] At that particular moment, the late Ebrahim Khan and the late Mohammad Hasan Aqa were in the area of Togh in the Dizak *mahal*. Mahdi Qoli Khan [his other son], with great speed gathered crack musketeers from among the population on the other side of the mountain, [and] together with his followers and others, assembled a large army which arrived at night in the presence of his venerable father, the late Ebrahim Khan and his esteemed brother, the late Mohammad Hasan Aqa.[360] The next morning, Abo'l Fath Khan with all his forces stormed Togh. The musketeers, renowned as crack shots, and the famed cavalry who were at the disposal of the late khan and his sons counterattacked and defeated the Qezelbash army, seizing all the horses and four-legged animals of their encampment,[and] killing and imprisoning many [men]. Abo'l Fath Khan then fled to the other side of the Arax.

Fath 'Ali Shah, upon hearing this, [43] censured and reproached Abo'l Fath Khan, and, hoping to bring the late Ebrahim Khan to his side by peaceful means and to discourage his submission to Russia, dispatched two or three khans as messengers. These khans were Karim Khan, Rahim Khan, and 'Abdollah Khan, who were instructed to subtly and affectionately deliver to the late Ebrahim Khan the shah's firm assurances and unbreakable oaths. They solemnly promised that the entire *velayat* of Qaradagh, with its income, even that which belonged to the shah,[361] would be entrusted to the late Ebrahim Khan and his descendants in perpetuity. In addition, two of the shah's sons would be sent to the fortress of Shushi as hostages of the late Ebrahim Khan. In exchange, both of the fortresses of Askeran,[362] which were located three *farsakhs*

---

[359] Ahmad Beg states that he entered from the region of Zangezur, *Karabakhskogo khanstva*, p. 95

[360] Ahmad Beg includes Khanlar Aqa, a younger son of Ebrahim, in the group accompanying Mahdi Khan, *Ibid.*, p. 95.

[361] Mirza Jamal does not specify whether these estates were *khalese*, or *khass*, that is property of the king, or *divani*, which were lands belonging to the central treasury. The distinction between the two was negligible, however, since the shah, technically, owned all the land, for details, see Bournoutian, *Erevan*, pp. 127-128.

[362] Donboli spells it with an *'ein*, *'Askeran*, *Ma'ser-e Soltaniye*, p. 150.

from the fortress of Shushi, on the road between Tiflis and Ganje, had to be given over to the [shah's] army, so that they could house a sufficient number of [the shah's] troops to block the road along which Russian troops might enter [Qarabagh]. In addition, the river which was situated one *farsakh* from the fortress of Shushi, and which had a barrier three *versts* from the fortress, were also to be given to the [shah's] army, so that both rivers,[and] all passages and roads to the fortress would be in the hands of the Qezelbash army, who would have to construct strong fortifications there to be able to halt the army of the great Russian State if it decided to attack the fortress of Shushi. A *sardar* with two to three thousand horsemen had to remain in Shah-Bulaghi to observe [the conditions] in Tiflis and Ganje and to commit murder and plunder in those regions. All [of the above] would be under the command of the late Ebrahim Khan and would have to obey his orders without question. The entire expense of the Qezelbash army would be born by the treasury of Fath 'Ali Shah. No soldier would be permitted to covet or expect even the most insignificant item in the *velayat* of Qarabagh. Everything which was indispensable for the army would have to be obtained through cash purchase.[363] [44] The goal [of all this was to make certain] that the impregnable fortress of Shushi, the fortress by the Khoda-afarin [bridge],[364] [which is] the gate to Georgia and the Shirvans, would not fall into the hands of the army of the Russian State.

Although the daughter of the late Ebrahim Khan, Aqa Begum Aqa, was the head of the [shah's] harem and the primary [wife], and Abo'l Fath Khan was held in great respect and had the title of *amir al-omara'* [at court],[365] nonetheless, the late Ebrahim Khan believed in the eternity of the Exalted Russian State and in the constancy and fairness of his majesty the emperor. He was certain that such a powerful state would always maintain its compassion [toward him] and that nothing would change the emperor's favor. [Therefore], he once again rejected the government of Iran and its favorable offers and again sent an envoy to

---

[363] Hence the customary requisitioning, which had devastated Qarabagh earlier, would be avoided.

[364] The Russian (*Istoriia Karabaga*, p. 92) and Azeri (*Garabagh Tarikhi*, p. 39) translations erroneously use the literal translation of Khoda-afarin ("created by God"). Their text reads: "the impregnable fortress of Shushi, created by God, the gate to Georgia and Shirvan."

[365] The title signifies the head of the *amirs* or field marshal.

Tiflis, and pleaded a meeting with Sardar Tsitsianov in order to conclude the conditions for his obedience.[366]

Sardar Prince Tsitsianov returned the envoy of the late Ebrahim Khan with great respect and gifts promising to meet in the spring in [one of] the regions of the *velayat*. Therefore, in the year 1805, on the first day of the month of May, the late Ebrahim Khan, together with his sons, the late Major-General Mohammad Hasan Aqa, Major-General Mahdi Qoli Aqa, Colonel Khanlar Aqa,[367] and other notables of Qarabagh, appeared before the great Sardar Prince Tsitsianov who, prior to their coming, had arrived and had camped by the Kurek River. [Ebrahim Khan] dispatched a trusted messenger to Salim Khan, the ruler of the *velayat* of Shakki, who was the hereditary and rightful owner of the *velayat* of Shakki and the son-in-law of the late Ebrahim Khan, and convinced him to appear with the elders of the *velayat* of Shakki before the great *sardar*. For several days they held fabulous banquets and welcoming feasts by the Kurek River.[368] After that the draft of the agreement was formulated.[369]

---

[366] That is, to draft the articles of making Qarabagh a protectorate and nothing else. Ahmad Beg here avoids the complimentary terms of Mirza Jamal and states that the council of Mohammad Hasan Aqa and his pro-Russian sympathies convinced Ebrahim, *Karabakhskogo khanstva*, p. 95

[367] Mirza Jamal again jumps ahead and mentions the titles prior to their actual conference. The titles were officially announced a few months later in September/October, 1805. His other reason for mentioning the Russian titles in almost every passage is to demonstrate his clan's loyalty to the Russians and the legitimacy of their income and position.

[368] Mirza Jamal uses the Turkish term *chay* here.

[369] Bakikhanov states that Ebrahim had to pay 10,000 (another manuscript of his states 6000) *ashrafis* (a gold coin weighing 190,894 grains troy) every six years and was to receive 500 troops, *Golestan-e Eram*, p. 187. Ahmad Beg has more details. He states that Ebrahim Khan had to cease relations with Iran and accept the authority of the emperor; not involve himself in the affairs of the other khanates; take care of the housing and animal feed of the Russian troops; and improve the road from Ganje to Shushi, to make it suitable for the passage of carriages. Moreover, his grandson, son of his oldest son, would remain in Tiflis as a hostage (more likely to protect him as his father, Mohammad Hasan, was the main Russian sympathizer). The sum mentioned here is 8000 rubles annually, to be paid in two installments, on February 1 and September 1. In exchange, Russia would protect his domain: a 500 man unit would be stationed there, he and his sons would receive titles, medals and salaries, and his grandson would be housed and fed in Tiflis in a manner which befitted him, *Karabakhskogo khanstva*, pp. 95-96. The treaty also stipulated that the right of primogeniture would be observed (this as will be noted below, caused problems later on).

The late Ebrahim Khan and Salim Khan, the ruler of Shakki sealed the agreement [with their name seals], and the great *sardar* accepted it with his signature.[370] Showing each other great honor and respect, they returned [to their respective lands]. It was agreed that the second son of the late Mohammad Hasan Aqa would stay in Tiflis [45] as a hostage.[371] [At the same time] the late Ebrahim Khan had asked that a Russian artillery unit be permanently garrisoned with him in the fortress of Shushi.

During that same meeting, the *sardar* sent a request to the emperor, asking that the rank of lieutenant general be given to the late Ebrahim Khan and Salim Khan, and [that of] major general to the late Mohammad Hasan Aqa and Mahdi Qoli Khan, and [that of] colonel to the late Khanlar Aqa. After four months, they were officially confirmed [from St. Petersburg] in these ranks and titles and began to receive the appropriate salaries.[372]

After returning from the Kurek-chay talks, on the order of the *sardar*, Major Lisanevich arrived in Khan-Bagh, which is ten *versts* from the fortress, with a group of chasseurs[373] and artillery.[374] At this time news arrived that the Qezelbash army was approaching the Arax River.[375] Flooding had occurred. The Arax River had risen considerably and there was no other way for [the troops] to cross except by bridge [Khoda-afarin Bridge].[376] Therefore, the late Mohammad Hasan Aqa took a group of the chasseurs, and the major (Lisanevich], and with the famed horsemen of Qarabagh went to meet the Qezelbash [army], which was in the vicinity of the bridge. Their object was to block the [the shah's army] from crossing into the territory of Qarabagh and ravaging tribes, villages, and crops of the *velayat*.

---

[370] Ebrahim had convinced the khan of Shakki to join their pact. Salim was married to a daughter of Ebrahim and his sister became a wife of Ebrahim Khan.

[371] Berzhe's translation reads, *Mohammad Hasan Aqa (not his son) was to come to Tiflis as a hostage,* "Karabag," 69 (1855), 298.

[372] Confirmed by Bakikhanov, *Golestan-e Eram*, p. 187.

[373] Mirza Jamal uses the Russian term, *eger*.

[374] Adigozal Beg puts the number at 500 and adds that the same number were sent to Shakki, *Qarabagh-name*, p. 106.

[375] Bakikhanov states that 'Abbas Mirza sent a 10,000 man army, under the command of Esma'il Beg Damghani and 'Ali Qoli Khan Shahsavan, who crossed the Khoda-afarin Bridge, *Golestan-e Eram*, p. 187. Donboli confirms the above, *Ma'ser-e Soltaniye*, p. 147.

[376] Mirza Jamal uses the term *korpi* here.

But the Qezelbash had outstripped them and had crossed the bridge into Qarabagh. Near the orchards of Jebrailu (Jebrail) they [Qezelbash] unexpectedly came across the Russian soldiers and the Qarabaghis. A major battle took place. The late Mohammad Hasan Aqa considered it more important to defend the fortress of Shushi. Therefore, at night he returned to the fortress with his forces. The Qezelbash army entered Agh-Oghlan,[377] which is situated four *farsakhs* from the fortress.[378] Close to five thousand of them came to the vicinity of the Askeran fortress and camped there. Their intention was to take the fortress from two sides.[379] The major (Lisanevich] informed the *sardar* [Tsitsianov] of these events. At that moment, the crown prince of Iran ['Abbas Mirza] was camped at the Chanakhchi region and was awaiting the arrival of the troops from Askeran.

[Meanwhile] Colonel Kariagin[380] and Lieutenant Colonel Kotliarevskii,[381] on the orders of the great *sardar*, appeared near Shah-Bulaghi with troops and artillery. The crown prince moved from Chanakhchi and took the field to repulse Colonel Kariagin. [46] He reached the vicinity of Askeran, fighting all the way. Since the Qezelbash army had taken and fortified all the roads, as and had taken as well the Askeran fortress, the [Russian] artillery and troops were blocked off, had difficulty moving ahead, and had to barricade themselves in the area. For eleven days,[382] this one unit of the Russian army[383] [Kariagin's group] fought the entire Qezelbash forces day and night. The fortification of the Russian army was also far from the water. After eleven days and nights, despite the fact that the colonel [Kariagin] and Kotliarevskii were both wounded, and that half of the Russian army was killed or wounded in battle, they, together with approximately

---

[377] Donboli spells it Aq-Oghlan, *Ma'ser-e Soltaniye*, p. 148.

[378] Donboli states that Esma'il Beg faced stiff resistance from Mohammad Hasan and the Armenians of Qarabagh and was ready to retreat when 'Abbas Mirza arrived with reinforcements, *Ma'ser-e Soltaniye*, pp. 147-148.

[379] It is not clear which fortress, Shushi or Askeran; it is probably Shushi.

[380] Colonel Paul Mikhailovich Kariagin served under Tsitsianov and partici- pated in the 1803 siege of Ganje. His heroic stand against the Iranian army (see below) earned him a decoration. He died on May 7, 1807.

[381] Peter Kotliarevskii was another protegé of Tsitsianov, who, together with Kariagin, were in charge of the Russian troops in Qarabagh. Both were young and brave men who had a rapid rise in the army of the Caucasus. Kotliarevskii became a Lieutenant General at age 29, see note 14 in introduction.

[382] Berzhe's translation has *fifteen* days, "Karabag," 69 (1855), 298.

[383] Berzhe's translation reads, *this unit of the Russian army composed of 400 men,* "Karabag," 69 (1855), 298.

three hundred infantry troops,[384] took their entire artillery, and with the help of Vani Yuzbashi, who is today Melik Vani,[385] who was their guide and who on that march had rendered them great service, withdrew toward Shah-Bulaghi fortress.[386]

In order to prevent the Russian army from entering the Shah-Bulaghi fortress, a large contingent of infantrymen from the Qezelbash army were stationed there. [Ignoring that] the [Russians] stormed the fortress that same night [of their arrival], taking the fortress from the Qezelbash, killing one of the khans and several of the Qezelbash. They paused there for three days and from there, again with the guidance of Melik Vani, withdrew to Ganje.[387]

[At that time] Fath 'Ali Shah himself, with the entire Qezelbash army, entered Qarabagh and camped six *farsakhs* from the city of Shushi.[388] Crown prince 'Abbas Mirza, after the withdrawal of Kariagin to Ganje, camped in the area of Shah-Bulaghi.[389] Meanwhile the great *sardar* Tsitsianov entered the territory of Qarabagh with Russian troops to repulse the crown prince and Fath 'Ali Shah. The crown prince, with the troops under his command, moved on Tiflis,[390] with the intention of destroying and looting Georgia, while Fath 'Ali Shah stayed on in the region of Agh-Oghlan.

---

[384] Mirza Jamal uses the Russian term for infantry troops, itself borrowed from a French term.

[385] Vani Yuzbashi was from the Avanian *meliks* of Dizak. His title of *yuzbashi* (head of hundred) or captain was given to him either by Ebrahim Khan or Melik 'Abbas of Dizak.

[386] Donboli is truly objective here, for he states that the Russians fought heroically. He also calls the Shah-Bulaghi fortress the Tarnavut fortress, which, as noted, was its other name, *Ma'ser-e Soltaniye*, pp. 150-151. E'temad os-Saltane confirms the role of the Armenians in this campaign, *Montazam-e Naseri*, III, 1426.

[387] Donboli also cites the role of the Armenians of Qarabagh as crucial in saving the troops, *Ibid.*, p. 152.

[388] Bakikhanov implies that the shah had arrived earlier, *Golestan-e Eram*, p. 187. Donboli states that the shah was in the vicinity of the fortress, in the Takht-e Tavus station, which was seven *farsakhs* away, from where he dispatched begs and khans to Shirvan, Erevan, and other places to bring various regions into submission. He himself was not involved in the war with the Russians at this time, *Ibid.*, pp. 152-153.

[389] Bakikhanov has him joining the army of Tsitsianov, *Golestan-e Eram*, p. 187.

[390] Bakikhanov has Ganje, which was defended well by the Russians and Armenians, *Ibid.*, p. 187. Donboli also states that 'Abbas Mirza went on to Ganje, where he was greeted by the Muslims of the city, some of whom returned with him to Iran, *Ma'ser-e Soltaniye*, pp. 153-155.

At that time, Fath 'Ali Shah received news from Rasht, that the army of the Russian State had moved from the Caspian Sea coast in the direction of the *velayats* of Talesh and Rasht. [47] Because of this news and the approach of *sardar* Tsitsianov, the shah withdrew to Ardabil.[391]

Sardar Tsitsianov advanced to Khonashin[392], located two *farsakhs* from Agh-Oghlan, where he learned of the withdrawal of the shah. From there he came to the Shushi fortress, where, after putting right some affairs, he took the three Qezelbash khans who had come as [the shah's] envoys to Ebrahim with the aforementioned conditions and promises, and with much pomp and full satisfaction left Qarabagh for Tiflis.

During the winter of the same year [1805], he [Tsitsianov] with the army of the Exalted State [of Russia], crossed the Kur in the direction of Shakki, with the intention of conquering Shirvan, Baku, Qobbe, and Darband.[393]

The late Ebrahim Khan, because of his sincere devotion to the Great State [of Russia], dispatched his worthy son, Mahdi Qoli Khan, with the Qarabagh forces and the sons of several begs, to the *sardar*, so that they would join the imperial army and perform the duties assigned to them. Salim Khan, the governor of Shakki, who was obedient to the Great State [Russia], made the necessary preparations and proper offerings, and escorted the *sardar* from the border of the *velayat* of Shakki to the border of the *velayat* of Shirvan.

Although, during the first few days, Mostafa Khan, relying on his unassailable site and his might and position, sent harsh replies to the *sardar's* [requests for submission] refusing to submit, in the end he realized that he could not resist the [combined] forces of Russia, Qarabagh, and Shakki. Furthermore, the Qarabagh army, taking advantage of the situation, had begun to raid and loot the villages of Shirvan. With Mahdi Qoli Khan and Salim Khan acting as intermediaries, he [Mostafa Khan], agreed to discuss terms of submission. He signed the same kind of agreement which had been signed by the late Ebrahim

---

[391] Donboli's account is slightly different. The shah may have left Takht-e Tavus, but it was 'Abbas Mirza who crossed the Arax to stop the Russian threat to the Caspian coast, *Ibid.*, p. 156.

[392] Donboli lists it as Khanshin, *Ibid.*, p. 144.

[393] Ahmad Beg gives an interesting piece of information here. He states that on October 25, Budagh Sultan of Shuragöl had submitted and hence the north-western section of Shuragöl, which technically belonged to the khanate of Erevan, but was claimed by Georgia, had fallen to Russia with Gumri as the border, *Karabakhskogo khanstva*, p. 96; also see Bournoutian, *Erevan*, p. 32 note 3.

Khan and Salim Khan, and he [48] outwardly[394] accepted the suzerainty of the Exalted State [Russia].[395] The supreme *sardar* then passed through Shirvan and moved on to Baku.

At that moment, the eldest son of the late Ebrahim Khan, Major General Mohammad Hasan Aqa, who had been ill, joined the Grace of God [died].[396] This confusing and anguishing event brought chaos and sadness to the *velayat* of Qarabagh. Certain individuals were inwardly not satisfied with the submission to the Exalted State. The death of the late Mohammad Hasan Aqa, the absence of Mahdi Qoli Khan from the *velayat*, as well as the illness, weakness, and age of the late Ebrahim Khan, led them to plot against the agreement and the treaty. Therefore, the supreme *sardar* reckoned it imperative to return Mahdi Qoli Khan with the Qarabagh army [to his father]. He dispatched him with full respect, appropriate gifts, and hopes, to Qarabagh. Having had a deep respect, devotion, and love for the late Major General Mohammad Hasan Aqa, he [Tsitsianov] expressed his deep sorrow and regret at the death of the late Mohammad Hasan Aqa, in a letter in which he demonstrated his kindness and [expressed his] condolences to Colonel Ja'far Qoli Aqa, promising his friendship and protection.[397]

Major General Mahdi Qoli Khan appeared before his honorable late father with the Qarabagh army and sons of the begs, and conveyed the kind and reassuring messages of the supreme *sardar* and set forth to remove and crush the plotters. He tried to strengthen the trust and devotion [of the people] to the Exalted State.

At that moment, news arrived of [what had occurred during] the negotiations of the supreme *sardar* in the *velayat* of Baku. Not suspecting that Hosein Qoli Khan[398] and his followers were capable of such a base and hideous act, the *sardar*, accompanied by the sons of two [49] begs, went to discuss [terms of surrender]. A certain Ebrahim Beg, with two other individuals, ambushed the supreme *sardar* and his companions,

---

[394] The word "outwardly" is repeated by Bakikhanov, *Golestan-e Eram*, p. 188; Donboli calls him a weak man, but states that the agreement was not taken seriously by the khan, that it was a "wolf's peace," *Ma'ser-e Soltaniye*, p. 161. Mostafa Khan eventually fled to Iran in 1235 (1819/20). In 1241 (1826), at the start of the Second Russo-Iranian war, he joined the Iranian army and reached the outskirts of Tiflis, where they were defeated.

[395] The agreement was signed December 25, 1805, Akty, II, p. 674.

[396] Mohammad Hasan Khan died from a lung disease, probably tuberculosis.

[397] Ja'far Qoli, was the elder son of Mohammad Hasan Aqa, who, according to the treaty, was to succeed Ebrahim Khan.

[398] Hosein Khan, the son of Hajji 'Ali Qoli Aqa, was the khan of Baku. After

killing them with bullet wounds,[399] then opened the gates and began hostile action against the imperial army. This mournful news greatly grieved the late Ebrahim Khan, his children, and the population of the *velayat*, for they did not yet know of the order [which existed] in the Russian government. They imagined that [Russia] was like Iran, where if such a supreme *sardar* died, it would have seriously disrupted the army and the state. In reality [in Russia] the death of even several *sardars* and military leaders in war with the enemy, would have absolutely no effect on the order within the army or the workings of that *velayat*.[400]

After the death of Sardar Tsitsianov, General Nesvetaev[401] took

---

the death of Tsitsianov, he escaped to Ardabil, received an income from the shah and died in 1845.

[399] Bakikhanov identifies him as Ebrahim Beg ibn 'Ali Beg Aqa ibn Mohammad Hosein Khan ibn Imam Qoli Khan Darbandi. The Khan of Baku was his cousin, *Golestan-e Eram*, p. 188. Donboli confirms the relation between the khan of Baku and Ebrahim, he goes on to state that a number of Russians who had accompanied Tsitsianov were killed or imprisoned. Tsitsianov's head and hand was sent to Fath 'Ali Shah in Tehran, but 'Abbas Mirza was not pleased with what had occurred. It seems that he knew of the plan to trap the Russian commander, but had hoped to capture him alive, *Ma'ser-e Soltaniye*, p. 162. According to Bamdad, Ebrahim entered the service of 'Abbas Mirza and in 1238 (1822/23) was appointed as the governor of Zur, *Bamdad*, I, 447.

[400] The term *velayat* is used as "state" here. Mirza Jamal is being too generous to the Russians. The actual amount of panic and disarray was greater than Mirza Jamal states. Bakikhanov states that the various khans who had agreements with Russia revolted, *Golestan-e Eram*, p. 188. Donboli confirms the fact that the Russians were confused and that there were a number of revolts in Ganje and Shirvan and that the Iranians began attacking certain districts, especially on the southern borders of Georgia, by the khanate of Erevan, *Ma'ser-e Soltaniye*, pp. 162-164. Baddeley, a pro-Russian source, using Russian accounts, admits the Russian retreat, J. Baddeley, *The Russian Conquest of the Caucasus* (New York, 1969), p. 71. The retreat was, of course, temporary and the Russians maintained their hold on Shushi, Nukha, and Ganje. Erevan and its great fortress now became the center of the Iranian defenses and remained so until 1827, for more details, see Bournoutian, *Erevan*, pp. 14-25.

[401] Major General Peter Davidovich Nesvetaev had served with distinction in the second Polish and Ottoman campaigns of Catherine the Great. He was sent to the Caucasus in 1804 and fought the Iranians near Edjmiadsin. He participated in the campaign in which Shuragöl was annexed to Russia (1805). He commanded the Russian army in Transcaucasia after the death of Tsitsianov. He fought the Turks in the Russo-Turkish war of 1806-1812 and died in 1808.

charge of the command of the army and the *velayat*[402] in the city of Tiflis. The late Ebrahim Khan sent a messenger with letters [repeating] his devotion [to Russia] and assuring them of his loyalty in every way.[403]

In the spring of the same year, which was 1806, the Qezelbash army once again began to cross [the Arax] into Qarabagh. Men were secretly sent to the late Ebrahim Khan with renewed offers [to switch allegiance to Iran]. Since, aside from Major Lisanevich's detachment of chasseurs, there was no other force in Qarabagh able to repulse such a strong enemy, the tribal pastures and villages would be trampled upon, precisely at a time when the grain harvest was approaching. Therefore, the late Ebrahim Khan reckoned it was wise to be conciliatory to the Qezelbash,[while at the same time] he kept the major informed of everything.[404] The major constantly assured and promised the late Ebrahim Khan that the army of the Exalted Russian State would soon arrive. In reality their arrival was greatly delayed [while] the Qezelbash army came within two *farsakhs* of the fortress. [Then] the late Ebrahim Khan resettled his household, who were in [50] Khan-Baghi, closer to the fortress.[405] A number of ill-intentioned people[406] made such slanderous [accusations] to the major [about Ebrahim Khan] that he [the major] went to Ebrahim's camp at night with a group of soldiers where, due to ill luck, the late Ebrahim Khan together with some members of his family and close associates were killed.[407]

---

[402]*Velayat* here signifies Transcaucasia.

[403] The sentence implies that since some of the other khans had turned against Russia, Ebrahim wanted to assure the Russians that he was not one of them. Interestingly enough, however, he was secretly negotiating with Iran.

[404] Bakikhanov states simply that Ebrahim Khan had turned to Iran and was making his submission to the shah. His son Abo'l Fath Khan, at his request, was coming with troops from Qapan to Shushi, and 'Abbas Mirza had crossed the Khoda-Afarin Bridge, *Golestan-e Eram*, pp. 188-189; Donboli states that Ebrahim Khan, after witnessing the generosity of the shah to those khans who had abandoned Russia in favor of Iran, decided to switch sides and sent his son-in-law to 'Abbas Mirza, who then ordered Abo'l Fath Khan to enter Qarabagh from Qapan, and Farajollah Shahsavan from Chanakhchi, while he himself crossed the Khoda-afarin Bridge, *Ma'ser-e Soltaniye*, pp. 169-171. Bamdad states that at this time the shah sent a number of commanders, led by Hosein Qoli Khan Qajar (later sardar of Erevan), but they arrived late and had to retreat, *Bamdad*, I, 247.

[405] Berzhe's translation states the opposite: *he moved his family from the fortress to Khan-Baghi and camped near there*, "Karabag," 69 (1855), 298.

[406] Mirza Jamal does not accuse the son and grandson of Ebrahim, who are his kinsmen, see note 409.

Major General Mahdi Qoli Khan[408] and Colonel Ja'far Qoli Aqa,[409] who were at the fortress at the time, did not participate in any action or move against the Exalted State, but tried to calm the fear of the populace.

---

[407] The incident occurred on June 14, 1806. Mirza Jamal's son, Reza Qoli Mirza Jamal Beg Ogli, in an unpublished manuscript, lists 17 individuals: Ebrahim Khan; one of his wives, Tuba Khanum (sister of Salim Khan of Shakki according to Bakikhanov, *Golestan-e Eram*, p. 189); a daughter, Saltanat Begum (a niece of Homay Khan Lezgi, according to Donboli, *Ma'ser-e Soltaniye*, p. 171); the 12-year old son of the khan, 'Abbas Qoli Aqa Kebirli; Hajji Khachan; 'Ali Beg; Mirza Ahvardi; Hummat Beg Harvandi; the sons of Qolimali Beg Sarijali, Javanshir and Hasan Aqa; the servant of 'Ali-Panah Harvandi; Javanshir and Mirza Naqi Afshar; the son of 'Ajam-'Ali Kebirli; Hajji Hasan and his two sons; two individuals from Shelli; and a number of Javanshir clan members, MS. Academy of Sciences of Azerbaijan, no. B-470/5224 in *Karabagh Tarikhi*, p. 43. According to Bakikhanov, Salim Khan of Shakki, whose sister was the wife who was killed, later avenged the death of his sister by killing a number of Russians. General Nebol'sin on the orders from Gudovich went from Ganje to punish him, forcing him to flee to Iran, *Golestan-e Eram*, pp. 189-91. The best account of the death of Ebrahim and the detailed reasons behind it is by Muriel Atkin, "The Strange Death of Ibrahim Khalil Khan of Qarabagh," *Iranian Studies* XII (1979), 79-107.

[408] Mirza Jamal uses the word *bandgan* (a variation of *bandehgan*) before the military title of Mahdi Qoli. The term, which can be translated as "overlord" or "master," appears a number of times in the text. This honorific has been left out from this translation.

[409] Ja'far Qoli, son of Mohammad Hasan Aqa, was the grandson of Ebrahim Khan; Donboli and E'temad os-Saltane accuse him of telling the Russians about his grandfather's plan, *Ma'ser-e Soltaniye*, p. 170; *Montazam-e Naseri*, III, 1481. Most sources agree that both Mahdi Qoli and Ja'far had a hand in the murder. Although Ja'far was only seventeen at the time, he felt that by right of primogeniture (stipulated in the Russo-Qarabaghi treaty) he was to succeed Ebrahim Khan. Mahdi Qoli, who was over thirty, according to Mirza Jamal was the designated heir. It is possible that being aware of the stipulations of the treaty, he hoped to ingratiate himself with the Russians and assume the control of the khanate. Although the Iranian sources do not mention the Armenians, Atkin, citing Russian sources, lists the Armenian Melik Jamshid (of the Shahnazarian family of Varanda) as one of those who spoke ill of the khan, Atkin, "Strange Death," p. 95. This account is quite possible, for Melik Jamshid and Meliks Abov and Feridun (of the Beglarian family from Golestan) were the offspring of the Armenian *meliks* who had fled Ebrahim Khan. Ebrahim in the 1770s and 1780s had repeatedly attacked the Armenian *mahals* and had caused the death of a number of their secular and religious leaders. Some of the *meliks* left Qarabagh and, together with their followers, settled in Georgia. They made contacts with the Russian court and participated on the Russian side in the First Russo-Iranian war.

They not only did not act against the major [Lisanevich] in any way but, on the contrary, they even helped to obtain provisions for the [Russian] troops, for food was in extremely short supply at the time.[410]

The Qezelbash army, under the command of crown prince 'Abbas Mirza, was camped at Agh-Oghlan. Barely fifteen days had passed since the sad events of the death of the late khan, when the Russian forces and artillery appeared in Shah-Bulaghi under the command of General Nebol'sin.[411] The moment this news reached Mahdi Qoli Khan, he immediately came out of the fortress with the famed Qarabaghi cavalry, attendants, and the sons of several begs.

Although the Qezelbash army was in the vicinity and on the roads, he appeared before General Nebol'sin, joined [his forces] with the Russian army and camped in the vicinity of the Askeran fortress. Colonel Ja'far Qoli Aqa, together with the major [Lisanevich] and the detachment of chasseurs stayed on in the fortress [of Shushi] to protect it.[412]

General Nebol'sin waited two or three days for the the crown prince and his army to attack, but they did not appear. He, therefore, decided to move against the Qezelbash army and to battle them, if the latter wished to fight; if [they did] not, to attack and to expel them from the territory of Qarabagh.

Having been informed of the movement of the Russian army towards [his camp], the crown prince [51] with his entire army moved to meet with them and to do battle. The two armies reached each other near the Khonashin station[413] and a battle ensued. Mahdi Qoli Khan, with his entourage, and the Qarabagh army constantly assisted [the Russian army] during the march, and during the battle took an active part in the rout and expulsion of the Qezelbash. The battle on the 15th of July [1806][414] in the Khonashin station lasted seven hours, and the Qezelbash army, [due to] the general's strategy, the bravery of Kotliarevskii, and the help of Mahdi Qoli Khan, was defeated.[415] Part of [the Iranian army]

---

[410] The effects of the famine and devastations of Aqa Mohammad Shah and the campaigns in Qarabagh had a terrible effect for a number of years, forcing migrations of both Armenians and Muslims.

[411] For details on Nebol'sin see note 11 in introduction.

[412] Donboli states that Armenian troops were also present in the defense of the fortress, Ma'ser-e Soltaniye, p. 172.

[413] The Persian word manzel in this context can be translated as a resting stop, a station, or a defile.

[414] Berzhe's translation reads June 13, "Karabagh," 69 (1855), 298.

[415] Donboli states that both sides fought extremely well, but since the Russians

was killed, and another part was captured, while the rest fled in the direction of the Arax. Kotliarevskii was wounded and some thirty officers and soldiers were killed or also wounded. The general and the army pursued the enemy to Qozlu-chay but did not find any trace of them. In full retreat with the Qezelbash army, the crown prince abandoned a considerable part of his heavy transport on the way, and in a period of two days crossed the Arax to the other side of the border.

The moment the news of the Qezelbash defeat arrived, Colonel Ja'far Qoli Aqa took Major Lisanevich, some of the renowned horsemen of the tribes, and his close associates and moved through the *mahals* of Zangezur to crush the Qezelbash army and to return all the tribes and the inhabitants of the villages that were being forcibly driven towards Nakhichevan and Ordubad by Abo'l Fath Khan and the other fugitive khans and begs of Qarabagh.[416] Using all their strength they rode day and night without stopping, even though the Russian infantry had a hard time keeping up with the cavalry in the mountains [and fell behind]. Finally Colonel Ja'far Qoli Aqa and the Qarabagh cavalry overtook the Qezelbash army near the mountains of Qapan and Ordubad. At the very start of the battle, the Qarabagh forces defeated a Qezelbash army of approximately two thousand infantry and cavalry in the narrow ravines. They captured a large number of them, took their horses, clothing, and everything else they possessed. When the Russian infantry arrived, [52] part of the Qezelbash army was already captured and the rest were on the run. The tribesmen and the villagers of Qarabagh who had been taken by force were all returned to their mountain regions near the fortress.[417] The crown prince was at that time [already] in the vicinity of the Arax River [and had left Qarabagh].[418]

The victory won by the troops of General Nebol'sin and Mahdi Qoli

---

had the river behind them they controlled the water. Lack of water and the stifling heat forced the Iranians to retreat, *Ma'ser-e Soltaniye*, p. 173.

[416] Donboli states that Abo'l Fath Khan would have succeeded in saving the tribes from the Russians (implying that the tribes had gone voluntarily), but that the Jebrailu tribe sent a message to the Russian commander (whom he calls a general and not a major) who then came with Ja'far Qoli, and halted the flight. The Iranian army would have still won the day had their ammunition not run out, *Ma'ser-e Soltaniye*, p. 175.

[417] These tribes must have been those brought by Panah Khan and Ebrahim Khan to Shushi and its environs in order to have some support against the Armenian meliks whose territories surrounded Shushi.

[418] Donboli's version has the same results but obviously not as enthusiastic or exaggerated, *Ma'ser-e Soltaniye*, pp. 175-178.

Khan against the crown prince, as well as the successful operation of the major and Colonel Ja'far Aqa, pacified the inhabitants of Qarabagh. The strength of the Russian army became evident and everyone settled in their own region and house and began to live in full confidence and peace.

In the winter of that same year (1806), *general en-chef*, Count Gudovich,[419] whom the most grand emperor, Alexander Pavlovich,[420] had appointed as the *sardar*, arrived in Tiflis. The letters of Mahdi Qoli Khan had already been dispatched by Major General Nesvetaev along with his own personal requests to the emperor. [Therefore, Gudovich], *after he had heard of the death of Ebrahim Khan* [421] called him [Mahdi Qoli Khan] to his presence to Tiflis. Mahdi Qoli Khan, together with all the elders of the villages, the tribal begs, and others went to Tiflis. On the day after his audience with the count, a grand ball was given, where the [count] handed Mahdi Qoli Khan the decree to rule Qarabagh, and the promise [to also deliver] a sword encrusted with jewels, and imperial banners, as stated in the treaty. After that, with many promises of future kindness and friendship, he [Gudovich] sent him [Mahdi Qoli Khan] back to Qarabagh.[422] The history of Mahdi Qoli Khan's rule began from that time and continued until October 1822,[423] which is of course known to your highness from the journals of the administrators of the Exalted State. [Therefore], there is no need for my devoted self to record it.

---

[419] Berzhe's translation reads, *General of the infantry*, "Karabagh," 69 (1855), 298.

[420] Alexander I, Tsar of Russia 1801-1825.

[421] "Karabag," 69 (1855), 298.

[422] Ja'far Qoli's right of succession was thus ignored. According to Bamdad, Ja'far Qoli's disappointment and his anti-Russian feeling made him suspect. He was arrested and was being transported to Tiflis, from where he was to be sent to Siberia, when by the Tartar River, he freed his horse and bolted into the river. After swimmimg across he sought refuge with friendly tribes and eventually reached Iran (1812). 'Abbas Mirza appointed him as the governor of Qaraje-dagh, *Bamdad*, I, pp. 247-248. It is probable that being so close to Qarabagh he kept in touch with the tribes and played a role during the Second Russo-Iranian war.

[423] Berzhe's translation ends here, "Karabag, " 69 (1855), 298. Mahdi Qoli Khan, as noted, was soon fed up with Russian interferences and may have flirted with the idea of shifting his allegiance to Iran. Russian suspicions and provocations forced him to flee to Iran in 1822. He fought against Russia in the Second Russo-Iranian war. He returned to Qarabagh in 1836, was forgiven, and until his death in 1845 received a pension from the Russian state. He is buried with the other Javanshir khans in Aghdam.

Chapter:[424] Facts [Of the Events] Which Took Place during the Period when these *Velayats* [53] Were Transferred over to the Rule and Protection of the Officials of His Majesty the Most Generous Emperor[425]

Despite the major losses which they experienced during the years of hostility with Iran [Russia],[426] in the year 1826, the officials of the Iranian government nonetheless broke the treaty of friendship and union which they had with the eternal State of Russia.[427]

Expelling His Excellency Prince Menshikov, who had gone to Iran as the [Russian] ambassador,[428] they (the Iranians] suddenly entered the *velayats* belonging to the Russian State. But their calculation was, in fact, incorrect. They did not realize that they could not withstand the might of the imperial army, and that once the Russian State's forces moved [against them], they would perish like straw in the stormy waves of the sea.[429]

In the first period [of the war], the late crown prince, with all his forces, laid siege to the fortress of Shushi. Although there was only a small force under the command of General Reutt' and almost no food, gunpowder, shells, cannons, or other supplies, the crown prince, despite his large force and artillery, could not, during the month-and-a-half siege, approach the ramparts of the fortress. [Finally], hearing that Amir Khan Sardar, who had experienced the might of the imperial army

---

[424] As indicated these additional chapters may have been written later. Some have titles, others do not, none of them are numbered.

[425] The Turkish translation has erroneously identified this chapter as Chapter Eight, *Karabagh Tarihi*, p. 31.

[426] This is a scribe's error. It should read "Russia," and refers to Iran's losses by the treaty of Golestan in 1813.

[427] Mirza Jamal blames Iran for breaking the truce and starting the Second Russo-Iranian war. In fact, most sources divide the blame equally, see Bournoutian, *Erevan*, pp. 21-24.

[428] Prince Alexander S. Menshikov (1787-1869) was the diplomat who in 1826 was sent to Iran by Nicholas I to bring word that Nicholas had become tsar and, more importantly, to negotiate on the border dispute between Iran and Russia. He refused to make any concessions, which was one of the reasons for the Second Russo-Iranian war.

[429] The sentence refers to the early Iranian successes at the start of the Second Russo-Iranian War, Bournoutian, *Erevan* , p. 25.

under the command of General Prince Madatov,[430] was being defeated in the *mahal* of Shamkhor, he ['Abbas Mirza] was forced to [raise the siege] of the fortress and to face and battle the imperial forces under the command of His Excellency Prince and Count Paskevich Erevanskii.[431] He reached the outskirts of Ganje; but he did not last an hour and was defeated. In a period of two days he [retreated], crossed the Arax River and withdrew to [54] Qaradagh.[432] The supreme *sardar* pursued them until the Charehkan station [but] did not come across even one Qezelbash soldier.

In fact, although, the military might of the victorious imperial forces was evident to the entire populace, in the year of 31 [1831], when His Excellency Prince and Count Paskevich Erevanskii, was appointed as the *sardar* and governor general in these *velayats*, he demonstrated the power of his Supreme Imperial Majesty's troops to the subjects of the governments of Iran and Rum. He calmed the dispersed and ravaged inhabitants of the *velayats* that belonged to the Exalted Russian State. Those inhabitants and notables of the *velayats*, who, [in desperation], had lost hope in the supreme emperor's sea-deep grace, and who had abandoned their homes and belongings and were scattered and in flight, were all returned to their homes and land. Their crimes and sins were deemed

---

[430] Valerian G. Madatov (1782-1829) arrived in the Caucasus in 1816. He defeated the Iranian army in Shamkhor (1826), thus halting the Iranian invasion of Tiflis, see note 18 in introduction.

[431] Mirza Jamal again anticipates the title given to Paskevich after he conquered Erevan in fall of 1827. Ivan Fedorovich Paskevich Erivanskii-Varshavskii was a count. He was born in 1782 to a Ukrainian gentry family and began his career in the famous Preobrazhenskii Guards. He fought the Ottomans and Napoleon and rose in the favor of tsars Alexander I and Nicholas I. In 1826 he was sent to the Caucasus to replace General Ermolov and in 1827 he became the commander-in-chief and administrator-in-chief in the Caucasus. He conquered the fortress of Erevan (hence Erevanskii), crossed the Arax and forced the Iranians to sue for peace (Treaty of Torkmanchay). Soon after he won victories against the Ottomans and ended the Russo-Turkish war of 1828-1829. In 1831, Nicholas sent him to Poland to suppress the uprising there (hence Varshavskii), a mission he accomplished with great brutality. In 1832 the tsar made him the Vice-Gerent of Poland, a post he held for some twenty years. In 1849 he became a field marshal and in 1854, he became the commander-in-chief of Russian troops on the southwestern front in the Crimean War. He was wounded and retired in 1854. He died in 1856.

[432] The Russian and Turkish translations have "Qarabagh" (*Istoriia Karabaga*, p. 99, and *Karabagh Tarihi*, p. 31).

like a drop of water which disappeared in the sea-deep generosity of the supreme emperor, who forgave their errors.[433]

Praise be to Allah, that all of them and other landowners, have gained their property and belongings and are living a quiet, peaceful, and secure life. Expressing their gratitude, they await the call to serve with devotion, along with the troops of the Exalted State. [Particularly so] since those Qarabaghis who had fought alongside the victorious imperial troops in Iran, Rum, and Daghestan, have obtained high rank and salaries, and none have been left without a reward [and decoration].

The End except for the Conclusion:

[55] I hope that the work of this devoted writer, who from the Muslim year 1205 (1790/91) to 1260 (1844), has been a loyal employee and official in the service of the khans of the *velayat* of Qarabagh, and has been present at most of the events [recorded], as well as the wars, and has written them down and has presented it to His Excellency, will result in the increase of favors and graces of the Prince Viceroy [Vorontsov]. I am hopeful for the favor of such a supreme, lofty, and grand *amir*, who has always made my loyal self happy, would not forget me from his noble memory. Actually, it is everyone's duty to serve him and wish him well. He showers all his devoted officials with generous favors. The one God is always pleased with well-wishers and makes them always happy and fortunate. Amen! [Allah] provide assistance!

It is better that a man leave a good name than a golden palace.

Conclusion and Resume:[434]

Since I have dedicated these few pages, containing the true facts about the land and *velayat* of Qarabagh and the rule of the late khans, Panah Khan and Ebrahim Khan, to Count and Prince Mikhail Semenovich Vorontsov, the viceroy of His Majesty the Emperor, and the source of all munificence and kindness, the supreme *amir*, who possesses mercy and

---

[433] Mirza Jamal alludes to Mahdi Qoli Khan and a number of other khans, who returned from exile and regained their property and pensions.

[434] The Turkish translation has erroneously titled this section as Chapter 9, *Karabagh Tarihi*, p. 32.

generosity, I have composed this poem in the fortress of Shushi.[435] It is a description [56] of his fine qualities, nobility, and greatness, and I have concluded it with a blessing.

Dedicated to him, who is famed For his grace
He is Count Prince Vorontsov
He devoted his entire time
Serving the greatest Emperor[436]
Whoever comes to his threshold with hope
Is sent away with favor granted
May his power and fortune increase, O Lord
May he always be content and happy in this world

End of Events
[written in] 1294 (1877/78)[437]

Chapter [on the Rule of the Khans]

The length of the rule of the late Panah Khan in the *velayat* of Qarabagh, after he received the title of khan and the decree from 'Adel Shah, son of the brother[438] of the late Nader Shah, naming him governor, was twelve years. The length of rule of the late Ebrahim Khan was more than forty-four years. [57] The length of rule of the late Mahdi Qoli Khan [given office] by the decree of His Supreme Majesty, was seventeen years and some months.

---

[435] The Russian translation has "Qarabagh," *Istoriia Karabaga*, p. 100.

[436] Mirza Jamal again uses the term *khaqan*.

[437] As stated in the introduction this is the date of this particular manuscript (manuscript C). The Azeri *Garabagh Tarikhi*, p. 46), Russian (*Istoriia Karabaga*, p. 110), and Turkish (*Karabagh Tarihi*, p. 32) translations have erroneously calculated it as 1875.

[438] The Russian translation erroneously refers to 'Adel Shah as the brother of Nader, *Istoriia Karabaga*, p. 101.

Chapter: On the Monuments and Buildings Which Were Constructed by the Late Panah Khan in Qarabagh

First: The fortress of Bayat which was built with baked bricks[439] and included a bazaar, bath, ramparts and [other] structures. At present [the fortress] is in ruins, with [some] unimportant remains.

Second: The fortress of Shah-Bulaghi, the mosque at the spring, bath, the city buildings and bazaar, constructed from stone and lime.

Third: The walls of the earlier fortress of Shushi and a building which at present is [used as] the granary for the army.

On the Monuments and Buildings Which Remain from the Late Ebrahim Khan

First: The large main mosque[440] built[441] in the Muslim year 1182 (1768/69). Later when it became dilapidated, it was renovated to a [condition] better than the original by his honorable daughter the late Gohar Aqa.

Second: The outer ramparts of the Shushi fortress, which were constructed in the Muslim year 1198 (1783/84). Their construction took three years. At present the trustees of the state have built new walls, [but] in some areas [the original walls of] the khan still remain.

Third: The two fortresses of Askeran, which were constructed three *farsakhs* from the Shushi fortress[442] in the Muslim year 1203 (1788/89) between two mountains, through which runs the Gargar River. If in these fortresses is placed even a small number of infantry troops in wartime, the enemy would not be able to pass through them and approach the fortress of Shushi.

Fourth: The building and rooms of the ravine known as Khazine. Constructed in a mountain cavern from stone, it has only one road to it. The interior of the cavern has been constructed with stone and lime.[443]

---

[439] Mirza Jamal uses the Russian word *kirpich*, which had entered the Persian vocabulary as *karpich*.

[440] The main or Friday mosque where the *khotba* is read.

[441] The Persian term *ta'mir* refers to both building and repairing. The date indicates that the former was meant here.

[442] The Russian translation has deleted "three farsakhs from the Shushi fortress," *Istoriia Karabaga*, p. 102.

[443] Judging from its name meaning "treasury," and its location, this must have

Fifth: The buildings of Khan-Baghi, which are located one *farsakh* from the fortress (of Shushi).

Sixth: The walls and canals of the orchard in Aghdam, with large cupolas on the grave of the late Panah Khan and his children.

[58] Chapter: On the Rules and Practices Which Existed During the Rule of Ebrahim Khan

All the tribesmen of Qarabagh, who were listed in the rolls and registers, formed the cavalry.[444] When necessary, infantry musketeers from the *mahals* and villages, along with their *meliks*, joined the army.[445] The tribes of Qarabagh were exempt from *touji* [446] and *mal va jahat* [447] taxes from their produce. The *mahals* and villages, however, paid the *mal va jahat* and the *touji* taxes annually. Occasionally, when Lezgi fighters were brought from Daghestan, then even the tribes paid the *touji*, as well as grain, sheep, and larger animals in order to pay the Lezgi and to make up for the loss of their horses. From those families who had members not listed in the registers as soldiers and retainers[448] and from those who were listed as soldiers and retainers, nothing was collected; they were exempt [from taxes]. The feed for their horses and the expenses for their gear were provided by the khan. Every soldier was attached to a specific household, which took care of the needs of that soldier and his retainers.

---

been the secret hideout for the khans' valuables, stored there in time of siege.

[444] The cavalry since Safavid times was always recruited from among the nomadic tribes, who, in exchange, were exempt from taxes.

[445] As demonstrated this was not always the case, some Armenian *meliks* cooperated, others did not.

[446] Touji is identified as a levy collected in cash from the peasants by the village headmen or *kadkhodas*. Its amount varied from khanate to khanate, for details see Bournoutian, *Erevan*, pp. 153-154.

[447] The *mal va jahat* (*mal-o-jehat*), which the peasants paid to the treasury, the landowner, or the toyul holder ranged from 1/10 to 3/10 of the produce or harvest. It was generally paid in kind. It was collected after the harvest, and included a tax on looms, fruit trees, domestic animals, wells, mills, and anything else which the khans wanted to tax, for details, see *Ibid.*, pp. 150-153.

[448] The word used is *nokar*, which in this context is retainer and not servant.

Chapter:

Every year, on the day of *nouruz*[449], which is a holiday, the late khan gave *khal'at*, monetary gifts, horses, and swords to all the commanders of the army, and to the *minbashis*.[450] Each, according to his rank, would bring gifts [to the khan], [including those] from the *velayats* of Azerbaijan, the *meliks*, and the *mahals*.

Chapter:

When the late Ebrahim Khan was traveling or had camped somewhere, most of the *minbashis*, *yuzbashis*,[451] begs, aqas, and those khans of Azerbaijan who were present, as well as some of the soldiers, workers, scribes, *eshik-aqasis* (chamberlains), *keshikchis* (watchmen), and *yasavols* (guards), had their breakfast, lunch, and dinner [59] from the kitchens of the late khan and their horses were given oats. Often, in the evenings, aside from live sheep, which were given to the *minbashis* and others, the kitchens of the late khan used (cooked) forty *puds* [452] of rice and thirty sheep. From these one can only imagine [the quantities of] baked bread, oat for horses, oil, and various sweets, etc. [used].

Chapter: The Income of the Late Ebrahim Khan

[The income of the khan derived from] *mal va jahat* from the *mahals* and villages either in the form of grain or in the form of silk cocoons, and other field crops, as well as the ploughs belonging personally to the khan.[453] I remember during one count, it became apparent that the late khan had as many animals and ploughs as did the entire population of

---

[449] The Iranian new year, which occurs on the first day of spring. This ancient Iranian custom was taken over by the various non-Iranian and Muslim rulers of Iran.

[450] *Minbashis*, as noted, is a Turkic term for tribal chiefs.

[451] The Turkic term *yuzbashi* refers to officers (captains) who commanded a unit of 100 soldiers.

[452] A Russian weight equal to 16.38 kilograms or approximately 36 pounds.

[453] The khan collected a *joft* or *juft-bashi* tax (a yoke tax) from every pair of oxen, see Bournoutian, *Erevan*, p. 152.

Qarabagh, and two pairs more. All the grain and other taxes in kind were used by the army, kitchen, harem, servants, workers, and guests. A large amount [of income, in cash and in kind, was received] from rents, *pishkesh*[454], and *ekhrajat* of Qarabagh,[455] the mint, and many presents of cash and kind were brought from the *velayats* of Azerbaijan.[456]

Chapter: On the Character and Behavior of the Late Khan

The late Ebrahim Khan was a hospitable man, who helped strangers, raised orphans, and cared about his subjects. [He was] proud, courageous, and generous, [and], being charitable, he distributed gratuities, favors, and food. He gave much offerings to the *'olama, seyyeds*,[457] and the poor. He demonstrated complete respect for the *'olama* and the *seyyeds*.[458] He helped everyone who sought refuge with him. The surrounding khans and begs of the *velayats* of Azerbaijan, Shirvan, and others enjoyed his favors, and he tried to oblige them and satisfy their wishes. He had a great passion for the company of beautiful women.[60]

Chapter: On the Thoroughbred Herds [of the khan]

The khan[459] possessed many fine thoroughbreds, other four-legged animals [horses], and studs. The great fame of the studs of the late khan had reached Iran and Rum. Most of the studs of the late khan were

---

[454] *Pishkesh* was a combination of tribute, bribes, and gifts presented during special occasions or when requesting a favor.

[455] *Ekhrajat* were indirect and extraordinary taxes collected mainly for the upkeep of officials, saving the khan from bearing the sole responsibility for the upkeep of his administration, see Bournoutian, *Erevan*, p, 152.

[456] Unlike some khanates, the taxes of Qarabagh were collected annually and were referred to as *saliane*, Bournoutian, *Ibid.*, p. 152.

[457] The *'olama* (ulema or ulama) are the religious hierarchy of Islam. The *seyyeds* are notables, who are descendants of 'Ali.

[458] The religious institutions were supported by the population at large and the income from *vaqfs* (religious endowments). The khans granted special income to important clerics, see Bournoutian, *Erevan*, p. 155.

[459] The Persian text has "Sarkar Khan" which, translated literally, means "Mister Khan." It is used as a title of respect to a person present or absent.

descended from the studs of the late Nader Shah, which were gathered from the *velayats* of Azerbaijan, Shahsavan, Shaqaqi, and from the khans of Khorasan. There were approximately some three to four thousand mares, who were kept together with the pedigree males. The number of sheep, goats, cows, and bulls was so large that it could not be counted.

Chapter: On the Officials [of Ebrahim Khan]

The officials of the late Ebrahim Khan, were his brothers and their sons, his children, the sons of his uncles, and were all noted begs. Each of them, in property and wealth, retainers, and splendor, was equal to the khans of other *velayats*. Among these were Mirza 'Ali Beg, the son of his uncle; Lotf 'Ali Beg, the son of his paternal aunt; and Fazl (Fazi?) Beg, 'Abd ol-Samad Beg, Kalam-'Ali Beg, and Qommat-'Ali Beg, who were the children of his brother and his children. Mehr 'Ali Beg and Ebrahim Khan were [themselves] the sons of Panah Khan. The begs of the Javanshir, Otuz-iki, Kebirlu, Damirchi-Hasanlu, Bargoshat, Qarachorlu, Hajji-Samlu, Kolani, and the tribes of the Qapans; as well as the *meliks* of the *mahals* of Dizak, Varanda, Jraberd, Talesh [Golestan], and Khachen, resembled the khans of some *velayats*, in their grandeur, glory, wealth, and property. Other begs, whom he had raised, educated, or reared, gained his favor through their bravery, service, and sincerety, receiving *rai'yats* and positions.

Chapter:
On the Officials and Workers in his Household and the Functionaries who Administered [61] his Khanate

The first and the most famous among these was the late Akhund Molla Panah, who used the pen name of *Vaqef*, and who was a wise and experienced vazir. He was well known in Iran and Rum as well. His wonderful poems in Turkish remain in the people's tongues today. His other respected officials, the *eshik-aqasis*, *nazers* (overseers), and other workers were all eloquent, competent, and talented people. After the events [involving] Aqa Mohammad Shah, and the [resulting] chaos and dissent in the *velayat* of Qarabagh, such famous and respected individuals, [as well as] the majority of the functionaries and supervisors of the late Ebrahim Khan, had all died.

Chapter: [On the Khan's Noted Descendants]

The grown boys[460] of the late Ebrahim Khan, who in his own lifetime, joined the grace of God, were: Javad Aqa and Mohammad Hasan Aqa, born from the same mother, a daughter of [one of] the begs of Jebrailu. After the death of the late khan, Colonel Khanlar Aqa [died], while Abo'l Fath Khan passed away in Iran. After that, Colonel Mohammad Qasem Aqa,[461] Fath 'Ali Aqa, Soleiman Aqa, Hosein Qoli Aqa, and Safi Qoli Aqa, also passed away.

At present are left in Qarabagh: Major General Mahdi Qoli Khan,[462] who possesses a plumed sash decorated with expensive stones,[463] and Ahmad Khan. Both of them were born of daughters of khans; Sheikh 'Ali Aqa [another son] was born from a slave girl.

The daughters of the late Ebrahim Khan who are presently living [in Qarabagh] are: Gohar Aqa, born from a daughter of a famous Georgian prince,[464] and 'Ezzat Begum, born from the daughter of Mirza Rabi', the vazir of the *vali* of Georgia. The *vali* of Georgia, Erekle Khan, was always interested in friendly relations and an alliance with Ebrahim Khan, but since he could not become related himself for religious reasons [restricted as a Christian], he gave three daughters of his vazir to the late khan [one married the khan] and [the other two] his two sons, Abo'l Fath Khan and Mohammad Qasem Aqa, so that [at least] in that way their friendship might be strengthened.

[460] The term *farzand* is usually translated as "child" or "offspring," but in most texts it applies only to boys.

[461] The Russian translation erroneously has Mohammad Hasan Aqa, *Istoriia Karabaga*, p. 105.

[462] Mahdi Qoli Khan is described here as being alive. Throughout these additional chapters, however, he is mentioned as "the late Mahdi Qoli Khan." Since Mahdi Qoli died in 1845, just prior to the composition of these chapters, such an error is understandable. See notes 22 and 25 in the introduction.

[463] This could have been a Russian or an Iranian medal, for he had received both. In all probability, Mirza Jamal refers to a Russian decoration which he does not identify further.

[464] The daughter of Prince Abashidze, see p. 97 in text.

[62] Chapter: On Why Mahdi Qoli Khan Became the Heir and Successor [of Ebrahim Khan]

During the first meeting of the late Ebrahim Khan with *sardar* Tsitsianov in Kurek-chay, the designated heir-apparent and successor was named the eldest son of the late Ebrahim Khan, the late Mohammad Hasan Aqa. The second son of Mohammad Hasan Aqa was sent as a hostage to Tsitsianov. Since Major General Mohammad Hasan Aqa died during the late Ebrahim Khan's lifetime, Major General Mahdi Qoli Aqa, the oldest of the remaining sons of the late Ebrahim Khan, inherited and became the heir-apparent. A document was prepared to which the late Ebrahim Khan and other notable individuals of Qarabagh affixed their seals. The late Ebrahim Khan gave this document to Mahdi Qoli Khan during his own lifetime, naming him his heir and granting him the title of khan.

For these reasons, after the death of Ebrahim Khan, Major Lisanevich wrote to Major General Nesvetaev, and in the year 1807, by the decree of the Supreme Emperor, the late Alexander Pavlovich, a standard, and a bejeweled sword [was presented] to the late Mahdi Qoli Khan and he was appointed as khan and governor of Qarabagh. The events at the time of the rule of the late Mahdi Qoli Khan can be obtained from the registers written by the officials of the Exalted State. They are known to your Excellency and there is no need for me, your devoted [servant], to present or to write them down. The End[465]

The transcript of the writings of the Late Mirza Jamal Qarabaghi is what is written here. Copied in haste! Forgive the errors!

And Peace [be with you][466]

---

[465] The Russian, Azeri, and Turkish translations do not include what follows, *Istoriia Karabaga*, p. 16, *Garabagh Tarikhi*, p. 52, *Karabagh Tarihi*, p, 36.

[466] The Arabic term of *wa-sallam* literally means "and peace." The term has occasionally been rendered in the West as "Amen."

Bibliography

Archival Material

Javanshir Qarabaghi, Mirza Jamal. *Tarikh-e Qarabagh.*
MS. B-712/11603, Academy of Sciences of Azerbaijan, Baku.

Primary Sources

a) Persian

Asef, Mohammad Hashem (Rostam ol-Hokama). *Rostam ot-Tavarikh.* Edited by Mohammad Mashiri. Tehran: Sepehr Press, 1352 shamsi (1973).

Astarabadi, Mirza Mohammad Mahdi Koukabi. *Tarikh-e jahangoshay-e Naderi.* Facsimile of the 1171 (1757/58) illuminated manuscript. Tehran: Negar Press, 1370 shamsi (1991).

Bakhikhanov, 'Abbas Qoli Aqa. *Golestan-e Eram.* Critical edition edited by 'Abdo'l-Karim 'Alizadeh. Baku: Elm Press, 1970.

al-Baladhuri, Ahmad ibn Yahya'. *Futuh al-Buldan.* Tehran: Bonyad-e Farhangi, 1346 shamsi (1967).

Donboli, 'Abd or-Razzaq Beg Maftun. *Ma'ser-e Soltaniye.* Lithograph of the 1241 (1826) edition. Tehran: Ibn-Sina, 1351 shamsi (1972).

Estakhri, Abu-Eshaq Ebrahim. *Masalek va Mamalek.* Edited by Iraj Afshar. Tehran: Elmi & Farhangi, 1368 shamsi (1989).

E'temad os-Saltane, Mohammad Hasan Khan. *Tarikh-e Montazam-e Naseri*, vols. II-III. Tehran: Donyay-e Ketab, 1364-1367 shamsi (1985-1988).

Fasa'i, Haj Mirza Hasan Hoseini. *Tarikh-e Farsname-ye Naseri*. 2 vols. in one. Lithograph of the 1314 (1896) edition. Tehran: Sana'i Press, n.d. (ca. 1965).

Ghaffari Kashani, Mirza Mohammad Abo'l-Hasan. *Golshan-e Morad*. Edited by Gholam Reza Tabataba'i Majd. Tehran: Zarin Press, 1369 shamsi (1990).

Golestane, Abo'l-Hasan ibn Mohammad Amin. *Mojmal ot-Tavarikh*. Edited by M. Razavi. Tehran: Ibn-Sina, 1344 shamsi (1965).

Hedayat, Reza Qoli Khan. *Rouzat os-Safa-ye Naseri*, addition to the chronicle of Mir Khand, vol. IX. Qom: Hekmat Press, 1339 shamsi (1960).

Khordadhbe, Abo'l-Qasem ibn 'Abdollah. *Al-Masalek va al-Mamalek*. Tehran: Maharat Press, 1370 shamsi (1991).

Mar'ashi Safavi, Mirza Mohammad Khalil. *Majma' ot-Tavarikh*. Edited by 'Abbas Eqbal. Tehran: Sana'i Press, 1362 shamsi (1983).

Marvi, Mohammad Kazem. *Alamara-ye Naderi*. 3 vols. Edited by Mohammad Amin Riyahi. Tehran: Elmi Press, 1369 shamsi (1990).

Mostoufi Qazvini, Hamdollah. *Nozhat ol-Qulub*. Tehran: Armaghan Press, 1362 shamsi (1983).

Nami Esfahani, Mirza Mohammad Sadeq Musavi. *Tarikh-e Giti-gosha*. Edited by Mirza 'Abdo'l-Karim and Aqa Mohammad Reza Shirazi. Tehran: Eqbal, 1363 shamsi (1984).

Saru'i, Mohammad Fathollah. *Tarikh-e Mohammadi*. Edited by Gholam Reza Tabataba'i. Tehran: Amir Kabir, 1371 shamsi (1992).

Sepehr, Mirza Mohammad Taqi (Lesan ol-Molk). *Nasekh ot-Tavarikh*, vols. I-II. Edited by Mohammad Baqer Behbudi. Tehran: Eslamiye Press, 1344 shamsi (1965).

Ya'qubi. *Tarikh-e Ya'qubi*. 2 vols. Tehran: Elmi & Farhangi, 1362 shamsi (1983).

b) Azeri

Garabaghi, Mirzä Jamal Javanshir. *Garabagh Tarikhi*. Bakï: Academy of Sciences of Azerbaijan, 1959.

Garabaghnamälär. Edited by Nazim Akhundov. Bakï: Yazïchï, 1989.

c) Turkish

Karabaghli, Mirza Cemal Cevansir. *Karabagh Tarihi*. Ankara: Kök Yayïnlarï, 1990.

d) Arabic

Ibn Hauqal (Hawqal). *Kitab Surat al-Arz*. Edited by J. H. Kramers. Leiden: E. J. Brill, 1938/39.

al-Moqaddasi. *Ahsan al-Taqasim*. Edited by N. J. De Goeje. Leiden: E. J. Brill, 1967 (reprint of the 1906 edition).

Ptolemy. *The Geography*. Arabic Translation (1465), manuscript 2610 Ayasofya, Istanbul. Franfurt: Institut für Geschichte der Arabisch-Islamischen Wissenschaften, 1987.

al-Ya'qubi. *Tarikh*. 2 vols. Edited by M. Th. Houtsma. Leiden: E. J. Brill, 1969 (reprint of the 1883 edition).

e) Russian

Adigezal'-Bek, Mirza. *Karabag-name*. Baku: Academy of Sciences of Azerbaijan, 1950.

Dzhavanshir, Akhmedbek. *O politicheskom sushchestvovanii Karabakhskogo khanstva s 1747 po 1805 god)*. Baku: Academy of Sciences of Azerbaijan, 1961.

Karabagi, Dzhemal Dzhevanshir. "Karabag," translated by A. Berzhe *Kavkaz* 61-69 (1855), 259-298.

Karabagskii, Mirza Dzhamal Dzhevanshir. *Istoriia Karabaga*. Baku: Academy of Sciences of Azerbaijan, 1959.

Opisanie Karabakhskoi Provintsii sostavlennoe v 1823 g. deistvitel'nym statskim sovetnikom Mogilevskim i polkovnikom Ermolovym 2-ym. Tiflis 1866 (without pagination).

Russia, Viceroyalty of the Caucasus. *Akty sobrannye kavkazskoiu arkheograficheskoiu kommissieiu*, 12 vols. Edited by A. Berzhe. Tiflis: Official Press of the Viceroyalty, 1866-1904.

Sharaf-khan ibn Shamsaddin Bidlisi. *Sharaf-name*, vol. I. Edited by E. I. Vasil'eva. Moscow: Academy of Sciences, 1967.

Tsagareli, A. A. *Gramoty i drugie istoricheskie dokumenty XVIII stoletiia otnosiashcheisia do Gruzii*, vol. II, part ii. St. Petersburg: Kirshbaum Press, 1902.

f) Georgian

Anonymous. *Kartlis Tskhovreba* (Georgian Chronicle). Tbilisi, 1959.

g) French

Chardin, J. *Voyages du Chevalier Chardin en Perse*, vol. V. Edited by L. Langlés. Paris: Le Normant, 1811.

h) English (original works and translations)

Dasxurantci, Movses. *History of the Caucasian Albanians*. Translated by C. J. F. Dowsett. London: Oxford University Press, 1961.

Dio Cassius. *Roman History*. Loeb Edition, vol. III. Cambridge, MA.: Harvard University Press, 1984.

Juvaini, 'Ata-malik. *Tarikh-e Jahan-gosha*. Translated by J. A. Boyle as *The History of the World Conqueror*, 2 vols. Manchester: the University Press, 1958.

Keppel, George Thomas (Abermarle). *Personal Narrative of a Journey from India to England*. London: R. Bentley, 1834.

Khorenats'i, Moses. *History of the Armenians*. Translated by Robert W. Thomson. Cambridge, MA.: Harvard University Press, 1978..

Minorsky, Vladimir (translator and editor). *A History of Sharvan and Darband in the 10th-11th centuries*. Cambridge: W. Heffer & Sons, 1958.

_____. *Hudud al-'Alam: "The Regions of the World," A Persian Geography, 372 A.H.-982 A.D*. London: Luzac & Co. 1970.

_____. *Studies in Caucasian History*. London: Taylor's Foreign Press, 1953.

_____. *Tadhkirat al-Muluk: A Manual of Safavid Administration (circa 1137/1725)*. London: Luzac & Co., 1943.

Monshi, Eskandar Beg. *Tarikh-e Alamara-ye 'Abbasi*. Translated by Roger M. Savory as *History of Shah 'Abbas the Great*. 2 vols. Boulder Co.: Westview Press, 1978.

The *Qur'an*. 2 vols. Critical Edition by Richard Bell. Edinburgh: T. & T. Clark, 1960.

Pliny the Elder. *Natural History*, vol. II. London: Bell & Sons, 1890.

Plutarch. *Lives*. Loeb Edition, vol. V (Pompey). Cambridge, MA.: Harvard University Press, 1955.

Rashid al-Din. *Jame' ot-Tavarikh*. Translated by J. A. Boyle as *The Successors of Genghis Khan*. New York, Columbia University Press, 1971.

Schiltberger, J. *The Bondage and Travels of Johann Schiltberger, a Native of Bavaria, in Europe, Asia, and Africa, 1396-1427*. New York, Burt Franklin, 1970.

Strabo. *The Geography*. Loeb Edition, vol. V. Cambridge, MA.: Harvard University Press, 1969.

Secondary Sources

Atkin, Muriel. *Russia and Iran, 1780-1828*. Minneapolis: University of Minnesota Press, 1980.

_____. "The Strange Death of Ibrahim Khalil Khan of Qarabagh," *Iranian Studies* 12 (1979), 79-107.

Avery P., Hambly G. et. al. eds. *The Cambridge History of Iran*, vol. VII. Cambridge: the University Press, 1991.

Baddeley, John. *The Russian Conquest of the Caucasus*. New York: Russell, 1969.

Bamdad, Mehdi. *Sharh-e hal-e rejal-e Iran dar qarn-e 12, 13, 14 hijri*. 6 vols. Tehran: Zavar, 1347-51 shamsi (1968-72).

Barthold, W. *Turkestan Down to the Mongol Invasion*. London: Luzac & Co., 1968.

Bosworth, C. E. "Arran," *Encyclopedia Iranica*, II (1986), 520- 522.

_____. "The Political and Dynastic History of the Iranian World (A.D. 1000-1217)," *Cambridge History of Iran*, vol. V, ed. J. A. Boyle. Cambridge: the University Press, 1968.

Bournoutian, George A. *The Khanate of Erevan under Qajar Rule, 1795-1828*. Costa Mesa, Ca.: Mazda, 1992.

Gaziyants, A. N. "K biografii Mirza Adigezal-Beka," *Doklady Akademii Nauk Azerbaidzhanskoi S.S.R.* 9 (1948), 405-406.

Grousset, René. *The Empire of the Steppes: A History of Central Asia* (New Brunswick, NJ, Rutgers University Press, 1970.

Hewsen, Robert H. "The Meliks of Eastern Armenia: A Preliminary Study," *Revue Des Études Arméniennes* (new series), IX (1972), 285-329.

_____. "The Meliks of Eastern Armenia II," *Revue Des Études Arméniennes* (new series), X (1973-74), 281-300.

_____. "The Meliks of Eastern Armenia III," *Revue Des Études Arméniennes* (new series), XI (1975-75), 219-243.

_____. "The Meliks of Eastern Armenia IV," *Revue Des Études Arméniennes* (new series), XIV (1980), 459-470.

_____. "Three Armenian Noble Families of the Russian Empire [The Meliks of Eastern Armenia V]," *Hask* (new series) (1981-82), 389-400.

_____. "The Meliks of Eastern Armenia VI: The House of Aghamaleanc', Meliks of Erevan," *Pazmaveb* (1984), 319-333.

_____. "The Kingdom of Arc'ax," *Medieval Armenian Culture*, ed. T. Samuelian and M. Stone. Chico, CA.: Scholars Press, 1983.

Lang, David Marshall. *The Last Years of the Georgian Monarchy, 1658-1832.* New York: Columbia University Press, 1957.

Lockhart, Laurence. *Nadir Shah.* London: Luzac & Co., 1938.

_____. *The Fall of the Safavi Dynasty and the Afghan Occupation of Persia.* Cambridge: the University Press, 1958.

Pakravan, E. *Agha Mohammad Khan Qajar.* Tehran: Franklin Publications, 1348 Shamsi (1969).

Reid, James. *Studies on Persia, Anatolia, and Central Asia, 1200-1750* (forthcoming).

Rhinelander, Anthony L. H. *Prince Michael Vorontsov: Viceroy to the Tsar.* Montreal: McGill-Queens University Press, 1990.

Roemer, H. R. "Timur in Iran," *Cambridge History of Iran*, vol. VI, eds. P. Jacskon & L. Lockhart. Cambridge: the University Press, 1986.

Ter-Grigor'ian, T. I. "Mirza Adigezal-Bek Karabakhskii," *Doklady Akademii Nauk Azerbaidzhanskoi S.S.R.* 9 (1948), 407-408.

Yarshater, Ehsan, ed. *The Cambridge History of Iran*, vol. III. Cambridge: the University Press, 1983.

Glossary of Selected Terms

aghach: Turkish equivalent of *farsakh*, measuring some three and a half miles

agha: a great lord, nobleman, head, chief master, commander; a eunuch

akhund: member of the religious classes, theologian, preacher; a tutor

'amale: worker, mason

amir (emir): a commander, chief, leader, lord, prince

aqa: the elder brother; the eldest, the chief of tribe or family

arkh: irrigation trench, canal

ashrafi: gold coin weighing 190,894 grains troy

ayalat: government, dominion; a major administrative division such as governorate-general, which equals the present-day *ostan*

beg (bey): nobleman, brother or son of a khan; civil or military administrator of a populous district

beglarbegi (beylerbey): provincial governor; governor general; military governor

begum: princess or lady of high rank

catholicos: Supreme Patriarch of the Armenian Church

chay (chai): river, in Turkish

chetvert: Russian weight measuring 3 liters for liquids and 210 liters for grains

dar ol-saltane: capital city; royal residence

divan: chancery

eger: Russian term for chasseur

ekhrajat: indirect and extraordinary taxes

eshik-aqasi: chamberlain

farsakh: Iranian measure equal to three and a half miles

hakem (pl. hokama): judge; governor; ruler

halal: legal; sanctioned by Islam

hammam: bath

'il (pl. 'ilat): tribe

javanghar: commanders of the right flank

juft (joft, juft-bashi): oxen, plough tax

kadkhoda: village or tribe headman

kargozar: official, supervisor

karkhane: kitchen

khal'at: robe of honor

khamse: the five Armenian districts of Qarabagh

khanum: lady

keshikchi: watchman

khan: governor, commander, tribal leader, ruler of a territory

khanate: province, a state ruled by a khan; similar to Ottoman *pashalik*

Khass (khalese): royal estates

khazine: treasury

kniaz: prince, in Russian

korpi: bridge, in Turkish dialect of Qarabagh (Azeri)

madrase (madrasa, maktab): school

mahal: district or county

mahalle: quarter

mal va jahat (mal-o-jehat): land and property taxes, generally paid in kind

manat: silver ruble

manzel: station

marhum: "the late"

meidan: square

melik (malek, malak): Armenian prince or feudal lord, secular leaders of Qarabagh Armenians

minbashi: head of one thousand, tribal leader

mirza: administrative official, secretary (if precedes the name), prince of the ruling house (if follows the name: e.g. Mirza Jamal, 'Abbas Mirza

molk (mulk): private property

monshi: scribe

mostoufi: an accountant, tax official

na'eb: deputy

nayeb ol-saltane: crown prince, heir-apparent, heir to the throne

nazer: overseer

nokar: retainer, attendant

nouruz: Persian New Year, first day of spring

padishah: emperor

pasha: Ottoman provincial governor, same as khan

piadeh: infantry

pishkesh: gift, bribe

pud: Russian weight equal to approximately 36 pounds

qezelbash: Iranian army

qeshlaq (qishlaq): tribal winter quarters

ra'iyat (pl. ra'aya): peasant

sardar: commander-in-chief, general, governor of a major border province

saqnaq (seghnakh): stronghold, lair

savareh: cavalry

sultan: Ottoman ruler; provincial grandee; commander (below the level of a khan)

toyul (tiyul, tuyul): land grant or its revenue in lieu of salary

tofangchi: musketeer

toman: Persian currency worth about one pound sterling

touji: taxes, generally in cash

uymaq: clan

vakil: regent

vali: viceroy, regent

vaqf (waqf): charitable or religious endowment

velayat: province

verst: Russian measure of length equal to 3500 feet

yasavol: guard, tax farmer

yeilaq (yailaq): tribal summer quarters

yuzbashi: village headman; head of one hundred; captain

zar kharid: purchased in cash

Index

Personal, Geographical, Tribal Names and Titles

About the Translator

George Bournoutian was born in Iran and received his Ph.D. in Armenian and Iranian Studies at UCLA. He is the recipient of an IREX Fellowship for research in Armenia, Georgia, and Azerbaijan and a Mellon Post-doctoral Fellowship. He has taught Armenian, Russian, and Middle Eastern History at UCLA, Columbia University, New York University, Tufts University, the University of Connecticut, and Ramapo College, and is currently Associate Professor of Russian, East European, and Middle Eastern History at Iona College. Professor Bournoutian, who is a member of the New Jersey Governor's Commission on Education, lives in New Jersey.

Also by George Bournoutian from Mazda Press:

The Khanate of Erevan Under Qajar Rule, 1795-1828
1992, xxviii+356 pp., maps, tables, appendices, bibliography, index. cloth, ISBN: 0-939214-18-0.

A History of the Armenian People, Vol. I: Pre-History to 1500 A.D.
1993, xviii+174 pp., 18 maps, 10 time-lines, 13 plates, bibliography, index. paper, ISBN: 0-939214-96-2.

۱

کیفیت حکومت و استقلال خوانین مرحومین پناه خان
و ابراهیم خان در ولایت قراباغ و بعضی از وقایع متفرقه

صورت مرقومه مرحوم   بسم الله الرحمن الرحیم میرزا جمال عز جناب قلاعی جبر الغیاثی سردار دورا

حمد بیحد و ثنای بی منتهاء دی عدد پروردگار عالمیان را سزد که کلاه سعادت و بزرگی را
بر سر هر که خواهد نهند و از هر که خواهد ستاند در حقیقت عزت و ذلت و اختیاری محض
از کرم عمیم و لطف قدیم است و در قسمت بندگی و شاهی الیس نوع دهی هر که خواهی
بعد الحمد و الثناء بر درگاه خالق ارض و السماء براراب دانش محور و مستربت که
دانستن و خبر دار بودن از وقایع و گذارشات گذشته و اوضاع و کیفیت هر ولایت
باعث ترائید بصیرت است و موجب نکثر منفعت فلهذا بتاریخ سنه سلمانی
۱۲۶۳ مطابق با سنه للمسیحیه ۱۸۴۷ که حالیه به عرصه کتابت الکتاب بولکوک و قوالیر
شاه امیرخان قرلا عز الاصلی تکلروف بر قلعه شوشی آمده بودند و با این مخلص حقیقی و خدا
قدیمی میرزا جمال جوانشیر قرا لائی که مدت مدید در خدمت و حضور خوانین قلاع صاحب کام
به بامر میرزائی و وزارت قراباغ اشتغال داشته و لهذا در حکومت ایث ن باز

از جمله فذ ملکدار

از جمله خدمتگذاران و کارگذاران دولت علیّه روسیه دقّت دارند که ام امورات مرجوعه قیام داقدام

میریکه درمقام صحبت آرزوی خیرخواهی وگداد اخلاص نسبت بحضرت میرکزل مسبح الجو و داکان

عظیم الشّان نجات المّالک بسعظم وحشمت دستگاه ماداذ الاحرا اللّعظام ولمّجانباص دعام نظر کبه

اعلیحضرت امپراطور بعظم دخاون اکرم فایمقام بادّه علیّما جناب پیدار الّ آونهّا نطیر وحبّب

انواع هاسیلاتغراف کمسیار میجائیل سمیولویج درا لطوف دام بعول عنایّه حضربقادر

رؤف علیهٍ الهّا رکعند میرکزل مظهرالیه بر دانستن وقایع وکارت هردلایتّ ریر

حکم نفو و حقیقت حکومت دبیّار رو ندررت خواپین کدشه میدتّام دارنند کر دبین باب شرح حقلم

آوررند وحقایتی وقایع دلایس قسم ربّاع وگذارش حشیار رقّ لدخواپین کدشه را مفصلا مشروع

ومعروض حضره جیاب ان امیر اعظم حباب کرم دارد لابیس مقبول ومطبوع اقلام موجب بحضیر رضا دخاطر

مبادرکبسّیا ان خواپهد شد وجون بنده بنا مراداخلاص داراله تخفو حضرصا المّسید الطّاو ومرحمه

کب رقایمقام مظّم الیه انکبود وسیله وخدیمتّ یعین دنش کبنی وسعادت خفو میدانم که درنظر انور

مشرایف جیاب ان امیر اعظم وخطیب حباب صاحبّزوکب حبّب کرم ذرّه وارخفو سلّجلوه دلّه بلّکه سماری خونشحالی

ومرحمتّین دلیان راحهّار سماورید یافت کنم پس مترکایّ علّ اللّه آنکه حقیقتّ بوّک ازقواریخ

قدیم دار ایّسّی خص مسّن وکاردّ ان اخیره وسندیده د دربّدتّ مّباه الّ اخفم دانسّه وخبر دارّنّه طبّم

بدوکی زباله دنفقصان بنجدحررران قیام داقدام بمود آمیدوارست که این نسخه تحفه درکاه لئان

دنیش نشه از جمله خدمات واخلاص مخلص حقیقی خواهدکردید ومن اللّه الاستعانة والتّوفیق

واین ادراق رامشتمل بچند فصل ساخته قدرهرفصل بذکر وقایعی پرداخته شه وباللّه التّوفیق والمعین

فصل اوّل دربیان اصل آبادی وسرحدّ ومیزان دیشمروشمر وشهر قدیم ولایت قراباغ

آنچه از تواریخ قدیم مزقوم هست سنور وسرحدّ ولایت قراباغ این هت طرف جنوبی رود ارس از ایل خداآفرین

میرود الی سنی کوپک که الحال درزبان اهالی مال قراق شمس الّدین ردمورجی حسنلو میشه واعناء انہ روستہ

باصطلاع ورسیه قراسنی موسّد یعنی قزل کوپره پیدا منذ وطرف شرقی رودخانه کُرست تاکه درقریه جوله

آب که درتو وارس ہیکدیکر ملحنی شه میرود بدریای خصرُری متّصل میرشود وطرف شمالی که سرحدّ قراباغ

ودیساست دیاه پل رود کوران هت ناآب کُر دهمه جا رود کر رود خانه ارس میرسد وطرف غربی

کوهستانات عظیم قراباغ هت که کوشرک سلاواریزوارکلووبکرید نہایت درعصا رسیده که

غینتاش وتغییر رودله ولبعی ارقعات پارتاهان ایران روم وترکستان بابین ولایتها سلّط باقره انو

سرحدّ علاحدّه نہار وقلعه ها رخته موسوم باسم دیکرکه امرو این ولایت سراباغ ازجمله مملکت ایران است

چون درزبان نوح پیغبر علیه السلام که طوفان شه ولبراز مدّتی که ازطافان کذشته بهو کا از ادلاد واحفاد

نوح علیه السلام دردین دلاتها که میان رود کر وارس واقع اواقع اند وعبارت شیه لذ نشر قلانس وکیه واردان

دیکجوان واور ہابال وبردع وبیلیان که درخاک قسراباغ اند واکالک هر ۲ ح زآت یسمند (الخ)

ولامنها دحاک ہا حکمران وصحب شه ۰ وآبار بعضه ہمدیا ناموخته کُه بیشتر موسوم باسم ایران که چودکه

نام دخولاد

نام خفا و اران لهیت و اول شهری که در ولایت قسطلاغ بنا شده شهر و قلعه بردعه است

که در سر رودخانه ترتر دو رسته از بخر رود کر دادم است و اسم آن شهر در قدیم ارمن و یا غیر ملت لهینه

نوردزمان خلفاء سابق بنی عباسیه که شهر بعد لولو را آباد نموده دارالخلافه که در آنجا ساکن

میشدند در آن زمانه که تاریخ اسلامیه در غزة ۳ هجری لو مطابق سنه المسیحی ۸۸۴

اهالی آن شهر مسلمان شده دلولو از آن شهر سلطان است که آنرا قفاز یارلغه که لقب یارلغان

ایران و فارس است ادبنا که گفت در تخمینا کهزار با فصل می رسد از رود ارس نهر عظیمی

آورده حصار و وسیع الفضای مسلمان را مشهر ساخته و سمت و اطراف از رود خانه

کند لمن تا رودخانه غرغر قرایا دعات نموده رعایا را جا ب سکنی مکدران مقرر کرده

نما مزارع و مراتع ربغ وزراعت دا آبار با بنا کردند و از قدیم الایام اسم

همان نهر عظیم بر لاس لبعه و حالا مشهور به کودر آخری شده است و تا عهد

چنگیزخان آن شهر و دهات و نهر آباد در شته ۲۴ قشون چنگیزخان

آمده شهر سلطان را محصره نمود و گراز جند ماه تبریز تسلط یافته خلق شهر ل

قتل عام کرده دها لی ولایت میلها و دهات قراباغ بکرست نا ت قراباغ

دشیروان متفرق شدند و مدتی باز همان شهر سلطان و شهر بزرک خراب

مانده تا وقتی که تیمور بارلاس از ترکستان بر سر ولایت مردم آمده و ایلدرم نایز

سلطان فرمان فرمای روم (دعوا که والی بصره دارد) اینکه معاونت کند شهر مبلغان را

با آباد کند خلق بسیار جمع نمده و نهر را با رشته نهر آورده جدا و آباد معمور رخنه

پس مدت آباد بود تا اینکه در عهد پادشاه آل صفویه و نادر شاه از تردد قشون به طرف

کرحستان دشت و دانات باز خراب شده خلق آن شهر پراکنده گشتند و الحالی

خراب است در حقیقت این نهر عظیم است و بسیار منفعت قهر زیر آب او هزار

غله و شلتوک و پنبه و باغ ابریشم را برجدبات هرچه کاشته شود بسیار خوب

بعمل آید بلکه از کشت و ریست کندم بسیت حسورت و بلکه زیاد تر حصول بعمل آید حسورت صد تک

و جا و رس که تخمینا اگر یک حسورت کاشته شود منی حسورت و بلکه زیاد تر حصول بعمل آید و

کاشتن هم آسان است که با اردوس کار و با کمال سهل میکارند و اگر در زیر این نهر

با ضابطه و نظام البته که پنجهزار و ششهزار زیاد خانوار با فراغت و رفاهیت

گذران میکنند که قریه و دهها مدغشه با کمال خوبی معشکل گذار میتوانند زیست کنند

نمایه و سوای این نهر عظیم حید نهر دیگر هم دارد که از اورس سپردن شده

در سر مهر نهر قریه های بزرگ صد باب و دویست باب خانوار باشنه فراغت

و آباد که از حصولات غله و شلتوک و پنبه بوست نفع کواره برند اگر چه

شماره مبلغان زیاد از سبعه کل میانش الحزاب شده اما از آن نهر ها در اودیه حکومت

خویی

خوانین مرحومین پناه خان و ابراهیم خان آباد لهجم امر که از سه اخزانند خوانین

مرحومین نفع کبوار لهوند و آنها مر آن نهرها بهترین تفضید سه کورک آدمی کوار آدمی

میمته آدمی که جو آدمی سردار آباج آباز آدمی تا شفای آدمی خان آدمی

فصل هم در بیان تبعیت و عمارت و قواعد قدیم دلایت قراباغ در عهد سلاطین

فروکس مکین صفویه که در ایران لهائد دلایت قراباغ ایلات و محلها خمسه ارامنه

که محال قراباق و ورزنه و خاحین وحله برد وطالش باشند تابع حکم بیگلرک کنوبه شده اند

وتاعهد مرحوم نادرشاه اکرچه خوانین کوچک درمیان ایل جوانشیر دادقوز ایک و برک طا وغیره

لهائد اما همه اینان درزیر حکم بیگلرک لیبا لطوال لهائد لوداراکه نادرشاه قلیا

تفلیس وکنجه وایروان ونخوان و قرا باغ را از تسلط اهالی و قشون مردم متصرف حق

آورده چندوقت قلیا باز دلایت شراغ درزیر حکم بیگلرک سیسا دلط بول لهجم کله

درزیر حکم سردار قوز باکجان کشته درمیان هر ایلی و محل باز خوانین دملک ان لهم انر

که هلاکت تلقیه ثابت هریا سار برام سردار قوز باکجان بعمر آورده اند تا زمانیکه

نادرشاه سزاد در سنه مسلمین ۱۱۶ مطابق سنه المسیحیه ۱۷۴۳ شد بقتدوس اسیدند

بها نقرار مسیحف که مذکورشد فصل سئیم در بیان نسب وحکومت مرحوم پناه خان در

دلایت قراباغ اصل ونسب مرحوم پناه خان ان از ایل جوانشیر قراق کمت از ادیای

سادوجلو که قدیم از ترکستان آمده اند آباء و اجدادلوئیان درمیان ایل جوانشیر مشهورو معروف

بوده اند ایک ۱۱۲ بهم

وصاحب اسم دیوان وصاحب مهلت دیوان لهواند وقتی که مرحوم نادرشاه ابدالله پی
قراباغ دکنجه دتفلیس وشیروان تسلط یافته درمیان ایلات وولایات کسری را
اورسید دکارآمد دکارداان دسته باسمه که صدرجمع برده ازخملٔه خدمتگذاران حضور
خفیه حشمه صاحب موجب حرام دمنصب کرده از الجمله بنا دخان زبان که درسان ایلات
به پناه عالی کس ردجلوی جوبشیر مشهد دلهب است دوهر کاروبار معلومه صاحب اسم
دوشقام جبک ودعوا از ابنال آحمه سبقت کننده خصوصاً در داوقات دعوای
نادرشاه مرحوم با ایل الشکر ای ردم رسالت ای نمهلو بنا براین که صدرخورده اهم
درسفر وحضر درخدمتگذاری درآستین کشیده درحضور شاه دصاحب مصمم ومدت شده تاباوقت
جمرجمه قیام واقدام مجمو حیدراک که بتنبو واد سه ردربروز مرجعت نادرشاه درمآثر او
زبار کشته از ابنال دالافران درمنصب دمرتبه برتری یا فته جناکه علامت بجلیان دصمردان
بیشه با ره ازبشیرار درخانهٔ شاهر وبا ره از ایلات درخفیه دکشار ردرحضور
نادرشاه درمرحوم زبان بیبد کی مرحوم بنا دخان کسراهم امرما اکه مراجع مرحوم شاه سد
ازبنا دخان متغیر ساخته اند پس بنا دخان حقیقت را دسته ازسیم جان جمع
دردستیکه سا درجراع ان لمه فرصت یافته چندنفر از اقوام دخلصان خودبکشته درسته ۱۱۵
پولابین قسرلباغ قرار کرده جون فرار کهان اوبرشاه معلوم کشته جابارع فرستنامه

بلکم درراه

که بلکه در راه کرفته شوند میسر نشده و فرامین با تاکید تمام بسردار آذربایجان و حکام گنجه و تفلیس و شیروان مرقوم شده که بنا به خان را در هر جا یافته شوند گرفته روانه حضور شاه زند

و خانه دعیل و سایر اقربا و الوام را اگرچه با رسته رکانیده و جریمه کرفته شد فائده نکرده مرحوم بنا به خان در آخر خانه اش اباغ شده با اخلاص تمام که (در کومت با ت قرابا دکان

در دولت بیشی در محال قلعه ادوا تکذار که د فر زند بزرک ا د مرحوم ابراهیم خلیفه خان که در آن

وقت قربت بنا نمشه که بهز ک در خر ان در خانه خوب ان لهمث بجز از چیز دقت از عقب

بزرک وار خود بقرا باغ آمده هم دقتی در حضور بر سر کذار که لهسب هر سه سال بدین منوال کذار

کمه تا آنکه در سنه مذکوره الفوق که ۱۱۲۸ تمارث را نقضی رسانیده بد در میان خلق

باز مانند قرا باغ بنا ت خان خوب اطل هر سه و از خوانان کار آمد بر سر قوم کوه در عبارت

باطرف کنجه و نخچوان و غیره کثیم هم جوانان دنحرص ان خوب اد که اوتتا درستی لهبذ صاحب دصر ولباس

دک و اسباب کرده (در این اثنا خبر رسد که ایلات خوت شیر و غیره که به کوچانیده بجر اسان کرده

بودند ینا ما خوبس کوچ کرده معاودت بوطن ینا رخه نمو می آید با همان جمعیت که در کوچینا ه خان لهبذ

آنها را بمقشه تا سرحد عراق و آذربایگان با ستقبال ایلات قرا باغ رفته و ا۶ ایلات و اقربا و جون

سلطنتی و جود و ا د یده و ا د را دیده و جمعیت نوکر د خاص ان را مث هرده کرده هم خوبهایها د ی سر در کشته بالا قن

با مرحوم پناه‌خان در آن خاک قلاع و هر کس بیوت اصلی خو شه و فارغ گشته اند چون ابلاغ ایلات همه
پی وضع وعمارت شده درزحمت کشیده و بهیچ وجه تمکن [...] مرحوم پناه‌خان بسیار از جوانان کارآمد اقوام خود
وایلات باخود منتفق و جمع از ولایت شیروان و شکی و کیه و لیزدی قرلاغ به آخر دیار مشغول شده
همه جوانان را صاحب وضع و لرست ساخته و الوف سایر خلقی را بابدل حال و کسب و خلعت و غیره را که ر ام
موافقت می‌سازی کرده اند با زخواست و قعر مطیع طاعت ساخته احد والذا الاجوانشیر و اولور ایکه و سایر
ایلات دها ت قدرت آن می‌دانستند که از امر و حکم پناه‌خان برون شود چون حکام شیروان و شکی
و کیه و استقلال پناه‌خان را درولایت قرلاغ شنیده و دانستند بجنگ آن مفطر و محیر دانسته هر
بالاتفاق بیوع مرحوم پناه‌خان معیشت شد و اتفاق که همه همین که از الهار خمسه ارامنه قلاع مطیع او
می‌نمودند از صلاح دیده که درمیان ایلات درجای مناسب بنای قلعه گذاشته شود که هر کار خوانین اطراف
بیوع او آیند لابد آنها و عیال خود و سایر اقوام و هر متکدران و دهاقین و بزدگان را در آنجای قطرت
نماید لجوار ممانعت در بنای قلعه بیات را که آکال درمیان خاک کبیر لواست که آن ها که ازان درقرب حصار
رحضدق محکم و بازار و حکام و مسجد درست که تمامی خانواران وا اهل وعیال خود واقوام و بزدگان و
بزدگان ایلرا بانجا جمع که دلار که اطراف و جوانب عتی از داری تبریز داده خلقی بسیار وجهان
صنعت آورده روند و مراد و مجت مرحوم پناه‌خان راشنیده با اهل وعیال وفا نه آمده
درقلعه بیات سکنی کرفند بنای قلعه بیات درسنه سلمان ١٦١١ مطابق با سنه المسیحیه ١٧٤٥

شده جراز استحکام قلعه نبات و کثرت جمعیت مرحوم بناه خان حکام شیروان دکک و صدرها کلیه

از جمعیت و قشون بناه خان میان بر همی که خانه هره و اتفاق که با قشون بسیار بر سر قلعه نبات بوقع

بناه خان آمده اند و محاصره مشغول کشته مرحوم خان با سواره رمی اقوام و ایلات و سلدار مالله

در موضع و ستاره روز یکدفوا زقلعه بیرون شده در میدان وسیع که میان قلعه و قشون دشمن لطیفه بست

طرح جنگ انداخته مرداکه ها که تعتبه ها شیروان دشک خالی شده لعلم معاقوب کرده هیچ

امری و کار رخ نمای شیروان دشک در منین نبرد مدت محاصره زیاد که درکمان کشیده در هر روز ضرر

مکی از غارت و سب داولاع و قشون خویش ان دیده لسیمان و برلیان وکوچ که هرکس مرحبت بوللف

جهد کرده در قورمتا معاقوت حاجی جلبر که حاکم داشرشک وکار اهد زمان جفله هست این کلاما را

کفه که بناه خان خان لهم حالاکه ما آمده و با و دعوا که دکار در منین نبرد هیچ هان معاقب

ممکیم ادرایشه کرده مرحبت که یک تس بعد از من مقدمه کا روستقلات دحک من بناه خان مرحوم

روبر زیادت نهار نوکر مطبع که حصه ارم اقلا آقلا ملک شا منظر یک که ملک قدیم محال

درندویست با ملکان میان جلببرد و طالس و درآق درمیان کدورت و حنا لفت داشته اند اکن

مرحم بناه خان را مصالحت دانسته قبول که در اصلاح دوستی مضا یقه کرده بناه خان هم اطلاعت

خان منتخص بزرگ دحتاب حرمت دهلت را لذا آمد اقبال دانسه اور برروز درحرمت درآم

ادمضایقه نکرد و ملک محال خاصین اکرجه چند رقت بحا لفت نوشمبر هست دبا رزده آخر

دلاخر سطری و منقال شده ملک علاحده که آباء و احدلو این ملکیت که الخالت

از روف مرحوم پناه خان مصوب شده همه اهالی خاصین مطیع و کذمات مرحوم (ارث) اقدام کویانه

اتا ملکان میل در عراق و چله بر دو طایفه جند سال با دشمنز و دعوا السیر برده آخر الامر با قدر دغارت

میرنداهیر که للازم لهمت بوه مطیع میشدند بعد از اینکه مدت پنج سال در قلعه ما تسکین

کهواه مازمطلحه حینین (دید دحول در اطراف و جوانب دشمن استباراست) از قلعه ما سکنی کون

د ابای شهورد قلعه ماس خنی از قاعده جتبی طاهری نماید پس بهلم میشوق قلوید درجایی و مقابلا

که منصر لکو هستانات قمراع با باشند تا که کهل ایلات قراغ از روی وقت دشمن در کوهستانات

صعوب و مکانهای محکم مال دو نیماری حفظ کنا میظطر نماید که از دشمنی ضرار نرسد جوانب اهالی خانین

که بالازی پرشئه بلولای جو ترکوت است ساکن میشند و جمه وقت با مرحوم پناه خان سالک طرف نی

عداوت دوشمنی میکودند اول دفع ماه ایسالیان را وجهه همت رخته با قشون سواره و بیاله

عزم مدافعه انا قریه اهالی مان خاصین بقوس هزار تفنکچی دعا ثواران چهه در حوال بالا

قایم در جا صعوب و محکم سقاف کهم که بعد از دوشمنی استند پناه خان مرحوم لورش بیسکر

انان کهانه مدت سته و در موالی او هم طرف اتش قایم و با اثره جدال در اشتعال لهودر

روز نیم پناه خان مرحوم سکر انان را متصرق شت باره از اهالی ذکر این را القند رسته

بجهه خوف و عبرت دیکران در سر دحوظه خاصین در سریعا از سر مقتولین بنا کل مینا در اکه

قوس سعد نیزه از سر این ان در آن منا رصب کهایه لکرارنی بمقدم که ارجا جنابی لصعب

مقداور دسکر حکم بقوس لاهزار تفنکچی لهو از بقوس پناه خان آمده اهالی الجرد و محال اهر خمسه را

خوف عظیم غالب شد که به اصلاح دوستی دل و دشمنی با جان با دارا که اندک اندک دفع بلک
حتم ملک مال حلد برد و ملک او کوب بیک ملک حال طلاش که هر حال این ملک قدیم

و موجب هرچه لفوذ و جمعیت کلی در اشتر مقابله دفع بلا بعد تلا آخر که تاب توقف
نیاورده مدتی در مکنها صعب المسالک و دره های عمیق و کوهستانات و رفیع المبر ره
جون دیدند که زراعات و باغات و دماغوایش لیان در دست توابع و قصونها مرحم
پناه خانل غارت و منکوب و خراب کهه کردان لیان به تفنگ میرسد ناچار
نزک دیار و وطن لها و باغات و مزارع لهه جلای وطن اختیار که به طرف کنجه فرار
کهدند و مدت همقتال سال در ولایت کنجه هور مان شد کر توقف کهدند و جون
پناه خانل را فراغت از مفاسدان و عدادت لها احا جن رو دلر ملک علاحده
به محال خاین لنصب قرحه همک باتی ما مذکال مطیع و منقار شده نز لبرار ان لنی
قلعه نرکلوت راکه لخاد شاه بولاغی مشهور است لهام لیس صلاح چپان دیدکه قلعه
بیات را موقوف که درشه بولاغی طرح قلعه در حوالی اسر حشمه بزرک انجا ولکنده
در اطراف ان حصار و سیع درجار مرتفع بنا که بازار و چارسو و حمام و مسجد
لعمیر کردند و تمام خانه ۱٤٤ لی ایلات و بزرکان دار ل اصنعت و محصصان و ملارنا
در سنه ۱۱۶۵ مسلمان بقلعه شاه بولاغی سکنی دله در آنجا ممکنن کشته اندردت

سته و چهار سال درسته بلاغی با استقلال تمام نشسته و آوازه استقلال مرحوم پناه خان که

روز بروز در شتابها رو یافته در زور و جمعیت حضور الیان باطراف و جوانب رسیده خوانین

شیروان و شکی و کنجه و ایروان و نخجوان و تبریز و قره داغ رسل در سایه پیش مرحوم پناه

خان فرستاده اظهار دوستی دلیکانگ کرده و با بعضی از خوانین بنا خویشتر گذاشته در تسلط

به ملالت زدکه روز قللق نخجوان و قبانات تعلق تبریز و جولا و در مغزری کانی قره داغ که در حکم

حاکم نخجوان و تبریز و قرا داغ بودند زا که به آنها خبر کرده و خسان سایر رعایا با قرا لاغ که یکان

و سلطانان لهضر منفعه همه مطیع و منقاد امر مرحوم پناه خان شدند که تا حال

بدا بقرار است فصل جهام در بیان صدور فرمان باسم

خانی و حکومت مرحوم پناه خان کبراز آکه مرحوم نادرشاه بقدر رسیده

علیقف خان برلو در لقم نادرشاه حفو سل عادل شاه لقب دله در جا مرحوم نادرشاه

بمسند دهی نشسته امیر اصلان خان سردار که از طرف عادل شاه مذکور در رحمت

آفور با کیان با مرسد دار منصو بشته در شهر تبریز توقف داشت اینکه استقلال

و شهرت پناه خان را در قلاع رسیده حفو خود اسب و شمشیر و خلعت فرستاده

با طاعت عادل شاه دعوت و ترغیب نمود مرحوم پناه خان با فرستاده گان

او لازمه حرمت و مهربانی بعمر آورده چند نفر از کدخدا یان نامی ایلات و احشام

و معتبرین

ومعتبرین کهبندهمراه فرستاده کان امیر اصلان سردار که راه غیوغیون هندر آن

وقت نبوده که بعنوان سردار صاحب شوکت و دولت با یکدیگر دشمنی و عداوت نمامه

بمقام ستیز و مقاتله آید و در اطراف و جوانب حوالین ان بضرر دلایت آنها هر چند در

ظاهر بنای الفت و دلفگستری و صداقت میکردند اما باطناً نیز در مقام بدخواهی

پناه خان مستعد بهندر بناءً علیه اظهار اطاعت بدولت عالیشاه هر کرده جوابهای

صداقت آمیز و تحف و هدایا فرستاده اظهار دولت خواهی کرده امیر اصلان سردار

اسکنه اطاعت و آمدن فرستادگان را نسبت بدولت عالیشاه هر حضرت عظیم

و پیوسته عرایضه بحضور عالیشاه نوشته در تاریخ سنه المسلمین ١١۶١ مطابق

باسنه للمسیحیه ١٧۴۵ از عالیشاه فرمان خانی و حکومت قندماغ باخلعت

گرانمایه و اسب با زین طلا و شمشیر مرصع با معتمد امیر اصلان سردار درقلعه

بیات بهندر رسیده و لیمیر اصلان سردار علیه تحف و هدایا بمرحوم پناه خان

هم فرستاده که وکلای خانان را که از طرف پناه خان مرکول سنه بجویند باخلع و الفات

و حرمت معطوف داشته مرحمتها کرده بجویند پس اول اسم خان و حکومت مرحوم پناه

خان با فرمان عالیشاه مرلوزله مرحوم بارث بیت کبراز ان مدت طلبا

نگکشیده و سمع مرحوم پناه خان رسیده که علیقلی خان را که عالیشاه میکفتند

شاهرخ میرزا پسر مرحوم نادرشاه کشته در خراسان بمسند شاهی نشسته و هرج و مرج

در سرحد عراق و لو باکان و فارس ظاهر شده در آن جا پادشاه خان مرحوم عزم همت

بسته که ولایات کنجه و ایروان و نخجوان وارده ملکرا بتصرف خود آورده خوانین

آنجا بهار اطیع خودسا زد در قلیل مدت بصره را باددر و لویهنرا با رسیدن و وصایی و خویشی

و قواست مطیع کرد در شهر نه بسیل محصصا درکاه تذکر ملی روحلوم حالم که استنه داره

خوانین زله کان کنجه هرکه را دوخواه سش که بامر حکومت منصوب میکرد و هرکه را خواست

عزل میکرد و چند نفر از اولاد خوانین آن ولایتهای مذکوره آمده در قلعه در بلاغی در نکو خور

زوال کنهاه اری کنه تا اینکه مستقلا ان محمد حسن خان قاجار در سمت مازندران و عراق لوزر

معلوم شده باز از صاحب کاران و کار داران حضور مرحوم بنا هخان اراده وشش درفکر امور

حکومت غافل نخفته مانرده و حسب الأمر مرحوم بنا هخان مصلحه جنان کفند که چون در قریب تمام

طهر از وفات مرحوم نادرشاه با علیقلی خان و امیر اصلان سردار سدارا ورابطه کماه و دوستی منعقد لو

حالا می نخوه با محمد حسن خان جنان ربط و علاقه هسی نشه در آخر این اطراف جندان خان خبر نداریم

و هردر نیت که محمد حسن خان را تحریک و لو دلا بنفاق بدفع ما کهارنه ولایات و جشم قلع بامل

قشون قزل باش لجه در قلعه شه بلاغی ناب مقاومت جنان دشمن قوی و خوانین اطراف

نیا بالله بالهره مستاصل بشیم پس علاج و اقعه سی از وقوع بابد کرد قلعه را با بد که در انرو

کاستامات

کوهستانات در جای یک صعب و محکم و ابدی و پایدار آنست بنا که شوم که مطلقاً... قوی قرار...
بمجرد کوتی قلوثه یکمت قطع دایما کسان لعه از ایلغه که در کوهستانات خواهشه وارذملها
خبرداری و درست رسی قطع نشود این مطلب را با ملک شا هنظر کرد هم وقت دو خیر خواه...
در میان که نشسه اند بنا بر صوابدید ور جنبا یک ملک شاه هنظر یک به بنای قلوذه شوشی مقیم شه...
و چند نفر از اشنا صردان وحجب ذف حضور خه فرمسار ملاحظه اطراف وجو آب جای...
که هور اندرون همین قلوذه که آب دریک که ست مکرم و سرچیمه کوپاک که کفایت به چندان جمعیت...
٨٠١٤ لی قلوذه نمر که کس کجایها منظنون جیا که کنده معلوم نمفذ که در اکثر جیا بها چه بجده آر...
این خبرا بعرض مرحوم بنا ها ن رسا نید نه خولان بانچند نفر از خاصان آمده ملاحظه کرده...
عزم جزم بر بنا قلوه کذاسته اند بنا تاریخ سلای سنه ١١٧ مطابی سنه المبحبه سنه ١٧٦٤ ام رعایا...
سا کنین قلوذ ت بولائی وخا نوادان عیان وشخاص وملک ن وسلار ان و که خدا ن ان ایلقا...
ولبضری دیا ت را که بنده در اندرون این قلعه ستنی دله که بمع آبا دای فبد از آن دینی
نبوده مکم آنکه اعلی قریه نشوشی در طرف سرقی قلوه درشش دیرث سا کند مزرعه وجای علف آنها
بوست هراز فراکت کوی خلی که همه و خصوصا خانه و عماد ت خوار ادر ت مظوص معین کرد
بنای حصا روبلور با اوستاران ماهر وکا رکرده ان هسیا روکا کمکیده که بهان آن حصا
اودیوار یک بنا مرحوم بنا پناه خان لجه خراب شه مکرد لبعض جا یها که آثار ولبقیه معلوم ست ولوذ از کمال الزه

قلعه محمد حسن خان قاجار که پدر آقا محمد شاه است با لشکر عراق و لور با خان بعزم تسخیر قلعه شوشتر و وطع
کوه مردم پناه خان از ارس گذشته دارد چهار فرسخی قلعه شد ٠ اور گرده آنچه بدر و فکر ها
بخاطر گذرانیده که مرکه مرحوم پناه خان به ارطاعت نیاید و بقلعه شوشی مستولی شده مدت یک ماه
نشسته قادر نشته که چنان لشکر لبیبا رکجرای قلعه آید ملک بسیار از اهر و اشتر و سایر جاها پا
و رو را با ما لی تو لا و و نسر اباغ و دخفیه و اکگار غارت که حضر ها کلیه بعنوان محمد حسن خان رسانیده
در این اثنا خبر استعداد لو کریم خان زند در ملک فارس در شهر شیراز بسمع محمد حسن خان رسید که
جمعیت تمام درست کرده در عزم تسخیر عراق و مازندران است با این حال قلعه کریری و تصرف شیراز دارد
و کنیز بغیره را گذاشته با سرعت تمام بطرف عراق و فارس و مازندران حرکت کرده و تا رسیدن بخین
خان کریم خان زند تمامی ولایات فارس و یاره و یاره از ولایات عراق و غیره بتصرف آقا مستعد
و آماکه مقابله محمد حسن خان شده دار بطرف محمد حسن خان نیز بجمعیت کلی از آلو و با کنی و کیلانات
و غیره بعزم دفع کریم خان حرکت بصوب فارس نمد ٠ اما از آنکه کخت و حالت ارعطا یار پرودر
عالمیان است چند نفر از خاصان محمد حسن خان لشکر خیانت افکام اور کشته و سرشن را
بریده بنزد کریم خان برده نمد رمناصب بلند و انعامات کلیه بمردند از آنکه که تقصص
بزرکا و سردار ان از جان کارها مذمومه بسردار ان میرسه قاتلان محمد حسن خان با راست
رسانده از انام و انعام رحمت محروم کرده و دیکران نسبت به ٠ و انعمت خبر کبخ چنین
خیانت نشوند و بلدار مسدمه محمد حسن خان ٠ ایقان افشاه اور می جا از جمله

سردار ها

سرداران ماکرث و لیهم از و لایت اردویه صاحب دلیره شده به تمامی آلوزباکان تسلط یافته
مرخید به مرحوم بنا هخان ایلچی های سخندان فرستاده به اطاعت انکار خود دعوت کرده مرحوم
بنا هخان اطاعت جان سرداران را بحقیقت کجمر بار و خفت دانسته کجوابهای درشت
فرستاکهان اورا معطوف داشته لبراز مرحمت و رونقه الجین فتح خان جمعیت تمام از ایاال
و لامیهار آلوزباکان و اردوی دعیره منعقد گشته لعزم قلعه کیری و تسخیر قراباغ و دفع بنا هخان
برسر قلعه توشر آمده درماک نرستخیر برابر قلمو اوراکه ملکان محال حله برد و طالش که بطنا
با مرحم بنا هخان عداوت دکشتند به نعو فتح خان رفته درحال قلمو مدت ششماه نشست
مورومر عید د روز درمیانه مرحوم بنا هخان و قسمان فتح خان مبادله و مقابله رد دله ازهرحال
قسمون مرحوم بنا هخان بلمشکر قزلباش فانی شده درین مدت فتح خان کامر از نیش نبرد اور
برروز عسرت وشکست خود بماته مه که آخرالامر یکبد فمه با تمامی فسو نخفو از اروراره وپیاره و
پیاده های محالهای ملکان مذکورین بهیت اجتماع و جمعیت تمام همته بورش لیبیة
از اردوهانه شوشر لصوب قلیه عنور کفوند تا نیم ویرله قلمو رسیده و از اطراف بنا هخان مرحوم
با جوانان کار آمده نامی و لفنکجیان قجاق ایلات و محلها ررنزه و خبس و از کو اف سرکرده
سواره های ایلات با اقوام رسید مرحوم بنا هخان حمله آورده به قسمون فتح خان شکست عظیم
دله درره های عیسی و معبرهای تنک بکرفتن و کشتن درست کنام تا اودرهای فتح خان از کشتن
و الکندن و کشتن درست مرتبنبد تخمینا بقریب هزار نفر از سواره و پیاله قسمو فتح خان

دیوان برزش مقتول نوسکینه و خانین بعاصر با هزار پر نشانی و پشیمانی در اوده رخنه توقف کرده

مرحوم پاه خان باکیف و کرفتاران قشون فتحعلی خان مظفر و منصور نقلعه معا او دت کرده و شیع

خان افشار لدرار مقدمه امیکنه و شکست قشون و کفو لکشه ن زمستان بنای سازش و مصالحه

کدشته انجری ها ی کا رد با فرستاده به سم مغلظ تعهدات کرده که پا ه خان کرفتاران

را اسر او قشون اور امرخص نماید و مقام اتحا و هم نشین باشند که از روی راستی صیه خود را فرزند

بزرک او ابراهیم خلیل آقا عقد و عنا کنه ﮐﻪ در خویش و هم نشین ابدر خواهم شد و هم مشروط با اکه

ابراهیم خلیل آقا را روانه نزدمن کنه صدر اور ها شیرینی خورده و صیغه ا خوانده و هم س

روز در بنا مانده معا او ت نماید و بکیته خان جمع بر مرحوم پا ه خان نسه نفر از اولاد ناماور و اقوام

خود را معا او ت ابراهیم خلیل آقا بعنوان پا ه خان فرستاده که می فطن نامید مرحوم پا ه خان

اعتمار بقسمه مغلظ فتحعلی خان و فرستاده اولاد و اقوام خود کرده ابرا هیم خلیل آقا را با و سه نفر

از کده اینان روانه اور ها ی فتحعلی خان کهه فتحعلی خان ازین خبر خوشحال شده از اولاد خود

چنه نفر را به استقبال فرستاده ابراهیم خلیل آقا را با اعز از تمام و همسا ب عشرت سا ز و لوازم

داخل اور ها کهه دیدرسا را بها نه نموده هر روز ابراهیم خلیل آقا را با عشر ی تمام اور اور ها کهه داشته

و مکرر آوهار معتمد و شیر ینی نقلعه نفیسا پا ه خان فرستاده چنا که غالات ایشان ہهت که لازمه لقارت

ظاهری بکهه فریب دلهن و بار صلاح کا رخش ن نمی آورده اکه که لازمه قبارت سر لو دران

و روز بعد آوهده نوشکیر ان و کرفنا اوان خور اخلاص کرده رو زسیم ابراهیم خلیل آقا را با کله و اهل

محبس دار ابوشته تاقلوه ارومیه در بیخ جا توقف که برخستد پس بنا به خان مرحوم وا عیان واقع
از این مقدمه بنا یت عکنی و پریشان و پشیمان و با یوسف شا آخر الا مرحبن از عکبیز و پشیمان نبانده
صبر نبوده لبکر خلاصی فرزند خود و دفع فتحه خان در تدابیر و مصالح شدند از آنجا که پروردگار
عالمیان و خالق آفریند نوع بشر در این در آن که ان معین و یا در رسان رود اران وحق
شناسانت حضور ذا توفی الضرت معجل آنانت که در عهد و میثاق دا ذار خویش ان
نابت قدم و راسخ دم بخشند واز مکر و حیله که آخر او منجر به نرانش درجبران ات کار نیو مردین
اثنا خداوند عالم استقلال ام کریم خان زند که در حضرت عراق و فارس صاحب داعیه شده
لبوه مرحمت کرده با فتحه خان مزبور رسانی پر خوزش و ستیز کذاشته بلکه از اقوام خود را نامرد
بدفع فتحه خان کرده با لشکر عراق و فارس روانه آور بایکان سخت و فتحه خان نیز تجدد و ستیع
این خبر با تمامی قشون بهای آور بایکان و اطرا ف و جو انب قبر از رود لشکر کریم خان لعزم ملاقم
بعنا بله شتافته در حوالی اصفهان تلاقو فرقین در تدله لشکر کریم خان معلوب و خویش
کریم خان که سردار قشون بهم در آن معرکه مقتول شده فتحه خان مظفر با رجعه بلکه بپای
ولایات عراق علاوه متصرف شده مرحبت نمود لجراز وقوع این حادثه کریم خان زند بقصد
انتقام اقلام از ولایت فارس با عساکر گران و لشکر کشی عزیمت آور بایکان و دفع فتحه خان
نموده و بقتر از دروه بهآور بایکان معتمد نیز در مرحوم بنا خان فرستاده اظها رلطف
و مهر بانی و اکنار کرده نوشته با بمن مضمون مرقوم کرده لبوه که فتحه خان با با ه اه بکه دشتم

بلکه خون ریخته و باشما آنچه ناکرده باله از نقض عهد و قسم کا آورده و لپسر مزا اردو مکرد غدر
وحیله به کفخه آورده مجبوس کرده ست بایدکه آنچه درآن درار درم وقت مضا یعک مکر که
هم انتقام و هم خلاصی پسر تو که خوشنال شبات لطف العیس حمیر ست پناه خان السکونه
سباب را کجه دفع دشمن دروغ کار و حیله ساز غنیمت دانسته با قشون آراسته د کوار با لی
ناهض قسر لاغ در حضت کور باکیا بنگه کریم خان رفته و کریم خان هم اکبر لازم لله از تعظم وعزّت
وحرمت و انعام مضایقه نکرده با اتفاق برنع فتح خان ل اطرف و لایی لارومیه کزم عنان
شند وفتح جان آنچه از ولایتها درزیر حکم خود لله با قشون کلّی دحمعیت تام لمقا بلر
آمده هرار لسکر طرح حنک انداخته آخرالامر فتح خان مغلوب قور قلعه اورومیه
مصدرکشته بلجبار چند روز بغیر از اطاعت چاره ندیده و از اطراف کریم خان
امید نوید هم دبه به نگه کریم خان آمده وقلعه اورمیه متصرف کریم خان در آمه
مستقر کود و کریم جان خود را وکیل بشاه لیران نام دلت نهاده بولی انکه
جون درایران همرز بلرنا بشاه مستقل نیت ناخروج و جلوس باشاه خود وکیل بارنا
هستم از آنگهه به کریم خان وکیل میکفتند ابراهیم خلیل آقا که در اروبه مجوس
لحه خلاص لهه و کبصورحق آورده اسب و شمشیر و خلعت و فرمان خانی وحکومت
قلاع را دله با اعزاز و ساسلام بقرلاغ راهی نموده و به پناه خان اورا لطف

و مهربانی و از راه مرید محبت خواهش کنند که باید چند وقت در نگو من باشد که تلافی
صدمت و امانت برای آری در حضور جمع ولایت شیراز که مرحوم ابراهیم خلیل خان دختر
خود را بغ شده اعلا قسم اع و سائر ولایتها مطیع و منقاد او شده در سند حکومت
خان مستقلاً و بدون اطاعت یکمر حکم از کسی کننده کوه من نشست و مرحوم بنا ه خان
مدت قلیل در شهد شیراز که دار السلطنه کریم خان بو مانده اذ موهد رسیده در شیراز جمبر
خدا وحهلمرشه نعش او را باحرمت تمام بقلاع آورده در ملک حلال و زرخرید دفن که
اخیار به اعظام مشورت مدفون کردند رحمة الله علیه و از کاره و وقایع که رو دله معلوم
و بعد از وفات بلاورثه مرحوم مدت دوازده سال و حکومت مرحوم بناه خان شه ده روز بر دو
فتح و نصرت و یکنمت دولت او هرطرف مرحوم بنا ه خان رو دله دا کثر و آلات لوز پاکیان
حکم که در ذ باطاعت او شده اند و کریم فتح خان را باخود برده تا احوال اصفهان
آنجا که بهشون کریم خان دعوا نمه و خویش کریم خان بقدر رسیده بود در آنجا نشو
خان را بقدر رسا نید و بانتقام خود رسید چنانچه با مرحوم بنا ه خان هم نقض
عهد کرده و قسم دروغ یاد نموده و حیله و تذویر کرده بجو بروز د کار رعالم برفوی
بسزای عمد خود رسانیده از لکم مکر و حیله و دروغ بغیر از ضرر مندامش خسارت
نفع کدار نشه چنانکه حقتعالی مندکان خود را از مکر و حیله و قسم دروغ و تقصی عه

نهر فرموده و تجربه رسیده که هر کس بدوست خفه و به ولی نعمت و بزرگ خفه دروغ
گوید و حیله و خیانت ورزد معرفت و مرحمت بزرگ را که پرورد کار عالم اورا
بزرگ کفته است ناشناس و چشم پوش کند در جزای آن غیر از خسارت و ندامت
حاصلی نمی یابد و الله یجزی جزاء ان خیر الخیر و ان شر افشر نمدلا.

فصل پنجم در بیان حکومت مرحوم ابراهیم خان و قواعد و وقایع آن زمان

مرحوم ابراهیم خان از تاریخ سنة المسلمین ۱۱۷۴ که بنا برحسا ب سنة المسیحیه ۱۷۵۶
تا سنة ۱۲۲۱ هجری برحسا ب سنة المسیحیه ۱۸۰۶ باشد در مسند حکومت
قراباغ بدون اطاعت و انقیاد به پادشاهان ایران و روم با استقلال نشسته
حکمرانی کرده و امرای ولایت به رشیروان و شکی و کنجه و ایروان و نخجوان
و خوی و قراداغ و تبریز و القبیل حتی مرحمه و قابلان که که سرحد عراق و آذربایجان
تا نذ کشته عزل و نصب خوانین و لامبها همه حسب الحکم و امر مرحوم ابراهیم خان
شده با والی ولایت اورا د داغستان که عمه خان بن نوصان خان بوست
خوشبین کرده خواهر مکرمه عمه خان را به عقد و نکاح خود آورده هر وقت که ضرور و دور کار
بهیمت از ولایت داغستان و لزکی قشون خواهش نمه با اتفاق عمه خان و سایر
سرکرده کان بولایت قراباغ آورده به هر جا که لازم می شد با سیر کردگان اولاد
خود و قشون قراباغ فرستاده و با طاعت خودی می آورده اورا

مع ذلك با خوانین ولایتها که ش همسول وقرا داغ دخور وکنجه با بستند هم خونشی
کرده خواه با زور و خواه با خوشیشر همه اطاعت ابراهیم خلیل خان را باپا ن ودل
قبول کرده لذ حنتی از ولایتها رتبریز وقرا داغ لبعض محلها را لبسر که کان نام بر بسم
انعام شفقتت که امه داز مدخفرآن نفع کبول رباشه و هلت و جلال ابراهیم ن
اگرچه ا سم پا ش هنیداشته اتا مانند مارث ان ابرلان شده ولر اولد و جفا د خوابین
ولایتها مذبور ه همه وقت درقلعه توشکر بر سم زوال درجه و درحق و مرحوم ابراهیم خان ساکن
کشته اند آزما نیک لبواز فوت کریم خان آقا محید خان لبسر خان حسن خان نا ظا
که در سه شهرشبراز زوال لهسمت فرار کرده دلقعا و سلطنت نمه چید سال لعد از کوشش
بعراق و فارس تسلط یافه شهرطران را دارالسلط خوخصه درسنه ١١٠٧ ا نسلطین
برلایت لفوربا کتا ن آمه تمام ولایتها طرف جنوب ارس را کحط تصرف آورده
سواد ولایت ابردان و طالش و بمرحوم ابراهیم خا ن که قبل از ان خلعتت و شمتشیر
دائب با دبن ولام طلا د فرساله به اطاعت خ دعوت که له اطاعت زبا ن و
نا رفت ظاهری داّمد دفرت اجر درسبا نه اکرچه بوقوع میر سید از انجم ابراهیم خا ن
عبدالقهبر عمورکله خورا با میرند ولها رلو که مرد کا ردان و نیرین زبان
له با لنقا و عنران زوال به نعلقا فرستا م لهند وشا هم با آهزام وکمال

حرمت در حضور خفیه نگهداری میکرده و وقتیکه در ولایت کرمان بالطبع خان زند

کہ دشمن آقا محمد خان بود و خوش نفس جوان رشید و سخی و صاحب داعیہ بوده و پاره امرا راکه

باعث برهم زده که باشد ادیانه با ابراهیم خلیل خان و آقا محمد شاه ظاهر مکشت

عبدالصمد کر کریان با میرزا اولی بهادر لو و چند نفر نوکر فرار که معاودت در روز املیک

کرده در کنار رودخانه قزل اوزن که جا باری میش از وقت آمده با لای قریہ سرجم

خبر کرده بودند با لو و لکواره را هہنار راکہ آمدہ با عبدالصمد دعوا کردہ عبدالصمد کر را با

زخم گلولہ ارز از انز زخمہ ارمنہ با رفقا خفیہ گرفتند و میرزا اولی و امرا انیز دستگیر کردند

عبدالصمد کر را انجا با همان زخم گلولہ مرحوم شدہ و سایر گرفتاران را با میرزا اولی الحضور

شاه بردہ بودند در شہر طہران محبس کردہ بودند و قتیکہ آقا محمد شاه در سر قلعۂ بیوشی

مربیو از طرف مرحوم ابراہیم خان که دا کا ہالتجی آمدہ و درفت مرکی بویندی میکہ فوم آقا محمد شاه

از سفارت مرحوم ابراہیم خان راغضبا که شدہ حکم نوشتہ لچہ که میرزا اولی را و اظہار

بردہن توب لسبہ انذا احتر بودند و سایر گرفتاران را که ہمہ دہ نفر بودند لقبذ رسید

احمدیو باقی نگذاشتہ بودند رحمۃ اللہ علیہم **فصل ششم** در بیان وقایع وفاتمہ آقا

محمد شاه چون در بیان ابراہیم خان و آقا محمد شاه دشمنہ کدورت و مبرہغذ که ظاہر شد

در سال ۱۲۰۹ با لشکر کران و عساکر فراوان بجہہ تسخیر ولدتہا ریقلیس

وایروان

دایروان وقراباغ دطالش بصوب آذربایجان آمده اولا علیقلی خان شاهسون را که ...

سرکرده آن آقامحمدشاه ... باساتیر خوانین برسر قلعه ایروان فرستاده وخفش با تمامی

لشکر عراق وفارس وآذربایجان وخراسان برسر قلعه شوشی آمده درکیفر سخ قلعه درنزل

فوجان اوردو کرده ودوائی تعلیس عالیه ارکلی خان وحاکم ایروان کهن خان وحاکم طالش

میر مصطفی خان همه با مرحوم ابراهیم خان ... هم قسم لبودند که اطاعت آقامحمدشاه را ...

دراعانت و آکار ... یکدیگر متفق باشند باره ایلات قسرلاغ را اسمت تفلیس وباره بصوب

شیروان کوه مصطفی خان هر درولایت شیروان منصوب کرده ابراهیم خان بجه فرستاده

با باقی ایلات وقشون را که درسیاه ... دفتر کهواز درکوهست ... قسرلاغ قوداز درون قلعه

سکنز دله بیاره دسواره لشیاره داز آنکه ... ومیلهاو قسرلاع جمع کهه با تواری کات کلیه آنباب

قلعه دادری باشته با توپهای بزرگ وکوچک مستعد قتال وجدال باشند ... مدت سه روز

آقامحمدشاه درحوالی قلعه لهم باجماع قشون کران قاردشته که ازدو خانه اطراف قلعه م

پنج دیرتی لقلوبی شوق بصوب قلعه عبور نمایند سواره وبیاره قشون قرلاغ دسرکرده کان

ایلات و دنیات وملکان محال درنده درنراق وخاین درپیشه ها وراهها وکهره

درست تسلط وعارت لقشون قرلباش کثام هرروز فوج فوج ازلهب واستره و

... سر و ساز بردرگ ت وکاروان غله که از ولایتها به اور حوالی آورده غارت کرده و اسیر نموده

بعضی در مرحوم ابراهیم خان برمی آوردند بدینگونه بعد از آن فاطر یکجا رومنا ط و مکتفی نشدبه بخش منات

داس خوب بدمنا ط بنا بر حساب پول آن قت بسیار میعر و خسته هورا طراف اور وحی خود

محکم دحوب بر جهاترتیب لعلف عار در مبارا قسون قلاع شبها به اور جه شبخون آلله شور

پیاله حمال درنده بکشب باجمعیت رفته یک برج برزگ راکه از تفنگجیان خاصه خفه آقا چپنه

مظفر نیمکردند متصرف درآورده درک عشهانی تفنگجیار القدر رسانیده و رهسه لغر زنده قمت

طلوع صبح بعد ورحوم ابراهیم خان آوردند روز دشب آرام به قسون قرلباشی برلوبنوسته

وجیاردفعه خفاش با قسون کله بعزم عبور کرده ان از رفوجانه لیجوب قلعه آمده ازنظرف میاله ها

چاپک و سوار برقوجان برکهکان بمقابله رفته بادعواوجگها برحبوانه مغلوب خفه مظف

کردند ناآنکه جولفخان حاکم کنبه با ملاک مجبون ملک محال حله برذک از مرحوم ابراهیم خان بردکردانشده

در ولا سکنبه درکنو جوادرخان بر بجوکفی سواآقا مپشاه آمده بنا برصلاح دران ازسر قلعو باهر ازرکت

وبرپشانی کوچ کهمکه بصدر بفلیس و تسخیر کرجستان حرکت کرذنه مرحوم ابراهیم خام قبل ازحوکت

شاه این خبر برلو لیماه والک کرجستان رسانذه که آقامپشاه ازتسخیر قلعو عابرکشته وضروراً

که ازقسون دچار برا برادوحصار کرده صلح دیده که بلکه این سگ خفوارا درتسخیر نفلیس دغارت

دهات کرجستان درست نماید درتوارک دفع فساد و قتل اولاوکشته آقامحدشاه و کربه رفتن

وآسایش چار برا وقسون خود درحصرمطه درست... آغذام ادوه که مدت یکاله

مبلغ رسالۀ زحمت را غنیمت دانسته از آنجا عازم تسخیر ولایت کرجستان و شهر تفلیس شدند چون

با ملک مجنون در هر جا میشود و قشون در همان شاه ۵ بودند لیکن از ورود سمت تفلیس در اندک وقت

شهر تفلیس سلطنت واعلای شهر و سایر دیار تحت رسد غارت و اسیر که و شهر آتش زده معاقه

لصوب آوریاجان کردند در هر جا ارکان زخواکرد زخوا قریۀ جوله ارس و کشته در جست معان ن فسل ق کردند

رمستان در را کاسپرریزد وقت بهار که قلوه اردان در ارسب هم مستخر کشته مانده بودند باز در رحت قارس

انقلاب شده شورش بسیار در جست کردن و غیره لبو بعزم اصلاح لان ولایت فارس عزیمت کردند در

بهار که شاه دوست ۵ فارس لبو مرحوم ابراهیم خان به دوال کرجسته هم تکلیف کرده و از داغستان

قشون آورده و شهر گنجه را محاصره کردند که باعث خرابی تفلیس شده بودند در ازای مدت جوله خان با راطا

کرده لیسر دخواهر خود را بمرحوم ابراهیم ن در وال دله شرطه و عهد کرد که از حکم داطاعت مرحوم ابراهیم ن

سیرون نشود و قوه و وقت دعوا هم ملک مجنون مقتول شد   در آن وقت که هنوز آغا محمد شاه در

سمت فارس و خراسان لبو سردار اعظم میارالی استف و ایران و عراف زبوف با لسکر گرا

و هاسن سلطنم حسب الامر و فرمان ایمراطوریۀ عظما لیقطریه وارد رخیت در بندشه قلوه دربند را

مستخر کرده وارد حوالی اشهر شماخ رکشته او در کو کند مرحوم ابراهیم خان با سبر خود ابوالفتح خان را

چند نفر از سبکزلقه لان قسرلاغ با لخف دبرایه و سبان لحبب با رضا از عربت تمام بحضور سبر دور

اعظم دلیران زبوف فرسام و از صمیم خاطر اطاعت و اظهار مخلوص و حداقت دولت علیه

روسیه کرده و عریضۀ عقیدت قریضه هم بحضور ایمراطوریۀ عظما و نوشته بودند سردار معظم الیه

آنچه لازمه حرمت و تعظیم بود در باره ابوالفیض خان و سایر بیکزاده کان قسم؟ ؟ نع بعد از آنکه دیگر خصه

مرحوم ابراهیم ؟ ؟ بلوا بمعیته فرستاده مرحوم خان والبیک آقا نسرخف لاز راه در بند و قر لادر روانه حضور

امپر الطور دیه عطا کرده وکف و هدایا قیمتی درما انفت در مرا؟ بکنفر کنیا زکیبه مرحوم ابراهیم خان فرستاده

امید وار مرحمت امری با ؟شا ؟ عطا؟؟ کرده بهر خوانین الطرا؟ را معلوم شه که ابراهیم ؟ نیز

خود را کحضور سردار اعظم فرستاده همه ثان در میر مصطفی خان طالش و مصطفی خان شیر وایی و

چولفضا ؟ ختر خوانین ایروان و نخجوان و خوی و قراداغ الجزا یا کحضور مرحوم ابراهیم خان فرستاده

لمهار که ما از صلاح دید مرحوم ابراهیم خان بیرون نمی شویم جنا نکه الطت ؟؟ دولت اروسیه ؟؟

صلاح دیده اند تحکا ما سالک طریق ادالت واطاعت با؟شاه مرحمت مدار اروسیه را

قبول خواهیم کعه مرحوم ابراهیم خان فرستاده و نوشتنی ست حوانین مزبور مجددا تما؟ روانه

حضور سردار اعظم زیا؟ف کردند ؟؟؟؟ اکرده بعظمت وشوکت والی کرجستان مند سایر خوانین

سیر دان و خور و ابردان و غیره ببنجه اوجاق قدیم و دو؟ است عراص والایت عظیم دکشت ا؟؟

باز در مهر مصالحی از صلاح دید مرحوم ابراهیم خان کنی در نظر کردند لمبسب اؤکه مرحوم عمه خان

حاکم آوار دا؟ستان و سایر بزرگان اکنا یا لمبسب خویشی و قرابت با مرحوم ابراهیم خان قطع

ومنقاد میشدند هرگاه حیا نا کدوزا درمیان والی کرجست و مرحوم ابراهیم خان بروقوع میرسید

بنا براثا زه مرحوم ابرا هیم خان عمته خان و سا؟ بزخوانین دا؟ستان با لشکر لبار لطرف

کرجستان

گرجستان حرکت کرده خزائن بسیار بعهدی آورده دندجنبکه در ۱۱۹۹ که دررّی درمیانه

والی مرحوم ابراهیم خان طاهرشده عمه خان آوار ،افسون لبا رکرجستان

حرکت کرده قلعه د سقناق دکومش خان سه ابتفرق آقله حلی لبا رنقدربرسانده

ماباقه عیال واطفال ساکنین آنجا را سیرکه داراطراف جواننده ای بسیار غارت

کمه بولایت آخسقه سبزدسلیمان پاش رفته زمستان درآنا مانده ازسلطان روم خلعت

والهام بسیار حاصل کنوند وقت بهار باز ازکرجستان عازم دغستان لهبذ قلعه واطفال را

کمه درسر حد دکورکاه لهم ازکنیازها ابا شیرضا کنیازبا اهی وعیال خو در پان قلعه سکنی

دکشت دقلعه محکم لهم محاصره کرده لهراز محصره بنقلو مسلط یافته لبا ری را ز اهی قلعه نقدربرسانده

سائراطفال دعیال قلورا سیردمال دهالس آن را غارت کمه لهجوزه دیکنیفر دختر

ابا شیرضا کنیا زرا باپاره سیاب رسم تحف دهدایا روانه نزد مرحوم ابراهیم خان کمه

لهنیز ابراهیم خان نجبالک لکاح خو آورده لهبنذ دیکنیفر پسر دیکنیفر دختر از همان دختر

ابا شیرضا کنیا زبرجعو آمدند دیکنفر دختر کنیا ز ابا شیرضا را خفته خان نکاح

کمه بجوازه حرم اوله   ازنتیجه با احتیاج دالغ مرحوم ابراهیم خان لبا میر بوضع

ذلکرش خوانین میردوان وسک دکنجه دایرودان دخوی وقرا داغ دجوان دطالش

و تبریر دعوانین سا هسون دستقوم در اطاعت مرحوم ابراهیم خان به تمرد و تخلف و قرار نهود

دال بقلیس نیز از راه اخلاص و حسب طا باطاعت دولت علیه اردوسیه رضا دلم ایلی و زلیصه

فرستاد به واهم جمیاً را اطاعت خص سین بدولت علیه شد و لهذر که مقدم دوات امر اصر

یه عظیمی رود لقسا اعظم زبوف ابوالفتح خان را با پیکر لقه کان وکده اند قراع با اعزاز و حرمت

والهم کنی موطوف دکست بایه چکم پارته مرحوم باول مساعدت خود راحال مرحوم ابراهیم خان کهو بند

ازین خبر از سر کلی رود لقه دهم سبب زیاده عداوت آقا محمد سا ه شر چونکه در خاطر داشت که

بلکه صدر کله خاص کنیه بطرزن ملاد میه مرحوم ابراهیم خان مطبح خفسا زد با سراعت وارک

مرحوم ابراهیم خان بدل جنگ و زراع بدولت دائم القرار روسیه قوت کشیده ازبار نا سلام

و ایران اورا بغیظ کنی افنه عزم جرم مدفع مرحوم ابراهیم خان لسه دقت بها با تشکر سپاه

یصوب لقور پاکه نا حرکت کهند جهنموت سه راه لے در با درودائم قسرابع از آفت سماوی

وارضی محصول علم و سار محبوباب به دست سیا مده قحط تمام رودلقه حسر منطه علم کمبر رسیده طر

که یک چپور ت کندم ب پار جب ب بول آلوفس مبلغ جهاردنج مناط بادشوار میدلقه کار

با نظفار رسیده دلشکر قرلباش و آقامحمد سا ه کبا رودو ارس کسیه ند از نجط آزوق و

زحمات چند سال دیگر توقف در قطه سوشی در مقا بل رجان بارسا ه قوی سکندلعه لاعه

با اهل وعیال و اولاد و احفاد و اقوام دعا مذ دعیاک سکها سعروف حملص و مللانا ن باتر

از قلعه کوچ که غرمیت صوب جار روتله کفند... درآنجا استقامت که اکر از داغستان ذکرحبان

وسائر ولایتها اعانتی و تدارک شود بمقابله آمده شوند والا از آنجا بداغستان خانه خویش خود

عمّه خان حاکم آذور رذته خود را ذرست... آقا محمّد شاه کفوظ دارند و از جمله خوانین که درآن زمان

دوجمهور ابراهیم خان لفوز در دجدایی حمیار که فار مرحوم فصیر خان داوراخان و عطا خان از آنجا همون

وسلیم خان حاکم ولایت شکی که او هم دارا خان لفوز ما سیها ری و لایت شکی وثه کول داولاد در

اخفا دمیان... و آقا محمّد شاه درکنار ارسی خبر بیرون شدن ابراهیم خان را از قطو شنیده تقریب

سه هزار نفر سوار ده ما مرکرده که آن فرسا کو لبو لاخبر دار لهم ملکه درراه کنی دکن اکر رسیده شوند دیان

لشکر مرسوله قزل باشی درحوالی کوربی لا دوتر بر به کوچ و جمعیت... دوجمهور درجم ابراهیم خان لفوز رسیده

دعوا کمه از کوچ و کلفت وسائر کوهها ضرر رشده لهو اقا یا رکشی وجهانس باز نار کوچ را اغات

عهم از آنجا معادوت کرده لهوذ... مرحوم ابراهیم خان از ذکر عبرمنفه از ولایت شکی کذشته داخل

خاک بلکان و جار شده کدخدایان در روسا ء جا روتله همه شان اکر جه از آقا محمّد شاه به آن

فرمان رسیده لهو که مرحوم ابراهیم خان در خوانین دیکری... ملکه شته نکذارد که ابصوب داغستان

بیرود اما جون اما احوا روبلکان در داریم در مدت ها رسید از ابراهیم خان محبت و الفا ما

کلیه خاطر که لهوز و دهم دقت درا طاعت و کنام امر مرحوم ابراهیم خان لهو در لعظ... وخبر خواهی لهوذ

در روه جهرام و مرهما ن نوذر بعمل آقله رضا مندی خاطر را بکار آوردند مدت بیت روز در خاک

بلکان ذقف دکشته لهوند که خبر مقتول شدن آقا محمّد شاه درا وردن قلعه شوستی

بمرحوم ابراهیم خان رسید و مقدّمهٔ مقتول شدن آقا محمدشاه چنان بود که ابراز رفتن

ابراهیم خان از قلعهٔ صوبو بلکان آقا محمدشاه بدرون مانع ذخلی قلبی شوشی شده مدّت یک

هفته مانده میکشت بجهه امری که رضا و خاطرش نبوده است به دو نفر خدمتگذار آن مقرّب خود

صفر علی بیک و عبّاس بیک نام ناخوش و غضبناک شده عهد کرده که اگر طلوع صبح کرده و

هر شما را سیاست عظیم خواهم کرد چون آن دو میدانستند که در کوته و فرموده او به وقت تغیّر

تبدیل نمی یابد از خوف جان خونبار قتل او را قبل از طلوع صبح از وم شمرده و قت طلوع صبح که

شاه از خواب بیهوشما باخنجر تیز ذبح شده شاه را بقدر رسانده در ها البته و بازو

بند و تاج و جواهر شاه را بکوته به نزد صادق خان اشقاقی رفته حقیقت ما با و ملا

کردند صادق خان از خوف شاه این قول را اعتنا نکرده از بسکه از طرف شاه اطمینان

و خاطر جمع نداشت و از جان خود به دقت برسان دهراس آن مربع این نقدر را حیله شاه تصوّر

کرده با دور کرد آخر الامر با نسیم ها ملاحظه خاطر جمع شاه کرده باز با کمال خوف برسنور

سابق آمده داخل عمارت مرحوم میناراول مایور محمد حسن آقا فرزند بزرگ مرحوم ابراهیم خان که آنا

محمدشاه در آنجا منزل کرده ذخ شده دربارها بالوب تمام بها اوطاق کوتهٔ جفته بیه کرده را

برد کشته سر فرو آورده آهسته آهسته داخل اوطاق شده و صفر علی بیک هر چیز بیک با و دلداری

دله باز خایف مستعد صفر علی بیک پیشتر داعلی شاه لجاو را او مرشاه را کشیده جسد مجروح او را

پاره پاره شده چنانچه با دمضهر فی الغور صادق خان تاب نگرده ایشان باز و بند و تاج جهانی راشته
بهمنزل خود آمده آواره دلکه شاه همرا بصوب کنج و کرجستان مقرر داشته سمت باشی قوابچ خو
و قنون سقاتی از قلعه مروش و ازجمله قاتلان شاه عباس نام را از ار انقت خو برده و صفر علی
از قلعه مانده فرار از فتن صادق خان براعت نکشیده بلوه که خبر گشته مقتول شاه در اندرون قلعه
شهرت یافته خوانین قزل باش هرکس را آمیه و پریشان با قوابچ خویش انکه بدرک نوح فوج
رو بکریز نهاده اند الا شهر نکنه هرکس را بدست آمده الحی ـ که دخل عمادت شده اند در وقت تاراج
اموال و کسباب و فرش و فروش و سایر بها طلا و نقره و جواهرات شاه همی محمد بیک برد
ملکه مرحم الابراهیم خان ارجوان شجاع در کشیده و مشهور لوجه جبر دارد چنین نفر ملازمان انکه در عمارت
گرفته هرکس که انکه بدرک رسیده بمه برده بلوه با باغی را از درت آدم ها که که آنکه از آلات جواهر
و طلا و ظروف طلا و نقره و فرش و غیره نقد و جنس مانده بلوه بهمی مقرر شده د ار عمارت شاه
قد حسن آقا حر و نقد کناذه و عمارت خو گرده در اندرون قلعه حکم دیوان مشغول شه وسرا آقا گده
که برده نبوند در مراقفت کنیفر از حذ مکذر ازان قدیمی با عرضیه خو به بلگان کذ متمم ابراهیم
فرسادنه فجراز انکه مربسپاه کرحضور ابراهیم خان رسیده دربت یقین شده که شاه واکشده اند نشاه
باحرمت نمام که از رویه نجابت و حرمت بعد غسل دله و کفن گرده با ملا ارخوب و معتبر
لازمه واحبات رامی دانسته فرستاده در مقبره از مقام بر عظام عظماء جار ذفون گردند

مدت سه ماه کمهم پاره موانع معاودت بصوب سراغ رود مذکوره در یلکهان توقف کردند از هر طرف
مخصوصاً والی گرجستان وجولوخان حاکم کنجه ومصطفی خان شیروانی تحف و هدایا فرستاده اظهار
اتفاق و یکجهتی میکردند چونکه چنان پاشاه که دشمن قدیم به وفات یافته وهمه خوانین آذربایجان
وغیره همه وقت عظمه و شوکت و نظام امر وحکم مرحوم ابراهیم خان را در وقت تمامی دیده به همه در اطاعت
لهو و مهیو می ستند که مش از همه بجهه خیریت جویان ایشان در صاد خاطر شریف ایشان را بابقه حضرت حکمه
مربوط دارند وخدمتگی در دینا بس قراباغ تا رسیدن مرحوم ابراهیم خان با مرحکومت مشغول بودند
مگر از توقف مدت یکی در یلکهان عمر خان اوار و سایر سرکرده گان داغستان با تدارک کان کلیه
از خورد نی و پوشیدنی و قشون بسیار به کمک مرحوم ابراهیم خان آمده لوازم خویشی و عهد بنی در روبه مهابه
و شایسته چنان امیر اعظم که کجا آوردند که بمکه نیتنها در باب مرحخان و اولاد نامدار و مکهار قراباغ
ملکه در باره خوانین شاه همون و اولاد سکهار ایشان از تعارف حرجر وخورد نی قصوری نکند داشته
بعد از نزک موت ها ماه لجراز ور دویبه خان با قشون داغستان ومرکرده کان دایا ایث کولن
وقراباغ از یلکهان غرمیت تحراباغ کنید ومرحم ابراهیم خان قبر از انکه غرمیت قراباغ که شود یلکهان
محمدیقی خان را که آن قتر محمدیقی آقا میکفتن باجد نفر از اولاد سکهای قراباغ روانه و
ماه نسیر جهه بهو در داخل قراباغ شده ۱۵۱ قراباغ لجراز ورده معظم الیه مرتکب یاره هفذا فنا
نشه از سری آواز تمرد بیرون شده ومحمدیک که زور جوانی و غرور و علاوه با عز در

چنان جهت

چنان جلادت و حباب که هر پاشهری بدت اور رسیده مبالا فریقه وسا دس شیطط نشده از در

مخالفت دا ماد لا عنیمی در آمده بود مبرقان مهدیقخان که با بکر الله خان د اضر قلاع شده

اکرچه ظام مهراحمد بک پاره روبه ومهربانی با بعد آورد ه لاف اخلاص نورستزنده که از اثبیس مرحوم

خان ببردل نشد اما باطن هوس حکومت لسپر اقام از اهبره واوبخش ولوف خانان و

خانان جمع که در فکر حکومت شده به ومهدیقخان لنجب ضرورت مدارا که پرده ارکا

عهدائتن که از پیش نمیرفت کاه درتسمتر از اطرافها دکاه در اندرون قلعه براه میرفت وجمیعت را

عرضه داشت سخفر مرحوم خان که منتظر بیوند اکر خبر مرحوم ابراهیم خان رسیده مرحم که

حسن آقا را که فرزند ارشد دبزگتر مین اولاد به با لصد نفر قشون لرک وسرکرده کان قراغ با

سرعت تمام راهی فرمهومد که آواره درقه مرحم خان را که دک شیده ارله دارد که ایلاقلاع را

کوچنیده لسبت ارس بیه درکا رارس توقف کهمهم از مخالفت زیر مجد د درقه مرحوم مجد حسن لعا

درته فرسخی قلعه درکرده گرس جمعیت مدرک وقشون د هراعانهان اولهسبرفت

آنها رسیده اهالی قراغ لهبرازمثاه قشون ومرحم آقار اهمهشان فوج دوج کدمت آقا

ودست بوسی آمده ایلات که جمع که یه درسیه ه وصحرا اجاکاه نه لف فرساله مدرک

کهضور خواستند اکرحه حمدرک دردفه اول خان لف دهرسان شده آخرلاله مخاطر جمع حاضرکه

بحضور مرحوم محمد حسن آقا آمده ودست بوسی بعد آورده با خاطر جمع در حضور بطه است وحمد بعد لذ
اسرار که در وقت استقلال آن خان یک باعث نزارت شده لهذا در برابر حقه که یک به یازده
وسیت آن آن امر مقیر مخارو دبیکان مهدیقلی خان که در اندرون قلعه لهذا برد در دو بتر مرحوم آقا
دکه نتین آن آن باقشون از زیر ابر قلق کا مشتق لهد کا را که عمو زاده او کرد بنده مجوس کرده بود
مرحوم حسن آقا ایلات قراغ را حال جمع والطمان لهذو همحه لهار احکمها نوشته همه را بمشغول
شدن کار ودر بار دکا سیر امر فرمودند تا آنکه ابراهیم خان با یک قشون ومتعلقان و
نصیران دعط خان ثنه مکون وارد ودخل قسر باغ مشدند فصل المقتم در بان
مقدما مجید که بهراز گشته شدن آقا گشاه ومعا فوت ابراهیم خان از بلگان بقرلاغ
رود له جبراز لکه مرحوم خان بقرلاغ رسیده در مقر حکومت قرار کرفت الا لی ولایت از
قحط درحمات برتیان آن دیا اوضاع و بسیاری از ابلت لعه ات متفرق بولایس کرجستان
وکنجه ولایردان وشیروان وانات حتر بولایتها ردم رفته و مان دولت نما تا نارت رفته اکرصه
خوانین قرب وجوار درطا هر خلاف اطاعت و دربستی میز دند اما باطنا صلاح خیرت حقلی ۲۶
طالب میشدند از آنجا مصطفو خان شیروان وقتیکه ابراهیم خان در ملک لهذا محمد حسن خان
بر لو وبرزک سلیم خان را آورده واعانت کرده در ولایت کش تا م حکومت کانت که مبالا
سلیم خان که دامار مرحوم ابراهیم خان است درکش نجکو کمش نشسته خلاف بکو متران رنه وحمه یک

جبراز لکه

چراز آنکه مرحوم محمد حسن آقا باوطائر حمیر دولود منتد سایر دعوانین درعیال این مسئله

مرحوم پناه خان خوف جان مطلقا نجی طر نمیر سید بخ از راه جوانی و غرور دولت کتبا زکبیر دفته

با محمد حسن خان ... لو بنار راشتر کناشت محمد حسن خان اورا فرصت یافته که من مرد کور...

وار حکم مصطفر خان بجان آمده ام دخترم را بتو عقد میکنم بزدمن آمده و به حکومت ولایت

ملک قیام مرئلی محمدک یا بگو نسخها فرلعینه شده از اولاد نامدار وعم بزرگ زادست کشیده

به کوة محمد حسن خان رفت محمد حسن خان بجبر دورتو محمدک را کرفته محبوس که تبمای آنکه از اخوان

اسباب دلقد جنس که ازنفع محمدک لهب صاحر که مصطفر خان که با محمدک درسال اول فتم

خوانلهب حریمید وبراو اورا درعوض پدر خود کشته لهب به محمد حسن خان آلقم فرستاده حمدک را

برده لقتر رساند وار آنجهته که مراو از لقه مرحوم ابراهیم خان را همچنین جدد که اکشته لهب خائف لهب

برشمر قراباغ دست که اه داز نطرف محمد حسن خان هم دشمن شده دجو لهفان حاکم کنجه بدستور

درمین اشا حضر رسیدکه قتل شاه که اورا با بخان هسردار میکفته وار طرف آقا محمد شاه درشراز

دولایت فارس والی لهب خبر قتل شاه دانستنده از آنجا ایلقا رکه دافر طهران شده

سخرمیه وکسهاب دکه باشاه ها صاحبی که درهسنده درشاهی نشست وله نطرف صادق خان

شقته قی منور که لذقلم نوشتی فرار کرده به آمد بکان سوی حاصر دیه لوای داعیه برداشته

وجمعیتی که بر سر خود جمع که معزم تسخیر طهران و آوردن خانوران زوال خویان عاد مسمت کشته

از آنطرف فتح شاه به مقابله آمد و شکست اسحاق خان دلو و او را فرار که بس الجی با کمال حرمت

به نفذ مرحوم ابراهیم خان فرستاده نفش آقا محمد شاه را خواسته و با طلبت ابراهیم خان البیار شرقمندی

که به دولت قسر اتباع با اوضاع و اطراف هم دشمن و بدخواه مرحوم ابراهیم خان صلاح در مدارا

دیده نفش آقا محمد شاه را با اعزاز تمام راهی طهران کرد فتح شاه آنکو نه روته که اندر مرحوم ابراهیم

خان را از آمد آمدن دانسته فرستاه کان را با انعامات دخلعت باز فرستاد خلعت و شمشیر و حکومت

قراداع اسلام نامی بدخر قراداغ واگذار عهده ابراهیم خان که انها رخوشی که بودند در باب کیفیت قاطر

جمع رفین صغیره عزیزه مکرمه خویلا که آقایکم آقا تب بجرم خانه مالیق دهند که با نور جرم ماشته

کرد مست در صلاح دره از آنطرف فتح تدارکات کلیه و خوانین عظام فرستاد با اعزاز تمام

آقا بکم آقا را عقد که با نور محترم و بزرگترین مجموع اهل حرم کود و بسر مرحوم ابراهیم خان را

کرد ابوالفتح خان بهند ابوالفتح آقا نمود کحضور شاه فرستاد از جملهٔ خوانین عظام محبوب داشته

محرم مجلس خاص خود ساخته هه وقت معزز و مکرم میداشت و اهل خلعت و شمشیر و اسب بازین

و اسباب طلا و سایر تعارف و تکلفات از فتح شاه بمرحوم ابراهیم خان درم درم کد من

آقا میر سید نار ما سکه اطراف میر اطهورا عظم هلس علیه عالیه روضه سرداری با قشون

وارد تفلیس شده در ولایت کرجستان مستقلا در شهر تفلیس میگنند نظار آنکه

هنوز فکر تسخیر

مهنر فکر نسیر ولایتها را برداشتن دکنجه و شیروانات و قرایات درخاطر مناء دولت اردبیه
شهظاهر نمود واز وقت یافته مرحمتمدار مرحوم مغفور مه ازالوت واصلاحی غانیا که بارضای عنت
دولت دایم القرار اردبیه درخاطر مرحم مغفور ابراهیم خان می کرد وحصوصیتر دروقت آمدن
میان را السف رنبوف ودلکه اقدم اران باصلاح دیدوالی کرجستان ه به وقت را بطه هفتمر
وصلاح وحیرمت بکه کرامنظور مید اشتند الجی مرحم ابراهیم خان با الجی والی بالانفاق
بهخفه عزاف عوزبح که درلمیه دمزدک سردار دبه فرستاده اطها را اطمینت واخلاص مردیت
دایم انفقرار اردبیه کهفه درمیان مراسله نوشته الجی بهخفه سردار که ازدولت علیه عالیه اردبیه
وارد نعلیس شده لمه فرستاده اند وازالوت قدیمی را کید کوند لجراز معاودت آن سردار آن قی
میان را قوال والسکه بسردار دامنصوبه مجدداً الجی وخفه دماریا کخدمت قوال سکه فرستاده لطاما
ورستد کوند درحقیقت میان را قوال والسکه فرستاد که مرا کاغز از تمام لکه دوسوقات وتکلفانت
خاصه فرستاده کامل مهر باشی درالله مرحم ابراهیم خان لعهمر آتفطویر آآ آنکه سردار عظم کبار
سیبیا نوف دارد کرجستان شده چون معظم الیه سردار عبور وحسب جرءت لبه باره
حکات لزکیه جارونله دیه کهند الجوفظان خاکم کبیر را دیه میان سایر سرداران متحمر شده
متنبه لزکیه جارونله وجوفظان مرا کجشته رحمت اهالی کرجستان للانه دنست قور
اواخرسنه المیتحیه ۱۸۰۳ برسر قلعه کنجه آمده وحصره کرد لجراز کیاه از حی حصره لکر وحیه جنفه شه
کهم فرستاده جوفظان را باطعت وانقیاد امیرالطور اعظم وسیردن قلعه دعوت کرده اند

نائب ونداشته شب یورش کرده قلعه استنجر خته وجولوفان باینکه لشکر لشگر او حبینقا اما مقبول

شده همه اهل وعیال او کسیرشدند واز اهالی شهر پاره بقدر رسیده و ما باقی سکنات مانده ازقلعه

کنبم جناب مابدلیسا وبع را بحضور مرحوم ابراهیم خان فرستاده طاعت یاش دایم المرحه اروسیه

دعوت گفته کهود مرحوم ابراهیم خان جناب مابور جدابادی خوش گفته با اعزاز تمام در سلسله جخح

مضطوف داشتند وفت بهار سال ۱۸۰۴ جنانکه محمد خان حاکم ایروان از فتحعلیشا وخالف

به دکلمعلی خان حاکم نجوان هم از مطمع شاه فرار که در ایروان لهذا الجری بینفر سردار سبا نوف

زستام اعانت خواستند که فتحعلیشا بحضورا که عباس میرزا ولیعهد سمت برسر ایروان مامور

گفته همرکا سردار نشریف آدرند و ما را اعانت فرمایند قلعه ایروان سبر دار دلهخهان طاعت

دولت علیه عالیه روسیه راقبول میکنیم بنابران سردار سیانوف تمام ایروان نشده دارا زوله مت

قرلباش ولیعهد نایب السلطنه با قشون قرلباش رسیده در سبا جنگ درد لعه قرلباش منکتر

شدند کبرار ور دولین جبر که در فتحعلیشا آمدن خود بدفع کمیاز سیانوف و تم مبار اکه

قلعه ایروان مبرکت دولت اروسیه برسد باجمعیت تمام وارد ایروان شده ازکطرف فتحعلیشا

دارکطراف قشون نایب السلطنه دارکطراف محمد خان دکلمعلی خان عهدخوردا که سردار سیته لبوئز

سگته در دلقل قلعه کدآی کهید واطراف قشون اروسیه را قرلباش ازجا وطرف

کرفته آروقه وعیزه سلاح مگذاشتند که بقشون اروسیه رسد بادجوه اینکه نه زحمات

بازنوانستند که بقشون اروسیه نسلطری یا فته شوند از هرجهر طرف مذر مارکلیه بود لعه آخر

الامر مسردار آسیا نو فرصلاح درمعنی دوت لصوب لقلس دیدند کوه علانم سردند و فتیه شاه
هم معاودت کنه لاهوب آورباکاه وطهران رفتند وقت معاودت از ایردان جناک رط
لهٔ سقر وآمدورفت التجر مرحم ابراهم خان را بنگویسردار ان اردسیه سشنیده لهند ابوالفتح خان را
بانجهر از قسول ابقرامع بنگو ابراهم خان سرسام اموركه کهند که آمده بیا رری واقعات مرحم
اقوام دارد ومرحم محدحسن آقا را حسید نفر از بیرلغان از قلاع روانه حصور فتیه شاه سا ذند و بد
مقام کم مرحم ابراهم خان درحال حیات بیت وکنف لهٔ ن سردند که هیج امری بدول لفل وصلاح
ابوالفتح خان در قرامع نسوه دربکونه لکف بات فتیه شاه مرحم ابراهم خان رکنده جواب باس رشت
به ابوالفتح خان نوسشتند که معاودت که دخفرحال قسرامع نسوه ابوالفتح خان امر بدر بزرکوار
قهبار کنه قسول قر لباس را کونشه جنا که مرحم ابراهم خان لهومرحم محدحسن آقا در قریه طوق لهور
دیراق بودند باسرعت نام از تفکلین قوجاق الا الطرف کوه وملازان کار آیخه
وغیره جمع کنه باجمعت نام دارد حصور مرحم ابراهم خان وبرلور بزرکوار خو مرحم محد حسن آقا
سده هال لب که صدیق خان رسید صبح ابوالفتح خان لقربه طوق باجمعت نام بردرک
کرده لفتیکیا ن قوجاق دکواره رایم که درحصورخان مرحم وفرزندان دکشتند هجم کرده
لشکر قزلباش را سکنه دهی سب وجا ربارادره لییان عارت که لیبار رستیکم
دکشته سده ابوالفتح خان فرار بالطرف ارسلان که فتیه شاه که این مقدمه را شنیده

باز از راه ملایمت هر سه نفر از خوانین را برسم رسالت به نزد مرحوم ابراهیم خان فرستاده
به ابوالفتح خان مذمّت و سرزنش کردند که بلکه مرحوم ابراهیم خان بالمرّه دست از دولت قزلباش
نکشیده تابع بدولت اروسیّه نشود و نامهای آن خوانین کریم خان و رحیم خان و عبدالله خان که
با زبان ملایمت و شفقت آمیز و تعهدات محکم و قسمهای مغلظه بحضور مرحوم ابراهیم خان فرستاده اقرار
و تعهد کرده بجهة که تمامی ولایت قراداغ را مع ملاحقات او که بپادشاهی میرسید واگذار ابدی نسلاً بعد
نسل مرحوم ابراهیم خان سازند و دو نفر از اولاد خود را در قلعهٔ شوشی بمرحوم ابراهیم خان زوال بدهند
همین که هر دو قلعه های عسکران را که در سه فرسخی قلعهٔ شوشی در سر راه تفلیس و گنجه است واگذار
قشون نماید که در هر دو قلعه قشون گذاشته محکم نموده راه آمدن قشون اروسیّه را مسدود سازند
و هم دو قراولخانه را در یکفرسخی قلعه است او را باسکر که در سه ورسی قلعهٔ شوشی هست واگذار
قشون قزلباش نماید که هر دو قراولخانه ها و معبرها و راههای قلعه در دست قشون قزلباش
بجهة سنگرهای محکم ترتیب داده هر گاه قشون دولت علیّه روسیّه بر سر قلعهٔ شوشی آمده باشد
نگذارند و یکنفر سردار با دو هزار از سه هزار سواره در شاه بولاغی توقف کرده که سوار از طرف
تفلیس و یا ایلطبول خبر دار بجهة تقتیل و غارت اطراف آنها اقدام نمایند و همه از اطاعت و امر
مرحوم ابراهیم خان سر نپیچند و تمامی اخراجات قشون قزلباش از خزینهٔ فتحعلیشاه باشد
دهند از ولایت قراباغ طمع و توقع ننمایند و آنچه از ضروریات قشون است از سیورسات وغیره با پول خرید شان

بکره همین که

بگیرند هیمں کہ قلعہ شوشتر کہ حصنِ حصین و قلعہ خدا آفرین ست موقعہ کہ جِسان و شیروان ابست
برست فنون دولت اردسیہ نرسد اگر چہ صبیہ مرحوم ابراهیم خان کہ آقا بیگم آقا است مند درخانہ
شمعہ ت ہ حرم بزرگ و اولین لہ دار القبو جا ن را امیر الامرا عفو حرمت تام کرد کہ دندر مع ذلک
مرحوم ابراہیم خان دولت علیہ اردسیہ را ابدی محبت و پارستہ امپراطور اعظم را دائم و با عدالت
تصور کردہ داطنا ز خاطر بودہ دولت بزرگ و صاحب محبت احبی دانستہ ت غیر مرحمت
امپراطوری نمیرسد باز بدولت ایران و مرحمت آثا نرا حکم گذارند جہدو ا ابلی بشد قلیس
در ستام با سردار سیانوف تمنا رملاقا ت و انعام شرایط اطاعت کند سردار کسیا ز سیا فن
درستام مرحوم ابراہیم خان نیہ با اعزاز و انعام تام معطوف داشتہ لہ صدر در بار در حوال ولایت
ملاقات خواہر شد بنا برآن در شنبہ ۱۸ اہر اول ماہی مرحوم ابراہیم خان با فرزندان خود مرحم بنا مرار بدر

چہ حسن آقا و بنا را لی مایو محمد قلی آقا و بلکبیر خا ندر آقا و سایر اعیان قراباغ بحضور سردار
عظم کسیا ز سیا نوف و قبدار در مصو آثا ن آمدہ در سر درمقخانہ کورک ا ور د و کردہ لہ از عزمت
لہ در و معتبر در ستام سلیم خان حاکم ولایت شکی را در حکومت ولایت شکی تلقی ابلہ ردا با مرحم برکم
حال لہ بود ترغیب دلہ با اعیان ولایت شکی بحضور سردار اعظم آوردند چند روز در کورک جا بی
هفتی تام و عشرت و مهمانی شد لہ برارآن در اغذلہ و عہد نامہ مرقوم کشتہ مرحوم ابرا ہیم خان
و سلیم خان حاکم شکی عہد نامہ را مہر کردہ بہ سردار اعظم قول کشیدہ با اعزاز و احترام و تکلفات
محمو پلہ بکبیر از آنجا مساعدت کردند و فرزند هرمین مرحم ؟؟ سن آقا راشرط کہ ندہ در قلیس

بعنوان روال گذرانید و مرحم ابراهیم خان نیکدسته از قشون اروسیه بانوکیانه خواهش که بوازدوقت
درنندهٔ ثواب در قلعه شوشی باشد و در آن مجمع رتبه بیارال لیتامذ بمرحم ابراهیم خان و سلیم خان و بیارال
مایوری که به مرحم محمد حسن آقا و محمد بیک خان و بلوک که بمرحم خانلار آقا و سطانمردار که بیوربیاغی
شده و لهرازینها رماه فرمان بهین القات و مرتب با موجب مستمری رسیده که لهرازیماه نوبت
ارمجمع کودک چنانچه حسب الامر سردار مایورلیسادیع با دسته یکورونویکیانه وزده خان باغریشدند
وده و بینه قلوپت (و در آن اثناخبر رسیده که قشون قرلباش وارد کنار ارس می شوند بنابرآن مرحم محمد
حسن آقا درسته یکورد مایورا بقشونه با سواری نامی قرلباغ غانم مقابله قرلباش شدند مدعا آنکه
چون آب ارس درنهایت لهه سوایک کورباکذرگاهی نداشت درحوال کورپله لهه بکذرندو لشکر قرلباش
درخنخاک قرلاغ نشوند ایلترودهبات دلایت و غله ورزعت باما لبود قرلباش میل بدست که
ارکورباطرف قرلاغ کذشته لهند که درحوال باغات جبرشلو لهمه رعسا کرارواروسیه و قرلاغ ببوغیشده
دعوای سخت بهم آمده منب صلاح درمفطر قلعه شوشی دانسته مرحم محمد حسن آقا باقشون معاولت
بصوب قلعه کرده لهند قشون نفر قرلباش وارد آغ اوغلان جهان زربر سنخر قلعه بنده و لقریب سنخر رفتقشون
کوال قلعه سکران آمده ارلعکم لهنده ازهرطرف بسنخر قلعه آمده شوند و مقدم را مایور بحضور
سردارنوشته لهند درزلانا نایب السلطنه ابران بقریه چنانچه منزل که منتظر درقوقشون بسکرانه
لهند حسب الامر سردار اعظم بلوکک فراکین باقشون ونوکیانه دلیه بلوکک فراکین قطارازیک درحوال
قلعه شاه بولاغ ظاهرشد نف نایب السلطنه از چنانچه کوچ که موقع بولوکک فرا کین رفتند

شده اند شاه بدین سبب این خبر دار و از آمد سردار سیانوف که سمت ایبی حرکت
کرده و سردار سیانوف با خوانین که در دور فرستخر آمع از غلبهٔ رفته در آنجا معلوم شد که
شاه کوچ کرده رفته پس از آنجا تقلبه شوشی آمده پاره امورات را قرار داده و کرده و سه
نفر از خوانین قزلباش که بجهت سفارت بنزد ابراهیم باز گرد و تعهدات که مذکور که بدآمده
بودند آنها را کرفته با کمال حرمت و رضامندی از قرار بلاغ لصوب تفلیس رفتند در زمستان
همان ایا ل عباسکر دولت علیّه از کرکذشته لصوب پتک و تسخیر شیروان و باکویه و تعید بدر
حرکت فرموده مرحوم ابراهیم خان را روی الفت بدولت علیّه فرزند ارجمند حقیقی آقارا
باقشون فراوان و پاره یکر که کان رد آنه حصهور سردار داد و متعهد شد عباسکر پارسای کذمات
متغیره اقدام نمایند سلیم خان حاکم شکی که در اطاعت دولت علیّه بود با ترارکات لازمه و
پیشکشها لایقه سردار را از سر حد ولایت شکی برگته ولایت شیروان رسانید در اول فهر
چند روز اکرچه مصطفی خان جوابها مغروزانه بماهر اعتماد جفا باجابها صعب و دولت و کنت خفی
سکهور سردار نوشته سراز اطاعت باز میزد در آخوذت بهرکرده تا بمقا دمت جان عساکر آرزمه
وقشون فراوان و یک خواهر آورد و قشون بلاغ فرصت یافته درین ساعت تا ردها شیردان
کشاراند بنا بردللش محمدیقی خان و سلیم خان لاف اطاعت را انقیا که بنز علیکه مرحوم ابرهم
خان و سلیم خان قرار دله وعلاوا مغشته لهذا بنا نقرار عهد نامه نوشته دخل کرده دولت علیّه

در طامشترد

در ظاهر مشره سردار اعظم از شیروان گذشته بصوب بلاکو به فرستند درین اثنا بنا را آل

مایور محمد حسن آقا فرزند بزرگ مرحوم ابراهیم خان که صاحب آذار بوده برحمت خدا واصل شد ند

این مقدمه کدورت و ملال آمیز پریشان وغلیک بولایت بلاغ و دله پاره شخصیکه در

باطن اطاعت دولت علیه را راضی منجوبند بسبب فوت ومرحم محمد حسن آقا وهر

شدن محمد نقی آقا از ولایت وبسبب ناخوش وکم قوت دمسر مرحوم ابراهیم خان از آن

شخصها علامات و آثاریکه خلاف قرارداد وعهدنامه بود به پرواز رسید پس سردار اعظم

معطوف کردن محمدنقی خان و قشون قراباغ را اصلاح دیره بالعراز و جهزام وافاتی

لایقه و امید نوید بقراباغ فرستاند وچنانکه با مرحوم بنا را آل مایور محمد حسن آقا از صمیم

خاطر محبت و درربانی بتمام داشتند از کمال یأس و نهایت تأسف از فوت مرحم محمد

حسن آقا مراسله محبت آمیز از نهایت مهربانی دولمداری بجناب حرمت مآب بولوکرگی حضور قوا

نوشته تقدیمات محبت و برسردار که پومده بنا را آل مایور محمد نقی خان باقشون و عسکرله کان

قراباغ وارد و حاضر مرحوم پدر بزرگوار رفته شده میقاات محبت آمیز ونوبات سردار اعظم را

حالا که بفتح و بدرفع بار رصفیه بین اقدام اشته قویم استحکام قواعد اخلاص جلوه خفیه

سعی بلیغ درین اثنا خبر رسید که سردار اعظم سینا ندف در ولایت باکرم بار رفته است

سردار بی بار آور در دز که چنان امر متنع و مذموم از حسین خان ولایت اده سرخواه بزد با بنفر

از بیکر لقه کان حضور به مقام مکالمه تشریف برده ابراهیم بیک خان نفر دیگر در کمین نهوانده
خفیه سردار اعظم در رفتا و اورا باز بعم کلوله بقندر رسانده ابواب حی لقنه نوشتمر بروی عساکر
پادشاهی کشاده اند   از این خبر بالله اثر بی شانی خاطر پیرجوم ابراهیم خان و اولاد داد و
اهالی ولایت قاصر شه چوک هنوز از نظام دولت روسیه خبردار نوامشه تصور قاعده ایرا
میکردند که اگر جهان سردار اعظم وفات یا بد در نظام قشون و ولایت خلال کة قاصر شه و حال
آنکه اگر چند نفر از سرداران و سرکرده کان در یکی م جنگ با دشمن مقتول شوند باز نظام کلی کة
علیه را خلل و درکار و ولایت اقتشاشی رو نمی دهد بلکه از وفات سردار کسی اند نون بنا را ال
نسویدیا ایوف در بلده تفلیس پنظام قشون و ولایت مشغول شدند   لقم مرحوم ابراهیم خان بامروت
جات اولت آمیز کبمت بنا رال رفته خاطرجمع در هر باب قاصر شه که دربار آن ال
که سنه ۱۵۸۱ بشتر قشون قزلباش بنا بر عبور الطرف قشر لاغ کردند قورخفیه لقم ة
بحضور مرحوم ابراهیم خان فرستاده امید نوید ة دلعل را برباکشفه چون سواله دسته بکور و
مامور لیستا وبچ قشول علاوة در قرلاغ نبجوحه بدفع جنا ان دشمن قور قار شوند و ایربت بینا
قرابع پا ماله مرشدند و قتی کهول عنه بم میر سید مرحوم ابراهیم خان بنانی مدارا باقر لباش
کذاشتند و هم مصالح را با بایور طالمی می کهف و مامور رفه رسید ان قشون دولت علیم او رسیه را
به مرحوم ابراهیم خان با تعهد و وعده می دکنف الحتی آمدن قشون بسیار و تاخیر شد و قزلباش
و قشون اانیان به مهر فرنگی قلم رسیده به فر و مرحوم ابراهیم خان دکوچ خنوسا که در خان

خان بکر جه

خان یاغی لیهوئندار کوچیده وسیرد یمک قلم اورد ند یاره اوسیزار بیجه سیاق به مایورکقیه لیوندکه
سب مایور با دسته قُنول بمهمزاک ابراهیم خال مرشدذ رفته از قضای ملک که تعییر یاوله
نمی باید مرحوم ابراهیم خان بابا یاره اموی وعیالی ومتعلقان خه در آنجا مقتول شده لیوئزر وبلکه
غنا رالی مایورحمیدلقجال وبلوکوبک حضوری آقا دراندرون قلم لیوند حرکتی دکار که خلاف
قاعده اداولت بدولت علیه سرو مرتکب شده دراصلاح وحشت خلق سعی شده واز جناب
مایور در هربار برمغایبریت مکرد ند بلکه جنا که غله وآزوقه کم یاب لیوند ارک ازقه قنول
سعی شدند وقنول قزلباش باعباس میرزا فاسر المطلبه در آغ او مغلان اودرکفه لیوند
لجمراز مقدمه کردرست امیزمرحم خال با نخه روز مزفته لبوکه قنول دقویکیانه باسرکقه یکه یزال
نبایا لبین درشا برلاغی مسلوم شه مجرد درقوخبر آمدن قنول محمدیف خان باکوارهای
امرقرلاغ وضدمملکدار ال وبابره میکرله باجنا که قنول قرلباش درهر اطرائ وراهها کرده
میکردند ازقلم میرول شره کجدمت میار الی لنبالبین رفته لبقنول هولس ادبه لتی شده
در حوال قلوم عسکران اودرجه کهذ وبلوکوک حضوری آقا با مایوردوسه لکیر درقلو مانده
مرمی مظهر قلوی شود ومیار الی لنبالبین هردسته روز منظرشدند که بلکه با مرالطه ایران
باقنول قزلباش برسر ایال ن آمد اثرظاهر شه بنا براان صلاح دیدند که حرکت بهجرب
قنول قزلباش که اگربدعوا آمده سود دعوایا یه دالا بیا بد برسر آنها رفته لدفاک
قرابغ بیرون وهررکنند نایب الطه حرکت قنول ادبیه را بطرف غنه دلمه

با تمامی لشکر خنه کوچ کرده بمقابله دمقانله دمقا آمرند دورحوالی منزل خونا نشین هر دو لشکر یکدیگر

رسیده نایره قتال اشتعال یافت مهدیقلی خان با متعلقان از قشون قزلباش در هر وقت راهنمائی

واعانت می کرد در قوم بکام دعوا بالا نفاق بدفع ورفع قزلباش سعی نمود که در پانصدهم ماه

ابول دیتر از خونا نشین مدت هفت ساعت که دعوا دجنگ هر دو لشکر به باندر سرنیاز ابل

درهما نجه قطلار ویکا واعانت مهدیقلی خان قشون قزلباش مغلوب پاره مقتول دوباره دستگیر

شده فرار بطرف ارس کوهر وقطلا روکا نیز رخمدارشده تقریب سی نفر از افرار دسالدات نخمدار

ومقتول شدند میازا ل قشون از عقب لهین آورلوجان لی رفته اثر نیافند ناین السلطنه

یا قشون قزلباش بسیار از آغردق ریخته لیواز فرار اردوعده هرروز از ارس یا نطرف

سرحد عبر که نمود نیجر در دوخبر شکست قزلباشیه جنانکه ابوالفتح خان وسایر خوانین

دفرار مان سهها نه سرلاغ نمامی ایلات دوباره دعات را کوجما نیده لسمت نجران واورد هال

می بردند بر کوک حهفرقه آقا ما جناب یا بدلیسناوی دلاد سوارها معلم ایلات ومتعلقان

بعهاشته ازراه جهان ویمکردر نجسه معطوف کردن رعایا قسرلاغ ودفع قشون قزلباش عالم

شدند دهرجه درتوه داشتند ات دورود نوقف نکه باوجهیکه سالدات پیاله درکوهستانات

دشوار لهی که از عقب رسیده سودر آخر الامر درحوال اکومسنانات قیان واوره یار قشون

قزلباش سوار نفر سرلاغ درخدمت بر کوک حهفرقه آقا رسیده ابتراری دعوا که در دره های

نزنگ بقریب هزار سواره وبار قشون قزلباش یلا شکست داله محهدا کرفته دلخت که

ازاب ولسباب ولباس عادی نفذ دهرجه که داشته از کسب که لهوزک سالدات از عقب

رسیده

رسیده تا مرقتون قزلباش را پاره پسر ویاره فرار یافته بوده وایلات ورعایا ی قرالاغ را
کوچانیده می بردند همه این از راسمت بسمت معاوت بجوار که هستان سمت قلم
کردند آنوقت نایب السلطنه درحوالی کن رارس یه ازکطرف قزلون یارال نی بالسین
باجمد یقی خان شکست بنایب السلطنه دله وازکطرف مایدر دوکو بنگ جعفر قنی آقا امگونه
کارها می آوردند اهالی قرالاغ را آرام شده بذورعا کرباره ایمن طی هرکست هرکس
درجا رردکل ن خف ن باآ ساییس وکمال رحمت آرام دقرار کرفته درزمستان همان سال
ازکطرف اسپهرالطور افخم مرحم الکس بذر باولیک یارال را انسف عراف عوم کم لبرداری
منصوب کشته وارد بقلیس شد ومرکله دنوشته مجد یقی خان سلا چنانکه یارال مایدر
قسیده الدف درعراغیه خف بوذر اسپهراطور نوشته بوذ کبذر جه لبشر بقلیس جهنا زرحه
مجد یقی خان یا تمکر کرد ایان دیکهای ایلات وغیره بقلیس رفته لجر از دیدن عزاف
روز دیکر مجمع عام شده فرمان حکومت قرالاغ مع وعده شمشیر مرصع وعلم باشا هی
که درعهد نامه مرقوم شده بوه بجمدیقی خان ن تسلیم کرد یا امید نویدها ی مرحمت
کی کون معطوف بغر لاغ کوند ومقد مات حکومت مهدیقی از تاریخ مزبور
تا ۱۸۲۲ ماه اوکبر البته ازذ فامرکیه کارکرذوان هلت علیه نوشته امج مط
را رشرلیعست حتیاج بعرض مخلص بذارد فصلی حقوت اوان زمان که این بلاتها

نتیجهٔ حکومت وصیانت بیگناهان اعلیحضرت اهمرا طور اکرم شده اند اکرم

در وقتهای دشمنی با دولت ایران ضیع و کلیهٔ خاطر محفوظ از امّا بعد از آنکه در

۱۸۲۶ کارگذاران دولت ایران نقض عهدنامه و نثر دولتی و اشتروانشان را که با دولت دائم

القرار اروسیه ببسته بوده شکسته و نیز بین الکتب کنسار منقوطه قسمه که کجه سفارت

بدولت ایران رفته لهو معطوف کجه غفلتاً در قفر و لا دیتهای کلیهٔ دولت اروسیه نذر

در حقیقت اقتدر، طرف که که بنا آورده لهو وند انستذ در متابعه بر عساکر یاپاشهی

تاب دوامی نیا آن هزار بنز که در وقت تلاطم امواج دریاعسا کر دولت اروسیه اینان

با نند حسن و فناتک معدوم خوانه مرشد در آوّل مرحله مرحوم نایب السلطان با تمام

قشون خفه بر سر قلعه شوشی آمده و با ذجهک که قلّت قشون در زیر حکم میرزا ال

دلوش و معدم خوراک و باردت و کلرله و لوب وغیره مدّت یکماه و نیم محصره که

با جان قشون و نوب خانه قا وارفته نذر که بسمت دیوارقلعه شوشی آمده بنود تا

آنکه مقدّر معلوب بشدن امیرخان سردار سله درگذشت شمکور از زورعساکر یاپاشهی

که در زیر حکم میرزا ال کنید زد هذف لهو شنیده از نیر قلعو لابّد چکوچ که بعزم مقابله و

مقابله عساکر یاپاشهی که در زیر حکم کنیز از اوز و عزاف لبوکوچ ایروانسکه له

ناحوال آیکا ایط بول رقه زنایه از یک عتنی با بیگمه معلوب شده درو علناً هاور در زر اراکسین بسمت

قمادا داغ عبور

قرا داغ عبور نموده و سردار اعظم تا منزل چوره کن از عقب آنها آمده و اجبر از قشون

قزلباشیه نیافتند درحقیقت اکرمه زدورعسکر منصوره پادشاه هر در افواه و السنه

سپند کان معلوم مرشد در آن سال ۳۱ که بیگلان والا مقام کنیا زانو بخواف

بسکویچ ایروهنسک در بین ولایتها با مرسد دار رسالا ری قیام نموده زدور عساکر اکبر

اعظم را امپراطور اکرم سو ۴ ه ۵ احرالتین علیتین ایران و روم ظاهر و معلوم کفار دا هالی

دله بتهای ملوق دولت علیه روسیه را که ئ آرام و پریشان لهبز آرام تمام د له

کس نیکه از اشخاص ولایتها وصحیان اودق از مرحمت دریا مثال امپراطور عظم

نا امید شده از ممالک و مترد کات خطایان در یک کشتی لهبز و فرار کشتی متفرق

لهبراز در برابر مرحمت دریا مثاب امپراطور عظم حرم و کنه اشیان را مانند قطره تصور

فرموه امیدوار مرحمت و عفو تقصیرات که هماہ اینمرا معطوف با مکان د اوطان

خطایان کنند که بخدائه همه آنها دساکرین مالک املاک و مترد کات خطایان شده

با کمال آرام و آسایش و خاطر جمعی میگذران دارند و سنگر گذاری که منتظرند که در

وقت حضار با عساکر دولت علیه به خدمتگذاری وجان نثاری اقدام دارند و زخنگ

ارتنجا ض قسلاع در سفرهای ایران در روم د د غستان با لفاق عساکر منصوره پادشاه زنیکلاور

اقدام که از صاحبان صاحب و موجبیبشه مذهج پا بره ناشند تمت سوالخاتم

امیدوارم که این نوشته جات مخلص را که از مدت سنه مسلمان ۱۲۰۵

تا سنه ۱۲۶۰ م در حضور خوانین مورد ولایت قسرا باغ مقرر مسکدار دکا رکذار

لبهده ام در داکثر وقایع وحکنهانتخاطر رسیده ام مرقوم و کحضور باهرالنّور دلعوم

باعث تزاید الطاف ورحمت کنیار نامسک خواهدشد و امیدوار

مرحمت جنان امیراعظم دقایمقام عالیمقام شده ام م اهمه دوقت مخلص

خوشگال فرمهد از از ظاطرشتریف محو و فرا موش نخواهدفرمهد که در حقیقت

خیرخواهی وخدمتگذاری جناب لیثال بهمکسی فرض دلازنمت والطاف لیثان

بعموم منانیان وخدمتگاران تام دکامل خدا ومذکیا نه ازخیرخوانان همه دوقت

رضایت لیثال نزا دایم خوشوقت وخوش طالع سا ونز آبین یمعین

نام میکو کرباند زلقمی به کرو ما نذرسای زرکذار ختمخ جون این جنده ادواق را

که مشتمل است بحقیقت خاک ایالت دلایت قسرالاغ وحکومت خوانین مرحوبین بناه

خان وابراهیم خان بنام مبارک مسکان منبع المجد والاحسان

امیراعظم حضب کرم رحم دل غراف وکنیار میخایل سیمونویج فایمقام امیرالطور

افخم ورا نصوف تام دبنا کمه لعوم در قلعه سوشی این قطعه را که نمونه ازاوصاف

جبیل

جمیل و نهایت و عظمت آن باقی مانده و ضم بدعای خیر شده

دو نیم مقام ختم کلام مرقوم شد قطعه منه   بنام آنکه در لطف بیت معرفت

عرافیت کنم نیاز و در تصوف   بخذ نکاری خاقان اعظم

همه اوقات خود را که ده مصرف ء   کسی که آمد بدر کاهش نهید ء

بعین التفاتش که معطوف ء   آلهی دولت و بخت ش فزون بار ء

همیشه در جهان مسرور و مشعوف ء

تمّت الوفا بعان

فی ۱۲۹۴

فصل مدّت حکومت مرحوم پناه خان در ولایت قسمراباغ لبراز

خطاب خانی در سیدن فرمان حکومت از عادل شاه برلود

زلعه مرحوم ناد رشاه دالقاب حاکمی هراز د ٥ سال لهه

و مدّت حکومت مرحوم ابراهیم خان چند دهجار سال دارم

بقیه مدّت حکومت مرحوم مهدیقلی خان با فرمان امپراطور
اعظم درقراباغ هفده سال وچند ماه بهم فضل

آثار و عمارتیکه از مرحوم بنا ه خان درقراباغ بناشده آوّل قلعه بیات است که
باکمال بوهمه بارار وحمام وبارو دیگرعمارت کهم به الحال خراب شده و آثار رجز ّهست
دوّم قلعه شا وبولاغر مسجد درسرچشمه دحّام دشهر دبازار بارنگ و آهک نیست
دیوار ساغر قلعه نوشئی وعمارت که اکال انبار رغله قشون است آثار وعمارتیکه
ازمرحوم ابراهیم خان باقی مانده اوّل مسجد بزرگ جامع است که درسنه مسلمین ۱۸۲
تعمیر یافته که بهصّه لکرّمه اس مرحوم کوهر آفا گید بد عمارت کهم خوبتر ازسابق
دوّم دلاح حصار قلعه نوشئی که درسنه مسلمین ۹۸ ۱۱ بناشده درمدتّ سّه سال باتمام
رسید الحال اماءهلت کبیر که آمد در بوضع مکان ننا آثار خان باقی است سیّما
هم ره قلعه را سکران است ه درسنه مسلمین ۱۲۳ درسته فرسخی قلعه نوشئر دریا نه کوه
که معبر ره خانه عزیز است که درووقتی دشمنی اکر جزو قشون پایم درآن قلعه با یشه دشمن
از آنجا گذشته بطرف قلعه نوشئر نمی تواند ره عبور نا نمه جهاکرمه عمارت و اوطا قها دره
خزینه است درمیان که درکناف مشتمل به یکراه است در اندرون مقاره با آبک درسک
تعمیر شده پنجم عمارت باریان خان باغیر است درریگلر سخی قلعه داقع است شسم حصار باغ آغدام است
مع کندی با رعایه در سر قبر مرحو بنا ه خان و سایر اولاد بناشده است ونهر بار آن

فصل در نظام و ضابطه ابراهیم خان و قواعد در ایام حکومت او ث نمام ایلات

قراباغ قشون سواره بودند با دفتر سیاهه و در وقت ضرورت از میان ودعات

تفکیک سیاهه ملکان ملا در قشون منتظر بودند از ایلات قراباغ توجیر پول و مالجهات

از حصول با زیافت می‌شد اما از جایها و دعات مالجهات و توجیر با زیافت در سال

می‌شد و وقتیکه کاکاه از دهستان قشونی لزکی می‌آوردند آن وقت بجهت قشون

لزکی موجب و عوض سب کمشده دعوت شده لزکی از ایلات هم توجیر پول و سیورسات

غله و کو سفقه و مال با زیافت می‌شد از ان خانوازان لزکی وقشون در دفتر بنه لجهام

و ازا ا ا لزکی وقشون که نام شان در دفتر مرقوم لجهه حنیری باز دشت می‌شد معافیه

علته کهب و کهب ب اان از سرکار خان میرسید بهریک نفر لزکر قشون یکبا خانه

نیز محول شده لجوکه کار و با ر آن لزکر و سواره و درست می‌نمایه فصل

در هر سال روز نوروز که روز عید سیاه به تمامی سرکرده‌کان نامی قشون و نوباشیان

خلعت و والانام و شمشیر از طرف خان مرحوم انعام می‌شد هرکس بقدر رتبه خفتی کشها

اودولت ها از آدربایجان و حاجیها وملکان می‌آوردند فصل وقتیکه برحوم ابراهیم خان

در سفر تبریز و یا در جایی اردو می‌کنند اکثر منباشیان دلیور باشیان و بیکها و

آقایان و اوزخوانین آدربایجان که در حضور خان تمامی حاضر است و شام و ذها رفیان

وجوب هارنین و پاره اهالی قشون وعمله ومیرزایان والمیک آقاسیان وکشیکیان و
یب دلالان هم ازکارخانه بیکوان خان مرحم می خوردند در اکرشهها بقدریش چهان پوط زیام
هرنغ دسرد بس کوسفد سوایاایکه کوسفد زنده به نبایشیان وغیره ولایهه شدمذ محض
درکارخانه مرحم خان مصرف می شد با تج مصارف خان پوخته وجوسپان دروغن وحلویات
اینقدرار بمرخنا لی آمذ **فصل** مدخنرمرحم ابراهیم خان الزا مالوجهات حاصلها
ودلات خواه ازغله وخواه البریشم واز مزارع کوما نها محصوصه خان حتی جفم یادام
کمیکده فوم حساب کوید جفتها رغله دکوآن محصوصه خان مرحم برابرجبنت وکبای انهار ا لا
قرارمیع شه بلکه مرجفت زیام تمامی اینقدرغله ومالوجهات مصرف قشون وکارخانه
مرحم خانه و نوکر وعمله ودلال می رند داراجاره جات دبشکشها و اخراجات قرارمیع
دصرا بکانه وازدلاتها رلقذ باکان نشکش ها ازلقد وجنس سایا می آوردیدند

فصل اخلاق وردستا رمرحم خان ابراهیم خان مرحم غریب دوست
ومهمان دوست ویتیم پرور ورعیت نواز وغیور وبردل وصحبت حان ونان داام
بجو وصدق ونذر ونیاز سادات عظام وفقراء سپارمی داونر وعلماء وسادات را
حرمت تمام می کوند وهرکس که باد بناه می آورد واعانت می خواست ازخوانین ومیر لقان
اطراف ودلایها رلوز بابان وشیردان وغیره در اجترام دانجام مرام این مساعی جمیله
ودکار داشته مقضی المرام می کوند ولمصحبت زمان خوش صدرت میرنام داشتند کفل

کبان الجی

اسبان ایلخی سرکار خاصه چارپایان و کسبان جوز والخی لشکرمید هشتند بقدر

رسیده بقه که آوازه ایلخی مرحوم خان دردلها میان ایران و روم شهرت عظیم که بعد

اکثر اسبان ایلخی مرحوم خان از اسبان ایلخی وازنژاد اسبان مرحوم نادرشاه بقه که

از زولاینها رکوز پاکان و شاهسون و شقاقی وازخوانین خراسان بخصوص و جمع نژاده

بعهد تقریب جهان و هزار و بکه زباله مالیان نزاینده درد برابر آقری رخاصه و خیب

می نظر مرد وحساب کوسفند کله خاصه وما وجا موش زباله به لقم غرقان

آورد فضله درکارگذاران ممالک نمرحوم ابراهیم خان و برلوها وان دربلورزلها

سلطان می ردف از اولاد وعمورزلها رخه صاحبان دولت ولذکر دجلالش که هریک برابر

خوانین ولادینها دیگرله از اکحله میرزاییع عمورلوخه دلطفها که عمه زلها خه وفضه برک دعالقه

برک دکاع برک و منع برک برلورزلها داد لدنهار دمدرع پک وابراهیم خان فرزندان بناه خانی لبعد

واز سکبار ایلداس جون شیر دادلمور ایع دکسراو ویبودر چ حسد لو وبرکش طا و قراجودلو دعای سالو

وکولالو وقبایات و ملکان جالها ردیزاق وورنده وجله برد وطالش دعا چین باز

مشار خوانین باره ولادینها صاحبان دولت وعظمت دجلالی وبهاس لبعد دساعیرسکبا که خه

پرورش للمه بیا برررشاد وضد مسگذاران داخلاص الینان ضحب دولت درعزیت ساخته لیها

مشهور لبز قصه دار جمله علم جات دکار گذاران درخا مه او ومتکفلان امورت بضالح

دولت او اولاد جم آخند ملایانا هست واقف کلیّه حروریز و بدّ تبر و صاحب کمال
مشهور و معروفت که درایران در مردم شهرت تام دارد و سایر کارگذاران حضرت حربت
دهمیک لکاسیان و ناظران و سایر عمله جات که هریک از هرکاردان و کاری و خوش زبان
لهرواد مقدّمه آقا محمدشاه دربنی بود نفرقه که ولایت سراغ جنان اشخاص به معروف
محترم اکثر علما ست و کارگذارا مرحوم خان تا نّا وقت بافته بود و فشر لهو دولت فضل
دولله نامدارش فرزند ان بزرگ مرحوم ابراهیم خان که درحال حیات حفظان برجس دوار قیل لند
جوا د آقا و محمدحسن آقا که از یک مادر اند لذهبت سکها رابل جبیر سلطاعلو بود و دیگر از مرحوم خان
بولکوبک خان لدار آقا و ابوالفتح خان در ایران مرحوم شه دلجع بولوک محمد قاسم آقا و دفه آقا
وسلیمان آقا و حسین قلی آقا و صفقا آقا و اکاک که باقی اند در قرا بع بیک خان سیار ال
ما بورحلی جبیر خلیلی و جقه مرصع مهدیقلی خان و احمد خان از دختر خوانین اند و شجاع آقا
از کثیر ست و این دو دختران مرحوم ابراهیم خان در حال حیات ست کروما آقا ست
که از حصّه نواطلقه نجبا و کرجسان تولدیا فشه ست و عزت نیم ست و از حصّه میرزا رسع
وزیر داله کرجسان نو آریا ینه چوبک داله کرجسان ارک خان دایما پایگار و لاسی
مرحوم ابراهیم خان برعنب لهو ادر و جون قرابت لسیب مغایرت مذهب متعذر لبوده نغر
دختر وزیر خوسا بجوم خان و ده نفر فرزندان ادد لهلهنه در ابوالفتح خان دمد قاسم آقا
هشه عقده کهربوند که عقد محبت بانبن سبب رابط باشه وصل

فصل سبب وراثت و دولت عندلیبگان مهدیقلی خان ـــ در اوّل
ملاقات مرحوم ابراهیم خان با سردار سپه نوف در کورک چایله مرحوم محمد حسن آقا
ارفرزند بزرگ مرحوم ابراهیم خان لهذا تسمه و دولت و دولت عندلیب بنام مرحوم محمد حسن آقا
لطف المیر جهانین محمد حسن آقا را برسم زدال وکرد لسردار سپه نوف لهذا چونکه
یناوال مایور محمد حسن آقا در حال حیات مرحوم ابراهیم خان مرحوم شده بناوال
مایور محمد قلی آقا بزرگ فرزند باقی مرحوم ابراهیم خان لهذا وارث و دولت عندلیبی و
باکاغذ ممهور با مهر مرحوم ابراهیم خان و سایر اعیان و کثنای شرلاع در سال
صحات حفو مرحوم ابراهیم خان مهدیقلی آقا دله دیکسم خان و دارائی حن طرح حسته
موالجزا راز مرحوم شدن ابراهیم خان بهمان سبب بایورالسندوچ کحضور بناوال بایورتسونیه
نوشته لهذا که فرمان امپراطور عظم مرحم الک نور با دلوچ و علم دستمیر مرصع
بنام مرحوم مهدیقلی خان صادر شده کحکومت دخان و قرا باغ منصوب فرمهد درسنه
شنه ١٨٠٧ و مقدمات ایام حکومت مرحوم مهدیقلی خان از دفاتر ترکه کارکرد را
طالبن علیّه نوشته اند معلوم را اشرلف من احتیاح بعرض و تحریر مودن نمیک

صورت مرقومات مرحمین جمال الدین الک مهابود که تحریر کرده ام مستجلا مرقوم
یا قابلی را عفو فرمایند
و السلم